AMERICAN ACADEMY OF RELIGION
CULTURAL CRITICISM SERIES

SERIES EDITOR
Björn Krondorfer, St. Mary's College of Maryland

A Publication Series of
The American Academy of Religion
and Oxford University Press

ANTI-JUDAISM IN FEMINIST RELIGIOUS WRITINGS
Katharina von Kellenbach

THE GREAT WHITE FLOOD
Racism in Australia
Anne Pattel-Gray

ON DECONSTRUCTING LIFE-WORLDS
Buddhism, Christianity, Culture
Robert Magliola

CULTURAL OTHERNESS
Correspondence with Richard Rorty, Second Edition
Anindita Niyogi Balslev

CROSS CULTURAL CONVERSATION
Initiation
Edited by Anindita Niyogi Balslev

IMAG(IN)ING OTHERNESS
Filmic Visions of Living Together
Edited by S. Brent Plate and David Jasper

PARABLES FOR OUR TIME
Rereading New Testament Scholarship after the Holocaust
Tania Oldenhage

MOSES IN AMERICA
The Cultural Uses of Biblical Narrative
Melanie J. Wright

Moses in America

AMERICAN ACADEMY OF RELIGION

Moses in America

The Cultural Uses of Biblical Narrative

Melanie J. Wright

UNIVERSITY PRESS

2003

OXFORD
UNIVERSITY PRESS

Oxford New York
Auckland Bangkok Buenos Aires Cape Town Chennai
Dar es Salaam Delhi Hong Kong Istanbul Karachi Kolkata
Kuala Lumpur Madrid Melbourne Mexico City Mumbai
Nairobi São Paulo Shanghai Taipei Tokyo Toronto

Published by Oxford University Press, Inc.
198 Madison Avenue, New York, New York 10016

www.oup.com

Library of Congress Cataloging-in-Publication Data
Wright, Melanie J. 1970–
Moses in America : the cultural uses of biblical narrative / Melanie J. Wright.
p. cm.—(American Academy of Religion cultural criticism series)
Includes bibliographical references and index.
ISBN 0-19-515226-3
1. Moses (Biblical leader) 2. Steffens, Lincoln, 1866–1936. Moses in red. 3. Hurston, Zora Neale. Moses,
man of the mountain. 4. Ten Commandments (Motion picture) 5. Bible O. T.—Biography—History and
criticism. 6. Religion and culture—United States—History—20th century. I. Title. II. Series.
BS580.M6 W75   2002
700'.451—dc21   2001052047

9 8 7 6 5 4 3 2 1

Printed in the United States of America
on acid-free paper

Preface

This book began as a doctoral dissertation at Oxford University, under the direction of Christopher Rowland. Thanks go to him for being a patient and tolerant supervisor, and to my examiners John Barton and Bill Telford. For their institutional assistance I am a grateful to the Bodleian Library at Oxford, the British Library, the Butler Library at Columbia University, Christ Church (Oxford), the Faculty of Divinity and University libraries of Cambridge, and Scunthorpe Central Library. Without the financial support of the British Academy, this project would not have been undertaken; I am thankful for their award of a postgraduate studentship.

On a more personal level, I wish to express gratitude to Mark Baker, Rachel Baker, Chris Carmen, Andrew Chester, Peter Clarke, Jane Doyle, Clare Drury, Jon Gifford, Nancy Isle, Robert Isle, Fazana Khatri, John Leigh, Don Stebbings, Andrena Telford, Jerry Toner, David Woodhouse, and the members of the Centre for Jewish-Christian Relations, Cambridge. They have read drafts of parts of this book, offered comments on issues raised, or heartened me with words of constructive criticism and support. Björn Krondorfer and Cynthia Read (and colleagues) of the American Academy of Religion and Oxford University Press were unfailingly patient and wise as *Moses in America* moved from manuscript to bound book. Finally, I want to register the debt that I owe Justin Meggitt, who has cheered me on over the years. I dedicate this to him and to Mollie Wright, who died shortly after the project was initiated but gave me the strength to see it through.

Contents

Moses in America

Introduction

> Then Moses, the servant of the LORD, died
> there in the land of Moab, at the LORD's com-
> mand. He was buried . . . but no one knows
> his burial place to this day.
>
> Deuteronomy 34:5-6 NRSV

Moses' biblical story lacks closure. On the eve of Israel's entry into the promised land, her leader, intercessor, and supreme man of God, assessed by the editor of Deuteronomy as greater than prophets and kings (34:10-12) dies. He leaves no known resting place, and his followers constructed no monument or tombs to serve as site of pilgrimage or remembrance.

Why is Moses' burial site unknown? Is the lost grave a legendary motif, designed to emphasize Moses' intimate relationship with God (as in the story of Enoch at Genesis 5:24)? Is it an attempt to guard against moves to establish an idolatrous shrine or cult in his honor, or to elevate Moses to the status of a demigod (against Exodus 20:3; Deuteronomy 18:11; 26:14)? Does the missing tomb merely evoke the universal and insoluble mystery of human suffering and death?[1] Whatever the intention of the Deuteronomistic editor, 34:5-6 leaves us with the sense that the Moses story is not yet complete or ended. Far from being "dead and buried," at the end of the Pentateuch Moses remains an illusive figure, at once on the boundary of wilderness and promised land, past and present. Not tied to any location or territory, he is seemingly free to roam across other landscapes and other contexts.

Throughout the Hebrew Bible and New Testament, the virtues of other esteemed figures are conceived in Mosaic terms. Jesus is the prophet like Moses at Acts 3:22 and implicitly in passages such as Matthew 2:16–21 and chapters 5–7. Indeed, Jesus' very name recalls Moses' successor, Joshua, who fulfills Moses' mission by leading Israel across the Jordan (Joshua 3:8). In postbiblical times, similar associations continue to be made. Early rabbis

evoked the God-Moses encounter as a means of legitimating their own reconstruction of Jewish religion (m. Aboth 1:1). Philosopher-halakhist Moses
Maimonides's (1135–1204) greatness was encapsulated in the popular medieval formula, "from Moses [of the Torah] to Moses [Maimonides] there was
none like Moses." And at the end of the twentieth century, in a country
where biblical values are often thought to have been overpowered by the
quest for the capitalist market and material prosperity, Martin Luther King
Jr. returned to Moses typology to express his conviction that, though he
should die, the goals he longed for would be accomplished.[2] In addition to
being viewed as a type of leadership, Moses has enjoyed fully extended and
elaborate "afterlives" in the artistic realm. Countless authors, dramatists,
and painters have represented his life.[3]

This study is not intended to be exhaustive in its approach to Moses in
America. Images of Moses, and the popular and critical evaluations of
those images, are continually being generated and reshaped: a definitive or
comprehensive account is an impossibility. Instead, I have selected a small
number of works, encompassing a variety of media and concerns. I have attempted to articulate (in the double sense of expressing and relating to one
another) the images of Moses created by three twentieth-century North
Americans: muckraking journalist and autobiographer Lincoln Steffens,
the novelist and anthropologist Zora Neale Hurston, and film director
Cecil B. DeMille. In their works, Moses in Red (1926), Moses, Man of
the Mountain (1939), and The Ten Commandments (1956), Moses is "redivivus," reborn to wander through what at first glance seem to be biblical
wildernesses but on closer inspection emerge as very modern environ-
ments. The Moses figures created by Steffens, Hurston and DeMille clash
with America's great twentieth-century Pharaohs, including militarized
opponents, such as the USSR and Nazi Germany, and those closer to
home who would oppress groups such as African Americans and women.

The discussion of Lincoln Steffens's Moses in Red takes as the starting
point for the analysis the book's apparently unexpected critical and popular failure. It deploys a considerable amount of archival evidence to consider the forces and concerns that shaped Moses in Red and to shed light on
its negative fortunes. For the first time, the book's recasting of biblical narrative is related to contemporary developments in historical criticism and
social gospel Christianity. However, the study is primarily concerned with
Steffens's use of the exodus story to explore the phenomenon of "revolution." Against the grain of popular rhetoric, which identified America as
the new Israel (both as promised land and as people chosen to witness to
God's will in the world), Moses in Red so designates the then new Bolshevik state in Russia. In this light, Steffens's failure to produce in Moses in

Red a popular reworking of the biblical narrative emerges as predictable rather than surprising. *Moses in Red* provides a reading of the Moses story so incongruous with those dominant in the early twentieth century that its lack of acclaim is inevitable. Steffens's Moses breaches the cultural agreement about the meanings of the exodus story in 1920s America.

Zora Neale Hurston's *Moses, Man of the Mountain* is not so readily categorized. Hurston's novel is deliberately complex in character, drawing on biblical narrative, African influences, and social scientific theory. Significantly, Hurston herself has in recent years attained an iconic status in American feminist circles. The discussion of *Moses, Man of the Mountain* therefore considers the implications of Hurston's identity as an African American woman for representation of the exodus. At the same time, I suggest that the author's anthropological training under Franz Boas is of fundamental importance. Hurston's familiarity with the perspective of cultural relativism leads her to present the biblical story as at once both unique and relative, the myth Americans live(d) by. The discussion of responses to *Moses, Man of the Mountain* shows once more the role that reader presupposition plays in negotiating the reception or (perhaps more accurately) the "secondary production" of the text. For those initial readers who did not share Hurston's anthropological awareness, the book's association with the African American folk tradition was a weakness: that community's account of Moses must of necessity be unreliable and inferior.

The final twentieth-century American representation of the Moses story considered in depth is Cecil B. DeMille's 1956 film *The Ten Commandments*. Here, the analysis of the film's content and reception draws on insights from film studies, particularly in relation to the history and status of the motion picture industry in mid-twentieth-century America. The Hollywood epic has typically been categorized as superficial and banal by biblical scholars and film critics alike, but the study argues for the rehabilitation of DeMille's Moses as a complex example of innovative biblical interpretation. For example, the ambiguity of *Commandments'* relation to its sources (including Josephus's *Antiquities* and Philo's *Life of Moses*) has been cited by some as indicative of its frivolity and arbitrariness toward tradition. I attempt instead to consider seriously the reasons for DeMille's inconsistent handling of ancient source materials. Above all, though, the film is characterized as presenting a "Cold War Moses," influenced by DeMille's desire to uphold "American values" in the face of Soviet strength and to present the threatened motion picture industry as the true champion of those values. The analysis of the responses to the film indicates that, while this was the most widely received of the three representations of the biblical narrative, statistical popularity is not evidence of any success on the part of DeMille in imposing his reading of the Moses story upon viewers. As with *Moses in Red* and *Moses, Man of the Mountain*, communities whose prior assumptions about the biblical story differed from DeMille's were often unsympathetic. Additionally, presuppositions about genre and the medium of cinema come into play. In particular, academia is seen to be (prejudicially) alienated from this phenomenally popular form of biblical representation.

The aim of this study, then, is not to judge the merits of Steffens's, Hurston's, or DeMille's Moses. Rather, it seeks to explore how their images of Moses function within particular contexts of production and reception. This twofold focus is discussed in more depth later. More generally, it also asks why, almost three millennia after he was "laid to rest" by the Deuteronomist(s), Moses was brought to life by these three "authors" and why they believed that their arguments (for arguments they were) were best advanced by the retelling of a biblical story. In this sense, I hope that the study will suggest a range of more generally useful techniques for others working in related fields, as they also attempt to grow the disciplines of religious and biblical studies. As John Riches has recently noted, the Bible continues to exercise tremendous influence in the popular culture of Europe and North America. In films, novels, and music, its language, stories and metaphors, types, and figures provide a vast resource, which is drawn on in a variety of ways, both consciously and unconsciously.[4] Examining the manner in which a particular biblical narrative has been appropriated by particular twentieth-century communities fosters sensitivity to the same processes at work in our own day, be that in the election speeches of political candidates, in contemporary Hollywood productions, or in academic debate.

Texts and Contexts: Methods Used in This Study

The methods used to examine images of Moses in America are akin to those employed in the material culture approach to religion, as developed (for example) by Miles and McDannell.[5] This perspective in turn is influenced by the discipline of cultural studies, which since the 1960s has been concerned not so much with objects deemed to be of aesthetic "excellence" as with culture more broadly or democratically defined as the texts and practices of everyday life. Miles, McDannell, and other students of popular culture argue that material culture (including books, film, and art) in itself has no intrinsic meaning of its own. It is only through a full examination of the historical contexts of material culture that it can be "read" or comprehended. In this study, therefore, the binary opposites of "auturism" and "reader-response criticism" are rejected as unhelpfully narrowing, one-sided forms of contextualization. Instead, the whole life cycle of the book or film, the circuit from production, to distribution, to reception, as well as the book or film itself, must be investigated.[6] In the words of Lawrence Grossberg:

> The meaning of a text is not given in some independently available set of codes which we can consult at our own convenience. A text does not carry its own meaning or politics already inside of itself; no text is able to guarantee what its effects will be. People are constantly struggling, not merely to figure out what a text means, but to make it mean something that connects to their own lives, experiences, needs and desires. The same text will mean different things to different people, depending on how it is interpreted. And different people have different interpretive resources, just as they have different needs. A text can only mean something in the context of the experience and situation of its particular audience.[7]

This approach does not deny that texts (or readers) have objective existence. What is disputed is that "text" and "context" (of production, or of reception or "production-in-use") are separate cultural moments. They are inseparable. One cannot have a text without a context or context without a text.[8]

The methodology for the study grew organically out of these principles. First, each chapter surveys the work in question and relates it to what might crudely be termed "religious" contexts (for example, the Bible and other source texts, North American religious trends) and then to "political" ones (events like the Cold War, questions relating to ethnic or gender issues.) At times, the contexts discussed have been somewhat artificially delineated from one another. However, this teasing apart of different elements is deliberate. Specifically, I hope that it enables the study to strike a worthwhile balance between close reading of the texts (attention to complexities of language and meaning) and sociopolitical analysis. These twin modes of analysis are intended to heighten appreciation of the sophisticated nature of these three oft-neglected works and thereby allow a nuanced estimation of the complex forces shaping and interacting with their images of Moses.

Second, the discipline of reception studies, which Staiger helpfully summarizes as the "historical explanation of the activities of interpretation,"[9] is employed to answer further questions: How were the authors' versions of the Moses story received by their contemporaries? How have they been evaluated by subsequent generations? Instead of proclaiming one reading of the work in question as authoritative, I aim to consider a range of the responses it engendered, particularly as they have been manifested within different communities of interest and interpretation (although, as suggested earlier, this work does not intend to overthrow the author in favor of the reader, to replace one tyranny with another).

Of course, analysis of such works as these is complicated by the fact that, unusually, Steffens, Hurston, DeMille, and their respective readers (or consumers) all possess a substantial preknowledge of the underlying biblical exodus narrative. As will emerge in later chapters, this is a reality that at once empowers and circumscribes the activities of both.

In short, then, this study attempts to hold in fruitful tension the roles of "producer" and "consumer," to value both as interpreters and creators, or re-creators, of the Moses story in twentieth-century America. It seeks to lay bare the dynamics involved in the afterlife of a figure who remains central to the identity of that civilization in all its rich diversity and, despite all attempts, unburied.

Growing Biblical Studies

I mentioned earlier that this project may be located within a more widespread trend toward the expansion of the field of biblical studies. Biblical studies as an activity in the academy grew out of eighteenth- and nineteenth-century attempts to separate the Bible from its interpretation as received and promulgated by the Western churches.[10] But despite this origin in an acute awareness of the interplay between "text" and "experience," biblical scholarship has been weighted heavily in favor of the former. Academic Bible reading as practiced in the West today is predominantly a form of literary criticism. For the most part, its practitioners deploy source, form, and redaction criticism and other related strategies in their attempts to reconstruct either the people or the events that lie behind the books we know today. In other words, much academic biblical study still bears traces of the Romantic quest for origins; it has tended to neglect questions of reception and the history of the Bible's influence as a source of both elite and popular cultural expression.

Consistent with the early shaping of the discipline, none of the works that feature in this study has previously received serious critical attention. In seeking to explain biblical scholars' ignorance of the history of their own discipline, John Drury listed the competencies expected of a biblical critic as follows: "The skills required are manifold and hard: knowledge of at least two ancient and two modern languages, of textual criticism and of testingly obscure episodes in history, of religion in its popular and philosophical manifestations, of a vast and sometimes barely readable secondary literature."[11] Drury was writing in the late 1980s, but even today most biblical professionals still view as peripheral activities the study of art, film, literature, or music that retells or depicts biblical stories and themes or the historiography of biblical studies. Although many undergraduate programs provide courses in Hebrew and Greek, fewer aim to teach students how to appreciate the distinctive nature of literary texts and artistic forms, so that they can offer intelligent evaluation of, say, a triptych by Hieronymus Bosch or Bob Marley's "Exodus."

Why does the academy attend to some "readings" of the Bible but ignore, or treat as trivial diversions, other interpretations and uses that have been of importance to just as many (or often many more) people? The answer lies partly in the origins of the discipline but also in the professional construction of biblical studies within the higher education context. In purely sociological terms, like other professions, biblical critics are an interest group. Limiting or restricting access to the profession makes it easier for them to improve their status and other rewards. While these kinds of "political" interests rarely figure in critics' own accounts of their research design and methodology, collective decisions about what and how to study tend to reflect the profession's strategic need to maintain boundaries between the Bible as an object of specialist investigation and the Bible as "a book studied in studies."[12]

This book tries to tackle head-on the history of, at best, benign neglect and, at worst, active condescension. It seeks to show that biblical studies should not continue to ignore the ways in which "ordinary people" think with the Bible. In stronger terms, I believe it cannot continue to do this, if critics genuinely wish to avoid their discipline's becoming an isolated intellectual exercise, increasingly distant from and irrelevant to the ways that those outside the academy are making meaning from and with the book.

Religion in America

This book does not pretend to be comprehensive. Looking at the work of Steffens, Hurston, and DeMille can hardly begin to illustrate all the particular ways in which so vast and varied a population group as twentieth-century Americans understood themselves and the Bible. But at the same time, it is impossible to write about particular images of Moses without some acknowledgment of wider discussion about the place of religion in America.

The persistence and vibrancy of religion in North America continue to exercise commentators. In contrast to most other Western nations, religion in America has not had the "prop" of formal establishment. At the same time, capitalism and the rhetoric of the market have arguably taken hold in the United States more strongly than elsewhere. But despite (or because of) this, American culture remains profoundly religious in character: "A pilgrimage to Graceland, praying football players, Jewish ritual in the Capitol Rotunda, cremation, and Christian Rock—all of these describe the landscape of American religion and mark the continuing fellowship of national identity and religious practice."[13]

One hallmark of American religious life that is significant for this study is the dynamic exchange between religious traditions and movements that were transplanted to or have emerged within America and the religious meanings applied to America itself. This transactional process is especially clear in relation to the place of the Bible and, more particularly, the story of Moses and the exodus within America. Since premodern times, much American political and social self-comprehension has been articulated in relation to this biblical narrative; many studies have traced its importance for the early Puritan settlers. Hebrew Bible images of creation and exodus exerted a formative influence on the pioneer worldview. And long before the New England settlers fled their European Egypts for a new home, Christopher Columbus had conceived of his New World travels in biblical terms, as one logbook record illustrates: "I was in great need of these high seas because nothing like this had occurred since the time of the Jews when the Egyptians came out against Moses who was leading them out of captivity."[14]

This use of biblical typology and metaphor was not confined to the early days of European settlement. As discussed in chapter 3, African Americans also took ownership of the Moses story, both during and after slavery. And as recently as his 1995 State of the Union address, President Bill Clinton famously spoke of forging a "new covenant" with the American people.

From the biblical story of the exodus emerge concepts at the heart of America's self-image: liberation, freedom from oppression, political and moral rebirth, divine providence, and promised land. There are also, as in Columbus's log, related images of trial and wilderness, endurance, and divine commission. It is, as Wentz suggests, almost impossible to describe American public life without recourse to imagery drawn from biblical narrative.[15]

Conversely, the transcendent meanings invested in the nation have shaped religious life in America. At times, the influence is marked and decisive. As will be seen in chapter 2, the historic identification of America as promised land led to the downfall of Steffens's attempt to argue that Russia might be seen as a new Israel. But in more general terms, too, the biblically based traditions of Christianity and Judaism have their own distinctively American forms. More consciously public and political than their sibling traditions elsewhere, they have adapted in response to their development in a society characterized by the interaction of biblical and secular energies. When Martin Luther King Jr. delivered his "I have a dream" sermon, he was not just building on a mountain of Christian tradition; he spoke in the shadow of the Lincoln Memorial and, in doing so, linked African American Bible interpretation with the president whom Sidney Mead has called "the most profound and representative theologian of the religion of the Republic."[16]

Neither the health of individual religious traditions nor the undeniable religious character of American public life should be mistaken for evidence of shared religious convictions and values in the United States. As Moore has noted, consensus-based views of American religion have been remarkably persistent. In part, the historian's tendency to emphasize unity over plurality, conformity over dissent, has reflected a long-felt desire to construct a more homogeneous nation. Even Thomas Jefferson's sponsorship of religious freedom stemmed from an assumption that legal tolerance would provide a stable environment in which people would voluntarily move toward a nondividing religious center: "The possibility that American religious energy would . . . expend itself with everlasting centrifugal force was one they tried to ignore."[17]

Probably the most famous twentieth-century writer associated with consensus interpretations of American religious life is sociologist Robert Bellah. Bellah described the development of a form of religious nationalism that he called "civil religion" in America.[18] For Bellah, civil religion was a religious system that drew upon and existed alongside other religions in America. It possessed a "theology" (a set of ideas about the American nation and its place in the divine plan for humanity), a set of "rituals" (or practices, such as the schoolchild's daily pledge of allegiance[19]), "symbols" (such as the national flag), and "saints" (figures such as Washington and Lincoln who played important roles in constructing America as a nation), all without the aid of formal institutionalization. Americans of diverse faith traditions (or of none) were able to participate in civil religion observances alongside one another in a way that both intensified commitment to the nation-state and reminded new generations of the values and motives that inspired the pioneers of the past.

Bellah's work was popularly read not only as describing the existence of civil religion but also as a call for its rejuvenation. (It is interesting to note that he wrote at the time of the Vietnam War, when a disturbing sense of national disunity was to the fore.) In the 1970s, Bellah himself wrote about the "empty and broken shell" of American civil religion, as if a previously solid community of meaning had suddenly fractured in the late twentieth century. As Moore notes, however, what scholars of American religion thought was falling apart in the 1970s "was not failing for the first time."[20] Perhaps "civil religion" never existed; had it ever been anything more than a scholarly construct, an unhelpful reification? John Bodnar's detailed work on public commemorations of war and statehood, supposedly the loci of civil religion, has shown how even these celebrations of the polity were in fact sites of competition and conflict, occasions of cultural exchange where diverse groups competed to establish their interpretations of history over those of others.[21] And Bryan Turner has suggested that, given what we know of the range of possible meanings that may be invested in texts, symbols, and rituals, "one cannot make the assumption that . . . they perform the functions ascribed to them" by consensus theorists of religion.[22]

This study is grounded on a similar conviction that "common myths do not have to be read the same way."[23] Both public discourse and popular expression in modern America make extensive use of the Moses story, but the private meanings of that story for individuals cannot be assumed to be uniform or readily accessible. This is not to say that consensus interpretations of American religion should be replaced by accounts of overwhelming fracture and disintegration. Rather, the story of American religion— and, indeed, the story of Moses in America—is a tale, as Albanese puts it, of "many centers meeting."[24] In their readings and reworkings of the Moses narrative, different groups of Americans engage both the biblical text and their fellow citizens. Exploring a shared narrative, they express ambivalence and acceptance, opposition and openness, toward one another. However loosely articulated and however lacking in an obvious public core, East Coast radicals, African American women, and Hollywood directors all find a shared source of power, meaning, and value when they locate Moses in America.

Back to the Future

Lincoln Steffens's *Moses in Red* (1926)

"*Moses* moves right along. I work at it every morning from breakfast." . . . "IT IS a good story. . . . I am so in the mood for the thing that I could reel it right off."[1] Lincoln Steffens was justifiably optimistic about his project to recast the exodus story as a narrative of revolution. By the mid-1920s, he was a figure of some renown—not quite a household name perhaps, but certainly a name known to many middle-class North American households. As a young man, he had been one of the first investigative journalists, or "muckrakers," to examine the relationship between business and urban politics. This study of graft and the squalor and injustice experienced by the laboring masses had both revolted and attracted a broad readership. More recently, notoriety had enabled him to gain access to world leaders such as Lenin, Trotsky, and Wilson. Among his friends were numbered fashionable intellectuals (including Hemingway, Pound, and Steinbeck), many of whom confirmed his assessment of *Moses in Red*. Fremont Older's remarks were typical: "I am sure the book is going to have a big sale, and probably will go into the movies."[2]

Moses in Red was a flop. Steffens's "good story" failed to impinge upon the consciousness of the reading public. By early 1927, his ebullience gave way to dismay: "The *Moses* is making no stir; it's not read, I take it. . . . I wish somebody would jump on it hard enough to get it read. Can't you stir up some Bishop to go for it and me?"[3]

For some three-quarters of a century, *Moses in Red* has remained at worst unread and at best read and quickly forgotten. Robert Stinson, one of Steffens's biographers, attributes this failure to the obscurity of Philadelphia firm Dorrance and Co. that published *Moses*. A warehouse fire also destroyed many copies of the book.[4] However, while mundane factors can account for its initial circulation problems, it is necessary to probe more deeply to explain the book's rejection by the reading public. Had there been either critical or popular clamor for *Moses in Red*, it would surely have been reprinted.

Perhaps the failure of *Moses* may be attributed to the declining fortunes of its author or to his attempts to draw somewhat labored analogies between ancient and modern—namely, the events of the exodus and the revolutions in Mexico and Russia. Again, these arguments are not compelling. Although the excitement of muckraking was long gone by the mid-1920s, Lincoln Steffens was still capable of arousing the interest of the reading public. His *Autobiography* (1931) was well received, gaining a Pulitzer Prize nomination and the honor of being abridged for high school students. Equally, although *Moses in Red*'s attempt at likening biblical and contemporary events may in retrospect seem forced or naïve, only a year earlier similarly crass parallels (between twentieth-century capitalism and the teachings of Jesus) were the subject of a phenomenally popular book, Bruce Barton's *The Man Nobody Knows*.[5] A survey of clergy conducted by Barton for the sequel to *The Man* also attests to the currency of the Moses story in interwar America. Respondents were asked to name the great men of the Bible and, aside from Jesus and Paul, Moses gained most votes (more than any other Hebrew Bible character).[6]

An attempt to solve the puzzle of the critical and popular failure of *Moses in Red* both answers and raises questions about the use of the Moses story in modern America. What can and cannot be said about Moses in this period? Why are some retellings regarded as legitimate adaptations, while others are dismissed as illegitimate corruptions of the biblical message? This chapter explores the relationship between *Moses in Red* and the popular political and theological trends of the early twentieth century. It considers how Steffens sought to go back to the exodus story in order to argue for a revolutionary future for the American people, and why his readers were so emphatically unwilling to do likewise.

America Reconfigured

Historians recognize the 1920s as a decade of American economic, political, and cultural reconfiguration. In the run-up to the slump and Wall Street crash of 1929, per capita gross national product increased significantly. Largely fueled by industrial and technological advances, this increase was accompanied by changing employment patterns, most graphically, a decline in the number of farm workers and an increase in the manual and white-collar sectors. While some 1.5 million laborers left the land in the decade before 1930 and traditional industries like textiles shed almost 50 percent of their workforces, the new motor industry mushroomed to be the largest in the country, employing almost half a million people. Coolidge's quip that "the business of America is business," sounds clichéd today, but set against the context of the nation's largely agrarian past, it was a radical assertion.[7] Industrialization brought with it urbanization and a boom in the production and availability of consumer goods—a major social and cultural revolution, as well as an economic one. Suburbia (in its modern sense) was born. Unsurprisingly, these changes provoked sharp controversy and social conflict. Did the nation's true spirit lie with the idealized simplicity of nineteenth-century, small town and rural America or with the brash consumerism and permissiveness of the city, as portrayed in modern advertising and the movies?

To many, it seemed that hidden, as yet unknown forces were ravaging the cultural landscape. Diversity and change brought in their wake a thousand threats to the older, seemingly self-evident truths that had shaped life in a lost golden age. These fears not only circumscribed behavior in the private sphere but also led to public, collective action in defense of "America." In the early 1920s a revitalized Ku Klux Klan attracted 5 million members with a brand of Americanism that entailed the physical intimidation (or worse) of Roman Catholics, Jews, recent immigrants, African Americans, and homosexuals. For Klan members, these groups were an alien presence that promised to warp the values at the heart of American civilization. Nothing less than the nation's future survival was at stake. In a similar vein, Henry Ford distributed antisemitic literature through his network of car showrooms.[8] In the civic arena, authorities, persuaded that the new rhythms of jazz constituted an offense against womanly purity (and, by inference, family life), banned the music from public halls in New York, Philadelphia, Detroit, Kansas City, and Cleveland.[9] Ostensibly for the protection of women, these measures bespeak a deeper unease concerning the shift in gender relations and a breakdown of older mechanisms of social control.

Not everyone felt threatened by the changing times. For the smart set of the sophisticated metropolis, "progress" was the watchword, and the small town values of the hinterland were either ignored or the objects of active disdain. Far from being a golden age of consensus, the American past was defined as an age that privileged white middle-class European males over African and Asian Americans, women, and the poor. As such,

its mores, and the assumptions on which they rested, needed to be disman-
tled or overthrown. At the same time as the Klan's membership was bur-
geoning, Marcus Garvey's Universal Negro Improvement Association
(UNIA) offered "race pride" to many thousands, as did new labor unions
like the Brotherhood of Sleeping Car Porters and Maids. In 1928 Oscar De
Priest became the first African American since Reconstruction to be
elected to Congress,[10] and while legislators pondered the corrupting influence of jazz on the "weaker sex," more and more women asserted their social and sexual independence. Many used contraception themselves and
donated funds so that their less wealthy sisters might do the same. The
American Birth Control League was launched in 1921.[11]

The 1920s were years of Prohibition and state legislation outlawing ex-
tramarital sex. Yet this was also the age of organized gang warfare, the "flap-
per girl" with her flesh-colored stockings, and the first screen sex symbols. It
is perhaps unremarkable, then, that many Americans considered themselves to be living in a new era and that scholars, too, were interested in
analyzing and rationalizing American life. The 1920s witnessed the development of a theoretically underpinned critical self-consciousness. Much social analysis was undertaken with specific reforming ends in mind. Scholars
hoped that by drawing attention to the problems born of rapid technological, industrial, and urban change, they might construct a reliable body of
knowledge on which the making of future social policies (such as the New
Deal, Roosevelt's 1933 economic recovery program) could rest. Helen and
Robert Lynd's sociological study *Middletown* searched for the essence of
American society and (a significant gauge of the concerns of the era) was
the first such book to be successfully marketed to the general public. At the
same time, the work of anthropologist Margaret Mead (*Coming of Age in
Samoa*) challenged established belief in constants or laws of human conduct
and promoted the idea of cultural relativism in the social sciences. Widespread discussion of related issues was also propagated among the emerging
American middle class through cheaper periodicals. *The Arena* and *Mc-
Clure's Magazine* made an audience of millions newly accessible to political
writers and social critics.

Lincoln Steffens was both a part and a stimulator of the trend toward
the expansion of social scientific discourse on American society. As a student of social theory and psychology in continental Europe, he had encountered attempts to construct a science of human behavior and organization. Influential cultural evolutionists like E. B. Tylor and Herbert
Spencer had argued that societies were functioning systems, susceptible of
scientific study. Spencer, for example, suggested that history should assume
the task of "narrating the lives of nations, so as to furnish materials for a

Comparative Sociology; and for the subsequent determination of the ultimate laws to which social phenomena conform."[12] Steffens retained a lifelong faith in Spencerian-style analysis, believing that the human world was subject to laws and that these laws were capable of investigation in much the same way as those operating in nature. While for the most part he did not hope to use the results of his observations to construct policies on specific issues such as deviance or employment, he was optimistic about the possibility of being able to explain shifting realities and thereby temper respectable fears.

The young Steffens conceived of himself as a teacher, an enlightener of the middle classes. (The unlearning of "myths" and half-truths acquired in school, and subsequent revelation to others of the fruits of true learning, is a recurring theme in the *Autobiography*.) As the son of a banker, he felt that he was in a unique position to mediate between radical labor groups and fearful, more conservative sections of the population. However, within a decade of his return to America in 1892, Steffens's belief that simple exposure of the corrupt links between business and politics would stimulate reform had given way to despair. He began to move toward the view that only revolution could rescue the American way of life, by destroying the corruption that swamped it and facilitating a complete reconfiguration of power. When communist-inspired revolutions shook Mexico and Russia, Steffens hastened to observe them. It was in the actions of Carranza and Lenin that Steffens saw the way to the renewal of America. "I have seen the future; and it works," he wrote to Marie Howe in 1919.[13] In short, it is this conviction that underpins *Moses in Red*. It is Steffens's offering to the 1920s debate about his country's destiny. Ostensibly a story about Russia and the ancient exodus, it remains a thoroughly American book.

The Bible and American Religion

Moses in Red opens with a lengthy discussion entitled "The Point of View,"[14] in which Steffens outlines sweeping themes: his theory of revolution, his views on reading the Bible, and the nature of true Christianity. It begins with an account of Arthur Ransome's suggestion that following the events in Russia all literature must be reread and assessed "in the Red Light of Revolution."[15] In Steffens's opinion, Ransome's words articulate a typical sentiment: "We all have had similar experiences. . . . [E]veryone that has lived through a deeply felt crisis either in his own or in the common life—a personal tragedy or a war, any disillusionment or any inspiring effort—has found his old favorites new—or dead. Our increased understanding sharpens our eyes and our ears for the seers and the prophets of old."[16] Everyone's experience and history teaches that person a living truth, and it is against this (rather than any received or book-learned wisdom) that literature, including the Bible, must be tested. Indeed, other forms of biblical scholarship are misfounded. Prefiguring postmodern approaches to the construction and interpretation of text, Steffens argues that any evaluation of the Bible that neglects the power of reader experience is in error. For him, the preoccupation of biblical scholars with textual and historical criticism betrays their shortsightedness. Caught up in petty details, they cannot appreciate the message or the cultural significance of the Bible. Similarly, the teachings of the churches fail to preach Christ because they are not grounded in the reality of life lived by the masses: "I soon ceased from expecting anything fundamental from the fundamentalists."[17]

When read against the experience of twentieth-century revolution, the story of Moses is held to "ring true": "Anyone who has gone through a revolution will recognize, not only the dramatis personae of the story, but the regular stages of its progress, the typical individual and mob psychology, the tragic disappointments and excesses, and the comic criticisms and excuses of every such crisis in the affairs of men."[18]

In summary, Steffens's thesis is that the Hebrew Bible story of the revolt and exodus of Israel is the history of a revolution and as such can both illuminate and be illuminated by the twentieth-century experience of communist uprising. Later I explore in more detail Steffens's overwhelming preoccupation with establishing analogies between politics ancient and modern. First, it is important to consider briefly the relationship between Lincoln Steffens's reading of the Bible and the readings of some other interpretive communities in his day.

No previous studies of Steffens's work relate *Moses in Red* to academic biblical interpretation. Steffens's reputation as a journalist and autobiographer is one reason that this dimension of the work is not taken seriously. His commentators have tended also to be drawn from these fields and therefore are generally not concerned to see how his book intersects with trends in the disciplines of theology or religious studies. Rather, the emphasis is on his credentials as a founding father of investigative reporting or of the modern, psychologizing biography. At the same time, scholars of religion have until relatively recently delineated the boundaries of their discipline in a way that has excluded the contributions of those who are deemed to be outside or marginal to "church" or "academy." Theological and religious studies have traditionally privileged certain kinds of texts and downplayed the contributions of women, the poor, and hosts of other nonprofessional critics who, like Steffens, Hurston, and DeMille, offer readings of the Bible not shaped according to the style and agenda of the academy.

However, Steffens's place in the history of biblical interpretation merits consideration. For Steffens scholars to ignore this aspect of his work is to overlook one of his most consistent concerns; he had an enduring interest in the Bible. At one point he considered writing a historical life of Jesus and read several of the other lives available at the time; some aspects of the presentation in *Moses in Red* are thrown into relief only by comparing them with conventional academic study of the Bible in the 1920s.[19] When reappraised from a religious studies perspective, Steffens's emphasis on the privileging of experience in biblical interpretation also shares much with some current hermeneutical approaches. *Moses in Red* provides an interesting example of an overtly political reading of the exodus, which, although it differs strongly from modern liberation theology in its pessimism about the capabilities of the masses and the emphasis on the person and role of Moses, nevertheless shares with liberationism a radical, programmatic dimension.[20]

Steffens presents his approach as standing against the work of his academic contemporaries:

> The higher critics might question phrases and passages, the scientific historians might declare the whole Book unproven. They could not move me. They are weak in their premises because they are limited in their inquiries. They depend upon old manuscripts and new-found texts; they search legal and official records and stand hard and fast upon the evidence of profane history, which is as unproved as the Biblical account of the trial of Jesus before Pilate. They overlook another source of evidence for Biblical, poetical and historical traditions and beliefs: the news of the day.[21]

This diatribe is so evocative of the early-twentieth-century debates surrounding the critical study of the biblical text that it is hard not to conclude that Steffens wrote with some of the lives of Jesus he had read in earlier years in mind. (Sadly, no list of these works survives.) However, when Steffens draws a contrast between the textual work of the higher critics and his own experience-based approach to the biblical text in *Moses in Red*, he is simplifying matters. In correspondence from 1923, Steffens refers to a visit or visits to Cambridge, England. Writing to Allen Suggett from London on 1 November, he describes the purpose of the journey, "to be near a library and some scholars who know bible texts and Old Testament lore and theories. It is for my *Moses*, which I'll finish this winter."[22] On 13 November he writes from "Alfredston," (possibly a misspelling of

Alpheton) in Suffolk. By 20 December he is in Cambridge, lodging at the Blue Boar Hotel, Trinity Street.[23] After the Christmas celebrations he tells Laura Suggett that while there he has "been . . . getting at books and men who tell me what is known about Moses"—perhaps in the university's divinity faculty, then located just a few yards from the Blue Boar.[24] Evidence thus suggests two trips to East Anglia in the winter of 1923, with at least one of them involving some time in Cambridge.

It is impossible to identify the men with whom Steffens met. Several of his date books have survived, but that for 1923 ends on 30 October, leaving no record of appointments during the crucial period.[25] A number of scholars were teaching Hebrew Bible in Cambridge during Michaelmas term 1923, including Nairne, Barnes, Kennett, Wood, McLean, Marsh, Cripps, and How.[26] Of these, Professor Kennett was lecturing on the composition of the Pentateuch, the topic with which *Moses in Red* is most obviously linked. But nothing in Steffens' book requires the author to have consulted him. A further possible contact is the dean of Sidney Sussex College, A. H. McNeile, author of one of the major English-language commentaries on Exodus. Some aspects of *Moses in Red* (in particular, the acceptance of the existence of different literary strata in the Pentateuch and the necessary existence of a strong leader such as Moses to effect a political feat like the biblical exodus) bear similarities to McNeile's,[27] but it is not possible to identify elements in the book that were necessarily gleaned from his work. In fact, unpublished correspondence from many years earlier remains the only definite link between Steffens and a contemporary biblical scholar, the Yale professor of biblical Hebrew, C. F. Kent.

In response to an article by Steffens about Christian social gospelers, Kent sent him a copy of his 1908 *The Student's Old Testament*. Kent employed modern "scientific criticism" (a phrase that would have appealed to Steffens) to the text of the Bible and presented the material in thematic collections, which were then further subdivided chronologically, under headings such as "Early Judean Prophetic," "Early Ephraimite Prophetic," and "Late Priestly." He denied that this approach undermined Christian faith, claiming that biblical traditions in large part derived their value from their reception, the use to which they were put by writers and teachers over the centuries. Kent was also optimistic about the extent to which a text that has undergone many revisions and additions might still preserve a record of human experience of the divine. Moreover, even an awareness of the extensive reworkings of the story of Moses during the "Late Priestly" era might deepen rather than detract from an appreciation of "the divinely gifted personality and far-reaching influence of the great prophet-leader, Moses."[28]

There are possible traces of the impact of Kent's research on the final form of *Moses in Red*. When Steffens writes:

> No doubt the priestly scribes, copyists and preachers edited copy, interpolating and cutting. We still do this sort of thing, and we do it better than the compilers of the old Books of Moses did it. They did not make clean copy. They left the scars of their blue pencils; they wrote a 'better' version of an incident and did not throw away the old one. The two or three accounts of some of the chief and most puzzling events, like that of the face-to-face meeting of Moses, the prophet, with God, remain quarrelling still in our text.[29]

he seems aware of some of the basic principles of source and redaction criticism, finding in the extant form of the biblical text evidence of an extended process of writing and editing of underlying narratives by different interest groups. The reference to the priests as being among the text's later redactors likewise evidences some familiarity with the findings of the historical-critical method. Most critics since Wellhausen place the priestly material (P) in the sixth century B.C.E., several hundred years later than the Pentateuch's other major sources, J, E, and D (ninth to seventh centuries B.C.E.).[30] Further incidental remarks support the idea that Steffens relies more than he cares to admit on biblical criticism. For example, he refers to the exodus and wilderness wandering as "the uprising, flight and reorganization of the Egyptian Jews."[31] This is, perhaps, an unusual turn of phrase to find used casually in a popular work like *Moses in Red*. The description of the liberated Jews as "Egyptian" may simply reflect Steffens's views on the extent of the conditioning undergone by those enslaved there.[32] It is hard for a displaced and enslaved people to resist the pressures of the oppressor-host's ideology and mores. Alternatively, Steffens may have been aware of the idea expressed some years earlier by McNeile, and later restated by Kennett and Albright, that not all those later known as Jews underwent the exodus experience.[33]

Thus, although Steffens claims to be unmoved by the historical critics of his own day, and even castigates their preference for minute textual study over experience-based readings of the Bible, he does not totally ignore the critical endeavor. Fundamentalists disliked the new criticism because of its challenge to belief in the literal revelation of scripture. In contrast, Steffens saw the biblical text as essentially reliable but found value in source and redaction criticism insofar as the interests of these disciplines coincided with his own conviction concerning the primacy of experience. Hence the approach of *Moses in Red* toward the biblical text at times bears some resemblance to that taken by several members of the Cambridge

University divinity faculty and to that of American scholar C. F. Kent, the only interpreter with whom Steffens can definitely be linked. However, some of the detailed conclusions of higher criticism, particularly its general pessimism about the historicity of the exodus event, are rejected in *Moses in Red* because the story "rings true" with Steffens's own experience of revolution in the modern context. Where "life" and "theory" contradict each other, the former must prevail: "Making every allowance for errors, priestcraft and politics in the Books of Moses, however, I hold to my [experientially driven] thesis that they give an essentially true account of a typical revolution."[34]

By the time *Moses in Red* was written, a significant minority of progressive theologians and preachers in America were advocates of the "social gospel." The social gospel movement was not defined institutionally or theologically, except in the very broadest of terms. In the late nineteenth and early twentieth centuries, it had followers in both Protestant and Catholic churches. Proponents stressed the practical implications of the Christian faith and the duty of believers to implement the Golden Rule as found in the Sermon on the Mount at Matthew 7:12, "So whatever you wish that men would do to you, do so to them" (RSV). The mission of the church was to build the kingdom of God on earth; hence divisions between thought and action, faith and works, and doctrine and deeds were to be rejected. Biblical understandings of justice should be applied without reserve to the modern social and economic order.

The concept of a Christian social order was, of course, not new. The social gospelers drew on earlier Christian social teachings as a means of tackling the particular problems inherent in an age of apparent spiritual and material revolution. But their convictions increasingly informed and were informed by the developing social sciences. Richard T. Ely, a founder of the American Economics Association (1886), was a social gospel advocate who contended that modern economics could be used to Christianize a society.[35] Social gospelers hoped that their programs would improve the fates of both society in general and their own religious communities in particular. The present social crisis was deemed to have damaged Christianity, as the poor became alienated from churches that increasingly blunted the message of Jesus in order to produce a religion palatable to the prosperous few. Although the social gospel was not an exclusively urban phenomenon, openly Christian commitment to progressive measures was in part viewed as a means of ensuring and demonstrating the continued relevance of the faith to a new, industrialized America.[36] "Religion, to have power over an age, must satisfy the highest moral and religious desires of that age. If it lags behind, and presents outgrown conceptions of life and duty, it is not longer in the full sense the Gospel," wrote Walter Rauschenbusch, most famous of the social gospel spokesmen.[37] The changes needed in the new environment were sweeping. Bold, systemic reform was better able to deal with the causes of injustice and poverty than the older strategy of piecemeal Christian philanthropy.

The social gospel's practical religion bears some resemblance to the approach Steffens advocates in *Moses in Red*. For Steffens, Jesus was a revolutionary anarchist: "The doctrine of Jesus is the most revolutionary propaganda that I have ever encountered. . . . Jesus denounced interest on money; He opposed the state; He was an anarchist, and His followers practised communism."[38] He also argues that the churches fail to preach Christ because they do not preach "revolution and social reform," nor do they teach the "love and understanding" that were "Christ's substitute for righteousness and force." Steffens believes that the churches' lack of attention to social problems is wrong not only in terms of what the Bible says but also in the light of modern social science, which has uncovered the impact of environment on the behavior of the individual: "If human acts have causes; not only reasons and not merely motives, but physical and social conditions to account for them, then Christ's commandment of infinite mercy, to judge not, is sound." These comments in *Moses in Red* are very much in line with the synthesis of traditional Christian belief and nascent sociology found in many social gospel texts.[39] Just as the gospelers argued for sympathy rather than stricture in dealing with the urban poor, so for Steffens the true imitators of Christ in modern America are not the Christian fundamentalists who condemn the immorality of the "lost" but the caring and practical social reformers he wrote about in his muckraking days.[40]

H. H. Stein's thesis notes several social gospel elements in Steffens's thought, including the fascination with the life of Jesus, whose original message for the poor and oppressed was seen as having been corrupted by the institution of the church, and the desire to build a just society. Stein concludes somewhat cautiously, "whether or not Lincoln Steffens was fully conscious of Social Gospel doctrines, what he offered was a conception of the Heavenly City of God on Earth."[41] This assessment of the writer's thought echos that made in Steffens's own day by *The Universalist Leader*, a journal of the American Universalists: "The Christian Church made Lincoln Steffens, and did a first rate job, for there is not one of the civic and social ideas which he embodies which was not preserved and taught by the church since ancient times."[42] Although Stein remains undecided as to whether Steffens was conversant with social gospel doctrines, there is strong evidence to suggest that he was. Many of the reformers Steffens encountered in his muckraking days were social gospel Christians. His 1909 book about them, *The Upbuilders*, has been characterized as depicting a "pantheon of political saints."[43] Steffens himself writes that the men exemplify "applied Christianity . . . putting into practice in actual life . . . the doctrine of faith, hope and charity." The description of Mark Fagan is typical: "The man is a Christian, a literal Christian; no mere member of a church, but a follower of Christ; no patron of organized charities but a giver of kindness, sympathy, love."[44]

Steffens did not simply write about the social gospelers. In numerous public addresses he joined their enterprise in seeking to offer not only a diagnosis of contemporary social problems but also something of a solution. One Bergen County, New Jersey newspaper reported how he had told the People's Congregational Church there that "until there is a unity of purpose for good and the acceptance of Christianity as the remedy there will be heartburns, dissensions and turmoil in all walks of life," but, on a more optimistic note, "you have it within your power to make Ridgfield Park a Heaven on Earth in about fifteen years." If the community lived according to the "principles laid down by the Nazarene" and united in faith, hope, and love, then they could achieve this utopia. The *Greenwich Graphic* reported a similar talk on "ideal politics" to a meeting of the Equal Franchise League. A sense of individual responsibility for others in the same community was the key to heavenly harmony.[45]

In addition to encouraging others, Steffens also engaged in practical theology. In 1910 he undertook what he would later characterize as an effort to apply the Golden Rule, by intervening in the sensational McNamara case: "I saw a chance to make an experiment with 'big, bad men' and with Christianity."[46] When two brothers, John and James McNamara, were accused of planting a bomb that killed twenty-one people in the Los Angeles *Times* building, Steffens attempted to achieve reconciliation between prosecution and defense by encouraging both parties to acknowledge their guilt. The McNamara brothers, who in more than one sense represented the laboring masses (John was secretary of the International Association of Bridge and Structural Ironworkers), must, Steffens argued, admit personal responsibility for the atrocity. The prosecution and victims, including the anti-union boss of the *Times*, must equally admit social guilt for abusing labor. Their contempt was forcing the masses into violent extremes to secure basic rights and conditions. Filler summarizes the rationale of the approach: "To Steffens it seemed that in standing behind a fiction of innocence, in demanding acquittal instead of telling the country why dynamitings occurred, the labor defenders lost something true and significant from their purposes and opened the way for lies that might finally enmesh them completely."[47] Steffens's involvement in the case was an extremely bold attempt to have social gospel principles applied directly to American public life. Although he had previously given a speech to the International Association of Chiefs of Police on the implementation of the Golden Rule in their work (through the humane treatment of prisoners, particularly juveniles and the homeless),[48] it was also his first such effort and, somewhat predictably, failed. The brothers changed their pleas to guilty, but the judge sentenced them to life imprisonment and called Steffens an interferer.

It is possible, then, to go further than Stein and say that Steffens certainly was conversant with the beliefs and thought of social gospel Christians. The fact that in the *Autobiography* he does not explicitly pay homage to their role in forming his own ideas does not preclude this conclusion. I noted earlier that in *Moses in Red* he chooses to present himself in opposition to traditional biblical scholarship, despite the fact that several aspects of his views on the final form of the Pentateuch are heavily indebted to the field. Steffens's self-important presentation of himself (in the *Autobiography* and elsewhere), as a lone discoverer of truths that he then reveals to others at (for them) life-changing moments, has long been recognized. He seemingly wished to guard against the possibility of posterity regarding him as merely a representative of what might be retrospectively deemed a trend and thus avoided explicitly identifying himself with one.

The verdict passed in the McNamara case did, however, mark the beginning of Steffens's disillusionment with the social gospel style of reform and hence his growing interest in revolution, which shapes *Moses in Red*. At a personal level, his ongoing association with the now convicted McNamara brothers made it harder to find mainstream publications willing to carry his work after 1910,[49] and his public speeches were monitored and sometimes terminated by federal agents and the police during the sensitive war years.[50] Always striving to place the emphasis on life experience rather than abstract theory, Steffens was convinced by the failure of his own practical "experiment" that the type of evolutionary reforming change envisioned by the Christian reformers could not achieve their end goal of a free and just society. Steffens's program accordingly shifted from Christ-inspired reform to more revolutionary action tinged with or justified by "biblical" principles. Thus while the approach in *Moses in Red* bears some superficial resemblances to the social gospel ideas its author held in earlier years, its core impulse is qualitatively quite different, as shown in the next section.

Finally, it is important to note Steffens's enduring ambivalence concerning the objective reality of God, which meant that even in the muckraking, reforming days, he could use social gospel ideas but should not be considered a true social gospel Christian. For Steffens, although "the theologians dispute whether to read it [the accounts of God's role in Exodus] literally or symbolically," "that makes no essential difference" to his own program. Like Ransome, Steffens believes that stories can have a power or a truth about them whether or not they are literally or factually correct. He is quite happy, should it please the reader, to "let Jehovah personify and speak for Nature"[51] in the sense of laws and processes that regulate the human and natural worlds. The eternal story or pattern matters most to him, not the characters who happen to be featured in any one of its configurations.

Politics

"All things considered, Moses in Red is a blemish on Steffens's record, both as literature and as political theory."[52] To make sense of these words, it is necessary to locate both book and author in the context of early Soviet-American relations. Horton's singeing criticism of Moses in Red is typical of the book's reception on either side of the Atlantic. Following Lenin's rise to power in November 1917, Western Europe and North America quickly swapped initial ambivalence for suspicion and then condemnation of the nascent Communist state in Russia.[53] This sea change had several causes. At the start of war in 1914, Czarist Russia was one of the Allied Powers. But Lenin concluded a separate peace with the Germans in the Treaty of Brest-Litovsk (March 1918): his Bolsheviks had promised the ordinary Russians "Peace, Land, and Bread." To protect stockpiles of Allied supplies and encourage the counterrevolutionary forces, fourteen Allied nations sent troops into eastern Russia. (American military forces would remain on Russian soil until April 1920.) The end of the war brought little improvement. The Paris Peace Conference (January 1919) participants sent the Bullitt mission (of which Steffens was a member) to Moscow to take soundings on Lenin's position, only to decide in the mission's absence that there would be no cooperation with the new regime.[54]

At a popular level, a distrustful attitude toward indigenous sympathizers of Lenin and his successors echoed the government position. In Connecticut, a salesman was sent to jail for calling Lenin "brainy"; evangelist Billy Sunday advocated lining socialists up before a firing squad. An Indiana jury took just two minutes to acquit an individual who had killed a "communist" man because he said, "To hell with the United States."[55] This anti-Communist "patriotism," which peaked first in the 1920s and later during the Cold War, helped propagate negative views of Steffens's work because he failed to replicate the often unthinking rhetoric of the age. One contemporary newspaper accused Steffens of "running a nursery for Revolutions."[56] He was the "Pied Piper of the Kremlin."[57] As the century progressed, *Moses in Red* was cited as evidence of how the Bolsheviks had transformed Steffens "from an ardent crusader for a better and wider democracy into America's foremost prophet of democracy's doom," although little account was ever offered of how this change had been effected.[58] At this time, anyone whose work appeared to actively support or simply defend the Communist experiment was automatically labeled as a dangerous subversive. As Cohen notes in his study of American foreign policy: "As Conservatives attempted to roll back the New Deal, especially labor gains, they appealed to fear of radicalism, labeled everything they disliked radicalism, everyone who opposed them a Communist, and blurred the lines between democratic socialism and communism, even between liberalism and communism."[59]

The image of a pro-Communist Steffens was also promoted by several of his many prominent intellectual and literary heirs.[60] A number of writers were to claim in later life that reading Steffens's *Autobiography* as young men had transformed them from liberals to committed upholders of the Soviet regime. Notable among them was Granville Hicks, the coeditor of Steffens's letters in 1938.[61] The two-volume collection of correspondence Hicks and Winter produced stands second only to the *Autobiography* in the influence it has had on the shaping of the academic and public memory of Lincoln Steffens. Although Hicks suggested elsewhere that Steffens was not a Communist,[62] the editorial decisions made when collecting the *Letters* have portrayed Steffens as staunchly loyal to the Soviet cause, particularly in later life. This image of the writer has rarely been questioned, because it seemingly accords with the experiences of the editors themselves: If Steffens himself were not a committed Communist, how could his writings have possibly inspired Communist commitment in some of his readers?

With both vociferous detractors and vocal supporters suggesting that Steffens was a Communist, it is hardly surprising that in the Cold War context even neutral figures found little to praise in the politics of *Moses in Red*. Walzer judged the essence of *Moses in Red* to be "a defense of Leninist politics" and "a complete vindication of Leninist politics, that is, of dictatorship and terror,"[63] and likewise Wildavsky, for whom Steffens "sought to defend Lenin and the Bolshevik revolution against charges of cruel ex-cess by arguing that they had done no worse than Moses."[64] To characterize the politics of Moses in Red in this fashion and identify its rationale as such is, however, to miss its emphasis.

Methodologically speaking, there are problems inherent in reading attitudes in the Autobiography and final correspondence into work of an earlier decade. Much divides the Steffens who wrote Moses in Red from the author of the Autobiography, including the failure of Moses in Red itself; the end of a long-term affair with Gussie Burgess, with whom he lived while working on the book; and marriage to Ella Winter and the birth of a son, Peter Stanley.[65] The published Letters are also problematic as indicators of Steffens's political views. The discussion has already demonstrated how editorial decisions, which, for example, excluded from the public domain much of the material pertaining to Steffens's use of biblical criticism and social gospel ideas and his general interest in Christianity, may mislead analysts. This is true also of Steffens's politics. The basis for a more nuanced assessment of the political viewpoint of Moses in Red must ultimately be a reading of the book itself, viewed without either the anti-Communist hysteria of the Cold War or the wish to find celebrity precedent for one's own political persuasions.

It is clear that Steffens moved in Marxist and Communist circles in America and Europe. Toward the end of his life, in private and in public, he undeniably called for propaganda on the Soviet behalf, signing an open letter backing the Communist presidential ticket in 1932.[66] But this cannot predetermine a reading of Moses in Red, particularly when set beside more ambiguous statements from the same period: "I am not a Communist. I merely think that the next order of society will be socialist and that the Communists will bring it in."[67] Do such words imply that Steffens was a Communist, or that the evidence this self-styled "scientist" of the social realm read off world events suggested that this form of political organization would become dominant? (By 1932 even Britain had flirted with socialist, or Labour, government.)

In the years following the McNamara dispute, a disillusioned Steffens found temporary refuge in New York's Greenwich Village, described by a contemporary as a place where "a woman could say 'damn' right out loud and still be respected."[68] It was here that Steffens participated in the discussion groups hosted by Mabel Dodge. Dodge's Fifth Avenue salon near Washington Square served as a hothouse for the Village's nascent radicals; its coterie included Louise Bryant and John Reed, Carl Van Vechten, Max Eastman, Emma Goldman, and Sinclair Lewis.[69] At a time when Steffens was increasingly convinced of the necessity for more fundamental solutions to the problems of modern urban life, the revolutionary ideas of the circle and the two giants they debated, Marx and Freud, inevitably exerted an influence. In later years, Steffens was to trace to the Dodge salon the origins of his ideas concerning the impact of the environment on the individual and the conviction that social problems must be actively tackled and not simply described.[70] "Made a radical by Christianity, Marx and Freud helped make Steffens a gentle revolutionary," judges Palermo.[71] For Winter and Hicks, "The reformer, who had turned to the study of revolutions, now became a believer in revolution as the only way to make 'all reforms' possible."[72]

These new interests were what sent Steffens to Mexico and Russia. He was alive to the failures and errors of both actions but remained convinced that as practical-experimental examples of attempts to overhaul societies, they provided the nearest thing there was to a blueprint for change in America. "The revolutions . . . especially the Russian—offered an opportunity to see how far men can get with their attempt to change the foundation instead of the superstructure of society."[73]

The Mexican revolution (1910) enjoyed only limited success. Its early leader, Francesco I. Maduro, was unable to manage factional divisions within the revolutionary party. After his murder in 1913, America intervened, to see Venustiano Carranza introduce a new liberal constitution in 1917. Perhaps because of its failure, little attention has been focused on Steffens's treatment of the Mexican revolt. However, it does provide two points relevant to the discussion of the political motivations behind *Moses in Red*. First, Steffens's study of the Mexican revolution suggests a general (what Steffens would have termed "scientific") interest in revolution per se, rather than in any of its particular manifestations. Second, Steffens's response to Mexico offers insight into the determining factors governing the production of his political viewpoint. When Steffens became interested in revolution, it was, as has been argued, for profoundly pragmatic reasons. Disillusioned by the failure of the practical experiment in reform (the McNamara case), he turned to more radical options. In his willingness to consider Marxist ideas about revolution as the only means of achieving a just and equitable society, Steffens was once again seeking to revise his earlier theories about the power of reform in the light of experience. This pragmatism always applied to Steffens's revolutionary theory. As in religious thought, "life-experience" should take precedence in political thinking. The experience-based approach of *Moses in Red* ultimately derides Marxists who will not do likewise and who resist any suggestion that they alter their doctrines in view of actual twentieth-century events. To reject an uprising because it occurs in a backward agrarian country rather than a sophisticated urbanized one and is therefore "not according to Marx" is ridiculous. If revolution does not occur in a highly urbanized and industrialized society, then the Marxist theory should be changed—not the revolution dismissed as invalid. Steffens cleverly turns the arguments of inflexible Marxists on themselves, justifying his approach because Marx himself changed his theories after observing the Paris Commune.[74]

In short, the evidence suggests that the simple dismissal of *Moses in Red* as Soviet propaganda is unfounded, as it fails to attend to Steffens's ambivalence on the political question. Although this finding may be intellectually "messy" or unsettling, it is arguably not surprising to discover that an author whose thought was so self-consciously grounded in experience as Steffens did not fall as squarely into any political camp as some of his commentators have suggested. As a pragmatist, Steffens could never have argued for a consistent Marxist program.

Kaplan points the way to a more reasoned analysis of *Moses in Red* when he notes that it was not the Russianness of the Bolshevik revolution but its universal aspects that interested Steffens.[75] Reconfiguration of power in society might be achieved in several ways, and Steffens's interest was to discern and analyze these ways (his beloved scientific method.) The prime purpose of *Moses in Red* is not, as was believed amid the anti-Bolshevik paranoia of the mid-1920s, to justify or defend uncritically the Russian revolution in particular but rather to understand that revolution as a "type" of human event and to discover its laws and modes of operation. This is the spirit of the lengthy "Point of View," which opens the book, with its abstracted generalizations about democracy and dictatorship and the origins of revolution.[76] Likewise, the main body of the book is not concerned with postrevolutionary attainment of an end goal, or the detailed legislation of Moses or the Soviet, but with the mechanics of revolution itself, the means by which revolutionary leaders are made and achieve their ends.[77]

To repeat, *Moses in Red* is a comparison that seeks to comprehend the dynamics of the biblical events and the Russian events and, from those, to move to an understanding of the principles of revolution in general. It is not a defense of the particularities of the Russian revolution by recourse to the biblical account.

Two particularities of the Russian revolution are frequently cited by Steffens's critics as indicating that *Moses in Red is* designed to function in its defense. These are readily identified in the earlier quote from Walzer's *Exodus and Revolution* as being "Leninist politics" and "dictatorship and terror." To support a reading of *Moses in Red* as a general treatise on revolution, it is therefore important briefly to consider how Steffens handles these two elements in the book.

Steffens certainly respected Lenin. Although dead by the time Steffens completed the manuscript, in *Moses in Red* he is presented as a living presence, a forceful, thoughtful speaker, whose words can persuade and enlighten. This is no mean accolade, especially from the pen of a man who, as a rule, liked to present himself in the guise of educator and instructor.[78] Lenin's ability to navigate the storm of revolution is contrasted favorably with the floundering attempts of his Mexican counterparts.[79] However, close reading of Steffens's analysis of the reasons for Lenin's success suggests that Lenin's actual function in *Moses in Red* is as evidence for the value of the author's own work. Lenin's greatest virtue is that he embarked on revolution armed not only with bullets but also with history books. "I never had with them [leaders of the Russian revolution] a conversation in which they did not refer to revolutionary history, and especially the French," claims Steffens.[80] In a key passage, Lenin is crucially presented as acknowledging the importance for the Bolsheviks of knowledge of revolutionary theory and practice: "What we need is a revision of all our theories in the light of the war, the peace and this and the other revolutions." The Russian leader concedes that as a man of action he has little time to study: "But if there were scientific men outside in America, England—Europe— they could look on and they could study, think, and tell us. We need criticism. The captains in all crises really need the counsel of the wise, thoughtful, sympathetic observers safely, quietly out of the storm center."[81] Here is a smoothly introduced defense of the apparent inaction for which Steffens and the rest of the Greenwich Village intelligentsia were so frequently derided.[82] As a rejoinder to those who criticized "armchair socialists," its message is that the writing of a book such as *Moses in Red* is not only justified but also required by those who seek to effect revolutionary change. Only the relatively detached analysis of someone like Steffens can do the necessary preparatory work for a successful revolution. To a large extent, Steffens's presentation of Lenin in *Moses in Red* seems intended to serve the author's own self-justificatory ends, rather than to praise Lenin.

For Steffens, in revolutions as in other forms of human activity, laws are of prime importance. Those individuals who learn the lessons of history and sociology may achieve temporary, dependent power. Lenin was only one example of such a figure. Elsewhere, Steffens gives praise to Mussolini, who has also read history, "not as the scholars do, for love of a growing body of knowledge . . . but as men of action, reading a record of human experimentation to find out what can be done and how."[83] Henry Ford is for him "a prophet without words, a reformer without politics, a legislator, statesman—a radical."[84] Someone capable of so praising Ford and Mussolini could hardly be termed an unswerving defender of specifically Leninist politics.[85]

On turning to the treatment of the terror of the Russian revolution, here, too, Steffens attempts to offer the kind of sympathetic criticism for which he has Lenin call in *Moses in Red*. Steffens felt that the evil of revolution (likened to the slaughter of the firstborn) was less bad than the horrors of the world war, which had killed and maimed indiscriminately: "In a war all the youth that are male go, and there are not only the killed but the wounded also; and the killed and wounded are sometimes all of one family, none of another, so that the makers of the war and the profiteers therefrom are rarely the sufferers. A war is a disorderly, long, miscellaneous, often indecisive process of killing, maiming, and destroying."[86] This same justification is placed on Lenin's lips by Steffens in the discussion of the so-called Red Terror (the victimization and murder of officials of the old regime, the wealthy, clergy, and others, which began in September 1918), rumors of which had so disturbed the allies at the Paris Peace Conference.[87] Steffens adds that horror appears to be an inescapable feature of revolution. However, this does not imply the kind of ruthless or bloodthirsty demeanor that Walzer suggests. Steffens stresses that revolutionary leaders do not always order atrocities, "they also deplore them." While deploring them, the role of the responsible revolutionary theorist such as Steffens himself is not to shy away from these events but to analyze and examine them dispassionately, with the ultimate hope that "perhaps, when they are understood scientifically, they can be avoided."[88]

To conclude this brief analysis of the political motivations behind *Moses in Red*, it would be naïve to claim that Steffens did not see the Russian revolution as extremely significant for both Europe and the Americas. It is possible, though, to hold that Steffens believed the uprising to be of fundamental importance, yet at the same time questioning the older consensus that interpreted *Moses in Red* as a straightforward piece of Communist propaganda. In the face of reform's failure, Steffens believed that only revolution could succeed in clearing the ground in readiness for the regeneration of American society. The Russian revolution was significant as the most radical (and in Steffens's day, most effective) attempt at sweeping away a corrupt system and restructuring a society on more egalitarian lines. He was embittered by his own fate at the hands of Western democrats (shortly after the Paris Peace Conference, he was excluded from Britain by Lloyd George, and joked that he could not leave France for America until the jails were more comfortable). It is hardly surprising that Steffens believed "Russia is an oasis now of hope in a world of despair."[89]

In an unpublished manuscript, "The Great Expectation," Steffens even voiced these sentiments in quasi-religious terms:

> First John; then Jesus. First the Kingdom; then, the King. First the people shall set up an order in which Christianity will be practicable; then and not till then, will the Christ come. . . . The Revolution was due all the people of low degree in the world. . . . This is the light which the gentle beast, the Russian mob, holds up shining in the darkness which will not, cannot comprehend: Love is possible. Make it possible. Peace can be. Let it be. Christ is coming. Prepare ye his way.[90]

The Paris Peace Conference indicated to Steffens that the old corrupt regimes remained intact in Europe and America, the eventual settlement being a "treaty of peace that was full of war,"[91] but as the previous passage suggests, he was far too pragmatic and far too influenced by social gospel ideas to advocate a purely communist solution to the problems of industrialized society. Indeed, he was too much a pragmatist to advocate any detailed program. *Moses in Red* is a treatise on the nature of revolution and an assertion of the value of those who, like Steffens, are equipped to do no more than seek to understand that nature.

Finally, the conclusion that *Moses in Red* does not attempt to provide a detailed political program for a new society sheds light on one of the puzzles inherent in the book itself—that is, why Moses? As has been noted already, Steffens believed Jesus to be the revolutionary anarchist par excellence,[92] whereas his initial impulse was to liken Moses to a reformer like Tom Johnson or William U'Ren (social activists profiled in *The Upbuilders*), an assessment still in evidence as late as 1925 in the correspondence to Gilbert Roe. Steffens was also aware of the problems inherent in classing as revolutionary a figure upon whose legislation some of the most conservative regimes had claimed to base their rule.[93] The commandments reflect patriarchal assumptions about the genders and accord high status to personal property, which causes difficulties for all those seeking precedent for radical politics in the Pentateuch. Nevertheless, Steffens chose Moses and not Jesus for his study of revolution. The reasons for this decision are several.

A survey of Steffens's treatment of Jesus (in *Moses in Red*, the prewar social gospel style of addresses, and during the McNamara case) indicates that it was the content of Jesus' program that fascinated him—opposition to the state, interest on money, and so on. For Steffens, these elements constitute the kingdom of God. But in *Moses in Red* Steffens is not dealing with "content" but with "form"—that is, with the characteristics and development of the phenomenon of revolution, rather than the details of any one particular revolutionary program. His program is merely to describe how humans act together to change society. The biblical exodus can clearly serve this purpose as an example of an actual reconfiguration of power. The exodus offers a far clearer picture of a liberating revolution, if not of a revolutionary leader or program, than the Gospels, where the death of Jesus is certainly perceived as liberating, but not in a way that humans may readily imitate, and where Jesus' teachings, although if implemented imply an overturning of the status quo, are not explicitly presented as such.

As a further ground for Steffens's selection of Moses rather than Jesus, it is also vital to refer back to the significant history of use of the exodus story in American political and social self-consciousness as discussed in chapter 1 of this book. Steffens was aware of this and most likely saw consequent merit in using the exodus story in his attempt to retail an understanding and acceptance of revolution to the American public.

Moses in Red is thus far from being a simple fable. Nor is it a mere piece of communist propaganda. Between its covers, Steffens is attempting to both conduct and justify a scientific examination of the phenomenon of revolution. By juxtaposing the birth of the Bolshevik state, already seen as anathema to all things American, with the story of Moses, which had for so long formed a vital element in American self-understanding and public discourse, he sought to stimulate in the American public a sense of the inevitability and the worth of revolution. To repeat an earlier claim, far from being a book about Russia, *Moses in Red* is a thoroughly American work.

Reception

In the introduction to this chapter, I described the failure of *Moses in Red* to attract a broad readership in either America or Europe. The first review of *Moses in Red* appeared in the British Labour party's *Daily Herald*. It was written by the paper's foreign correspondent, Norman Ewer, an associate of Steffens.[94] In fact, most of the book's reviews were written by Steffens's sympathizers. As such, they were somewhat bland and uncritical. Typical in style are the notices that appeared in the *Miami Herald*: "The only new thing I have seen in Socialist literature in many years": the *Emporia* (*Kansas*) *Gazette*: "*Moses in Red* is a pointed, unexcited, clear-visioned little book. And so long live Lincoln Steffens and his bright red fountain pen"; and the *San Francisco Call*: "*Moses in Red* is amazing, stimulating, convincing, a typical product of one of the most interesting thinkers of today." *Current History* shared Steffens's perspective, concluding a discussion of the book with the conviction that: "If the believers in the Bible could be led to grasp what it says so plainly, then perhaps . . . we might all of us really righteously face together the universal foe, ignorance, and gradually, by evolution, not revolution, reach, recognize and be fit to live long in the Promised Land, a heaven on earth."[95] While supportive, such praises could do little to introduce the book to the general public and broaden its readership beyond liberal to left-wing circles. The only remotely critical review, with the exception of the *New York Herald-Tribune*, which cautioned that "the analogy [Israel-Russia] is sometimes pressed too far,"[96] was that of Rabbi Stephen Wise, twice president of the American Jewish Congress.[97] For Wise, both the title and the contents of Steffens's book were "lurid." "*Moses in Red* is an attempt bizarre, withal not insignificant, to show that revolutions are of a piece, inevitable," he declared. Wise's analysis of the book was not blindly critical but insightful. Although the point was undeveloped, he did suggest that for Steffens "Moses is Lenin rather than Lenin Moses," picking up on the subtle implications of the book's subtitle, *The Revolt of Israel as a Typical Revolution.* (Revolution, and not Israel, is the referrent.) Wise also notes, "The book is in a manner of apologia for the old muckraking of the author" (again, recalling the suggestion that Steffens's portrayal of Lenin, for example, was shaped by the author's desire to defend his own apparent "inactivity" regarding the practical implementation of his revolutionary theories). Nevertheless, at a fundamental level, Wise was not able to accept Steffens's thesis on revolution, finding insurmountable problems in his perceived defense of Soviet violence and apparent dismissal of the Pentateuch's halakhic content.

Although all but four hundred copies of the book were destroyed in a warehouse fire, there was no reprinting, and *Moses in Red* remained out of print for more than thirty years until the collection *The World of Lincoln Steffens* made it once more accessible to readers in 1962.[98] Even Wise's criticisms (the closest thing to the book being savaged by a bishop, as Steffens had hoped it would be) failed to spark a lucrative controversy.[99]

Surprisingly few scholars have attempted to offer a real analysis of the reasons for the book's early critical and popular failure. Horton comes closest with his enigmatic remark that "*Moses in Red* simply came too late to be well received (although it could be argued it came too early)."[100] He suggests that following the end of World War I there was a general desire to forget the past, and so interest in the Bolshevik revolution was in decline by the time *Moses in Red* appeared in 1926. Likewise, the book was too early because it appeared when capitalism seemed to present few problems to the ordinary citizen. If Steffens had written such a work in the later

1920s or early 1930s, when severe economic depression was experienced in North America and Europe, his revolutionary program might have attracted more support.

Horton's suggestions are interesting but perhaps not entirely accurate. First, it is debatable whether a 1920s readership would have regarded the Russian revolution as a past event that bore no relevance in the postwar world. Certainly, the 1920s were popularly conceived of as a new age, but the evidence points to a sustained interest in the new Soviet state. Second, Horton's analysis generally appears to rest on the interpretation of *Moses in Red* as a call to popular, communist-inspired revolution, which might find favor with the masses in time of economic depression but was unlikely to meet with much success in a period of expansion and prosperity. The arguments against such an understanding of *Moses in Red* have already been rehearsed. It may be further emphasized that Steffens's account of revolution is hardly one that gives hope and encouragement to the "masses." He is overwhelmingly pessimistic about the abilities of ordinary people to achieve their own liberation, believing it impossible for them to break from the mental and emotional shackles of their exploited past.[101] Writing of the golden calf in Exodus, Steffens notes:

> The Children of Israel were going back to their old gods, the gods of Egypt, which may seem petty and altogether foolish in our unaccustomed eyes. But it is little things and foolish that a people see or miss and care about, not the big things. . . . It was little things that the Russian people lacked and yearned for in the Russian exodus: trading and the gossip in the marketplace; the sight of the rich and the gifts of their charities; a Tsar to bow down to and petition with prayer.[102]

To borrow Horton's language, *Moses in Red* came too late, not because the American public had ceased to be interested in Russia but because American attitudes toward the new state had changed from recognition and support to mistrust and condemnation. Kaplan quotes Woodrow Wilson's initial welcoming of the Russian revolution: "it [the autocratic rule of the Tsars] has been shaken off and the great, generous Russian people have been added in all their naive majesty and might to the forces that are fighting for freedom in the world, for justice and peace."[103] In contrast, by 1926 the American consensus was that the new Russian state represented the greatest existent threat to freedom, justice, and peace. In this climate, a work such as *Moses in Red* that presented the Russian revolution in a sympathetic light was hardly likely to be well received.

Horton's preconceptions about Steffens's politics were shared by much of the general public in 1920s America, and this is perhaps the most significant reason for the failure of *Moses in Red*. As noted earlier, Steffens's intervention in the McNamara case and his association with Lenin earned him the suspicion of many in America, including many among his potential readership. Already dismissed as a Bolshevik sympathizer, Steffens was unlikely to obtain a fair hearing from mainstream society.

Steffens himself placed a lot of emphasis on the importance of reviews when he attempted to understand the lack of success of *Moses in Red*. The letter to Jo Davidson quoted at the start of this chapter suggests that he believed a sensational review would stimulate interest. Reviews are frequently an important element in generating public awareness of a book. The lack of review interest in *Moses in Red* in part stems from Steffens's reputation as a radical, which made mainstream publications reluctant to handle his work. However, it is hard to convincingly attribute the failure of *Moses in Red* solely to negative "prejudice" on the part of the potential readership.

A series of unpublished letters held now by Columbia University indicate that long before *Moses in Red* was published, it was the subject of a controversy more intense than that engendered by any of the 1926 reviews. Having finished writing the book in early 1924 (shortly after Lenin's death), Steffens began to search for a company willing to publish it, initially hoping that it could appear in serial form in *Century Magazine*. Glen Frank, the magazine's editor, accepted but then sent a telegram in late October 1924 stating, "cannot serialize or publish Moses."[104] Despite his diplomatic suggestion that a revision of *Moses in Red* was required so that the book could be "as big as its underlying conception," the explanatory letter Frank sent on the same day indicated that it was not he but the managing board of the magazine who were unwilling to be associated with the project.[105] So, when *Moses in Red* finally appeared through Dorrance and Co. some two years later it already possessed a troubled history. A letter from Albert and Charles Boni additionally cautioned Steffens that any book issued though Dorrance "is started off under a severe handicap."[106] The choice of a subsidy publisher was an unhappy move on Steffens's part, necessitated by the refusal of larger publishers to handle a "revolutionary" piece. Despite the appearance of buoyancy upon *Moses in Red*'s publication, Steffens and his close friends were aware that the reading public might be similarly unsympathetic. Their correspondence discussing projected perceptions of the book points the way toward a realistic assessment of its failure. Arthur Ransome tried to interest English publishers in *Moses in Red*, but embarrassed rejection letters claimed that it was too audacious for them to accept.[107] Edward Filene attempted to promote the book in a covert manner and liaised with Dorrance and Co. over the organization of a list of syndicated columnists and others to whom review copies might be sent. Even he, however, felt a need for discretion and was uneasy about his association with *Moses in Red*. In a letter bemoaning an error that had resulted in some of his most conservative acquaintances being sent a copy of the book, he asserted that "it will probably result in their being afraid of me for the rest of my life because they will not understand the book which will offend all their folklore thinking."[108]

If Steffens's book is compared with a contemporary work in the same genre that *was* successful, further evidence emerges to suggest that Filene's assessment of *Moses in Red* was correct. Steffens's representation of the Moses story differed too greatly from popular perceptions of the meaning of the Exodus-Deuteronomy narrative (specifically, its meaning for American society) to be well received. Bruce Barton's 1925 *The Man Nobody Knows* was a huge success, selling a quarter of a million copies in its first eighteen months. Its popularity prompted a sequel, *The Book Nobody Knows*, and earned for Barton the role of consultant for the DeMille film *The King of Kings*.[109]

Analyzing *The Man* and *Moses in Red*, it is clear that, stylistically speaking, the authors of both are at times anecdotal and somewhat overbearing. The two works are also remarkably similar in structure, in that they both draw simplified parallels between the career of a key biblical character (Jesus or Moses) and a major current phenomenon (capitalism or revolution). Indeed, Barton's comparison of Jesus' ministry with modern capitalism often seems far more tenuous than Steffens's attempts in *Moses in Red*. Jesus was, he argues, "the founder of modern business." That he conceived of himself as a businessman is evidenced by his words on being discovered in the Temple as a boy (Luke 2:49); modern business philosophy is in reality grounded in his teachings, particularly in the Sermon on the Mount, which is portrayed as the root of the modern shopkeeper's "we're here to serve you!"[110]

Despite resemblances of style and structural arrangement, significantly different spirits animated *The Man* and *Moses in Red*. Bruce Barton's treatment of the biblical story did not challenge middle-class America but reassured it. In Filene's terms, Barton upheld "folklore thinking." By tracing its capitalist qualities back to Jesus, *The Man* claims for America an identity as a truly Christian society. In the words of one scholar, "Barton legitimizes big business, both for himself and for his audience, by finding a precedent in the Christian doctrine of individuality and Jesus' 'life of service.'"[111] *Moses in Red*, by contrast, presents as Bible-like the Russian revolution, an event felt by the majority to be profoundly un-American. It is easy to see how attractive a work such as Barton's might be at a time when Americans were becoming increasingly aware of the injustices and unrest in their society, through the growth of mass media and the social sciences. Here was reassuring evidence that, far from losing its way, American civilization had finally reached the point of fully embodying the teachings of Jesus. Here was an argument for an end to soul searching and the need for change, a statement in favor of the status quo. In contrast, Steffens's *Moses in Red* demanded a radical rethinking of the nature of American life. It suggested that America could no longer be considered the new Israel and that its special status as God's chosen nation had been lost to Russia. The idea that America had lost its identity as the land of freedom and liberty made unpalatable, unpopular reading.

The earlier part of the Cold War period in particular saw a partial revival of (negative) interest in Steffens and his "Russian" writings. During this era, the Soviet Union was demonized in North American public life, and with it, so were its Western sympathizers.[112] Steffens's exaggerated reputation as a communist meant that he attracted some especially vehement criticism. Setting aside one rather insipid use of *Moses in Red* in a composite work that aimed to recount "the legends of Moses" with elaborations and interpretations drawn from a variety of eras and contexts, the book's Cold War fortunes can be described only as poor.[113]

For von Mohrenschildt, "deliberately, dogmatically, Steffens accepted the Russian Communist dogma and tactics based on the proposition that the end justifies the means, while remaining naïve and uncritical about Soviet realities." He had once been a figure worthy of considerable respect, but "the major effect of his Russian experience was to blunt Steffens' critical faculties."[114] Rollins characterized Steffens as a writer who "had little to offer, except cynicism" and was "blinded to the complexity and frustration of life." He analyzed the modern experience only to draw "sterile conclusions."[115] Writing as recently as 1990, Pipes claimed that Steffens should be grouped with Upton Sinclair and others as a "mediocre writer" who toed the Communist party line, and in consequence "became a celebrity and even a best-selling author."[116] This remark is inaccurate. *Moses in Red* did not achieve celebrity or financial gain for Steffens. The book did not halt the decline in his popularity that began with the failed intervention in the McNamara case and was reversed only by the success of the *Autobiography* in 1931.

All the scholars whose negative assessments of the politics behind *Moses in Red* were discussed in the previous section wrote during this same Cold War era. A major cause of Cold War criticism of *Moses in Red* in particular (and Steffens in general) was the apparent emphasis it placed on the strong leader figure, be it Moses, Lenin, or Mussolini. In a post-Hitler,

Stalinist world, strong leadership of the type that Steffens advocated was associated with the horrendous slaughter of innocent millions and the curtailment of the basic human rights of those who survived. Steffens was criticized for posthumously supporting such activities.

This Cold War analysis of Steffens is logically understandable but does not do him justice. It is worth recalling that Steffens emphasized the value of a strong revolutionary leader as what seemed to him to be at the time the most effective manner of achieving the objective of a just and equitable society, which he so desired. Throughout his intellectual career, Steffens adapted his ideas in response to actual events. It is perhaps, then, inaccurate to claim with certainty that he would have retained his support for dictator figures in the light of the Holocaust and the Stalinist persecutions of the 1930s, through the 1950s. Not until the year of Steffens's death (1936) did news of Stalin's persecution of Bolshevik heroes at home and abroad reach the American public. When it did, the American left was split into those who defended or did not condemn events versus those who opposed them. Steffens's associates aligned themselves with both parties (Granville Hicks and Max Eastman, respectively).[117] There is considerable evidence that where Steffens was aware of acts of barbarity and oppression (i.e., in the light of his "life experience"), he reconsidered his political philosophy on leadership, changing his views on Mussolini and vociferously condemning Hitler's fascism. Stalin's nonaggression pact with Hitler in 1939 may well have prompted a similar reconsideration of the Soviet reality. As the Cold War recedes, scholars may be able to undertake far more nuanced and less overtly prejudiced studies of figures such as Steffens, and new assessments of *Moses in Red* will be offered.

Conclusions

This chapter has told the story of Lincoln Steffens's 1926 book, *Moses in Red*. On the one hand, it has offered an interpretation of *Moses in Red* and of the hermeneutical strategies its author employed in writing it. However, the story of *Moses in Red* is not just the tale of Steffens's personal engagement with the exodus narrative. It is also the story of an encounter between Steffens's readership (actual and potential) and his text. As much as a story of writing and authorial intention, it is also one of reading and production-in-use (or of nonreading and production-through-neglect).

Responses to *Moses in Red* have been overwhelmingly oppositional. Either the book has been ignored, or it has been criticized (to a large extent unfairly) as a simple fable or crude piece of communist propaganda. This fraught reception history (I hope) suggests several things of importance for this study as a whole, for, while this manuscript resembles a series of extended essays (and may be read as such), if the arguments in them are in some way successful, then they will suggest a larger narrative pattern.

Most obviously, exploration of *Moses in Red* provides evidence of the continued but contested importance of the Moses story in modern American social and political discourse. As an account of a this-worldly redemption effected by humans themselves, the exodus story is particularly appropriate as a precedent for all who (like Steffens) seek to encourage people's efforts toward change. For those who aim to preserve the status quo, the story can also justify their position (as Steffens is well aware.) In this case the role of Moses as legislator rather than as revolutionary leader is exaggerated.[118] These tensions of interpretation are inherent within Exodus-Deuteronomy, which shows Moses in a variety of functions and guises. Hence arguments about the text's political implications will persist throughout the period covered by this study.

Moreover, the issues surrounding the reception of *Moses in Red* begin to illuminate the nature of the communally determined limits to what are deemed "acceptable" or "legitimate" interpretations of the Moses story. In the 1920s, from a cultural studies perspective, the shifting ideological construction that is American (or any other) culture was characterized by instability and uneasiness. In this context, in suggesting that the events of the exodus prefigured the Bolshevik seizure of power in Russia, Steffens's *Moses in Red* in effect represented a blowing apart of the cultural agreement about the meanings of the exodus story in and for North America. Whereas dominant American culture, from the Pilgrim fathers onward, had read America as Israel (both in the sense of promised land-territory and people chosen to give moral-spiritual light to the nations), *Moses in Red* claimed that this identity belonged to respectable America's number one ideological opponent, the new Russian state.

What might crudely be termed Steffens's "mistake" is, then, that he believes that he can make revolution acceptable by associating it with the most respectable story of all, the Bible. But his readership's prior assumptions and ideas about revolution are such that he offers them a representation of America's iconic text so incongruous with established readings of the exodus story that it cannot succeed. For an author like Steffens, who continually stresses that people read and judge texts in the light of life experience, such an error of judgment is both significant and truly ironic.

Finally, a study of the hermeneutic strategies employed by Steffens (and Hurston and DeMille) cautions against simplistic attempts to differentiate forms of interpretation. In an effort to counter the tendency to differentiate "elite" from "popular" consumption of literature in the study of early modern France, the cultural historian R. Chartier has argued, "We must replace the study of cultural sets that were considered as socially pure with another point of view that recognises each cultural form as a mixture, whose constituent elements meld together indissolubly."[119] I hope that the reading of *Moses in Red* offered in this chapter has begun to suggest the necessity of breaking down older ways of categorizing and distinguishing "scholarly," "academic" (and implicitly "more legitimate or valuable") interpretations of the Bible from "popular," "lay" (and implicitly "less legitimate or valuable") ones. For example, much of what Steffens writes about the need for experientially driven hermeneutics indirectly prefigures and is in dialogue with professional biblical scholarship. But Steffens is never included within the perimeters of that kind of academic discourse. The shift in historiographical assumptions that the present book argues for could provide a route to richer, more nuanced (perhaps more plausible) biblical studies.

If Moses Was a Mulatto

Zora Neale Hurston's *Moses,*
Man of the Mountain (1939)

When in 1912 a disillusioned Lincoln Steffens became part of the Greenwich Village set centered around Mabel Dodge's Fifth Avenue salon, he was effectively ratifying a long-standing association with those at the heart of the American radical movement. Max Eastman was editor of the magazine *Masses;* William Haywood, a leading figure in the IWW (International Workers of the World); Emma Goldman, one of the most famous anarchists in the United States; and William English Walling, the first chair of the executive committee of the NAACP. Within a few years a typhoid death in the new Bolshevik state would earn another member of the group, John Reed, the questionable honor of being remembered as the first American Communist martyr.[1]

By the standards of later decades, however, the group displayed a striking social conservatism. Many of the male rebels had the privileges of an elite education and sizable private incomes behind them. The female members were often less conventional in practice if not in background. They were more likely to challenge publicly double standards in morality. They advocated birth control and an end to traditional conjugal roles and generally experimented to a greater extent with homosexual and open heterosexual relations. Even so, while the radicals were united in a desire to explore the possibilities of forming the vanguard of a revolution in consciousness to be achieved through the arts and literature, as well as by more narrowly political means, their conception of those who would serve in the roles of cultural and political leadership was often circumscribed by a prejudice against those of other ethnic or socioeconomic groups. To recall once more Art Young's aphorism, women might well have been able to swear aloud in Washington Square, but entry into the radicals' number was still largely barred to New York's African American population. Dodge's salon, open to interested whites, accepted "Negro entertainers" by invitation only, as part of a self-conscious plan to introduce "diversity" to the regular circle: "While an appalling Negress danced before us in white stockings and black-buttoned boots, the man strummed a banjo and sung an embarrassing song. They both leered and rolled their suggestive eyes and made me feel first hot and then cold, for I had never been so near this kind of thing before."[2]

Not all of Dodge's contemporaries shared her uneasiness in attempting to integrate ethnic and racial issues with political and aesthetic ones. The participation of the entertainment duo in the salon's activities had been suggested by Carl Van Vechten, a lively and serious socialite cum novelist, music critic, art patron, and photographer. In the 1910s and 1920s Van Vechten served as a bridge between Greenwich Village and the personalities of the Harlem Renaissance. Demographic changes in the postslavery era had seen Harlem develop as a city within New York City; it became the cultural capital of a newly confident African America. (Its "renaissance" was a broad movement encompassing literary, dramatic, and artistic outpourings, as well as commercial growth.) Among Van Vechten's Harlem friends was Zora Neale Hurston (1891–1960).[3] He would later remember her as "picturesque, witty, eclectic, indiscreet and unreliable. . . . It was she who invented the sobriquet 'Niggeratti' to describe the young writers of the [then] so called Negro Renaissance."[4]

Hurston arrived in New York in 1925. She embarked on an erratic career, which included the publication in 1939 of her own contribution to the radical literary debates of prewar America, the novel Moses, Man of the Mountain (1939). Moses cannot be considered Hurston's most successful book in terms of either authorial art or popular reception. Their Eyes Were Watching God (1937) has received far greater acclaim, having been vocally praised by Alice Walker in the 1970s. An earlier fictional work, Jonah's Gourd Vine, and the folklore collection Mules and Men have also attracted more frequent attention. Nevertheless, Moses, Man of the Mountain may be considered Hurston's most demanding and politically charged book. More important, however, for the purposes of this study is its contribution to an understanding of the nature and purposes of the representation of Moses by and to twentieth-century Americans. The book presents a multifaceted, often ambiguous Moses to its readership. Steffens's Moses in Red, although accessibly written, belongs to the genre of the political treatise. As such, it pursues the goal of exploring the exodus story as an example of revolution in a fairly straightforward and single-minded (almost two-dimensional) fashion. In contrast, Hurston exploits to good effect the relative freedom of the novel form. Here the Moses story is not used to argue a single point; many debates and contexts are alluded to and touched upon in greater or lesser depth. Like *The Ten Commandments*, *Moses, Man of the Mountain's* reworking of Exodus-Deuteronomy is richer and more vibrant, if less readily epitomized, than *Moses in Red*. On the one hand, Hurston's Moses stands in the tradition of a long history of African American use of the biblical story, stretching from early slave days through to Martin Luther King Jr. and beyond. And like Sigmund Freud, whose study of Moses also appeared in New York in 1939, she portrays a racially ambiguous liberator.[5] At the same time, Hurston's novel forms a part of the history of women's responses to the Moses story. Any willingness to follow African American conventions in regarding the exodus as paradigmatic of the American slave experience is tempered by a need to engage with the implications for women of the specifics of the biblical text, a text that, while promising liberation, also problematizes women, subordinating their voices and concerns to those of men, specifically to Moses, *man* of the mountain.

Difficult Freedom

Though decades had passed since Abraham Lincoln issued the final Emancipation Proclamation freeing slaves throughout the United States of America, the battle for Americans of African heritage to gain social, economic, and political equality with their white co-patriots persisted during the interwar period. Reconstruction had seen the granting of voting and other civil rights to African Americans, but much was still to be done to eliminate prejudice and discrimination. The newly emancipated found themselves at the mercy of the white South as sharecroppers, if no longer as slave laborers. As late as 1910, three-quarters of African Americans were party to land labor contracts that effectively tied them to a state of peonage. Property, literacy, and "grandfather clause" tests were imposed on would-be voters with the explicit aim of disenfranchising the African American community. "Jim Crow" laws promoted segregation in public places including schools and health care facilities. Atlanta courtrooms even had Jim Crow Bibles so that white witnesses would not have to swear on the same copy as their African American counterparts.[6] Such measures were supported by modern "scientific" rhetoric. In the vocabulary of Darwinism, African Americans were characterized as primitive, child-

and animal-like by their "sophisticated" white detractors. Hence, their retrogressive influence upon American society should be curbed. Culturally, this ideology found expression in the new cinematic medium, most notably in D. W. Griffith's 1915 film *Birth of a Nation*, which depicted the Ku Klux Klan's efforts to preserve the honor of white women from African American men who roamed like beasts, lawless through the South.

With the end of World War I the African American community was in the midst of a period of even more acute turmoil than that experienced by white America. In times of economic pressure, African Americans were the targets of organized hate campaigns and random violence executed by ad hoc lynch mobs. A combination of agricultural decline in the South and industrial expansion in the North further encouraged almost a million African American workers to undertake the Great Migration, yet their indispensability to new manufacturing industries did not secure esteem or even decent living conditions in cities like New York, Detroit, and Philadelphia. Soldiers returned from the European trenches to segregated ghettos and race riots.[7]

Throughout the early twentieth century, a growing and increasingly divergent body of African American theorists and activists sought to rationalize and ameliorate the situation. In 1895, Booker T. Washington urged African Americans to take a gradualist approach to advancement and find worthy occupation at "the bottom of life." But this scheme (and Washington's conciliatory tone) was losing favor by 1910.[8] It did not achieve the equality Washington hoped for and tended to reinforce white stereotypes and agendas. Clearly, more radical strategies were needed.

When in 1908 *New York Post* editor Oswald Garrison Villard called for a conference to renew the struggle for political and civil liberty, those who corresponded to that appeal included Lincoln Steffens and W. E. B. DuBois. DuBois advocated a bolder campaigning program for rights, to be led by the intellectual "Talented Tenth" of the African American community. Through his National Association for the Advancement of Colored People (NAACP), franchise-restricting measures were fought in the courts; the cultural hegemony was challenged.[9] Ultimately, however, DuBois's elitism and the romantic pan-Africanism that characterized his thought both failed to attract the masses and disillusioned the more privileged members of his community, who were distrustful of the communism and voluntary isolation he seemed to represent. By 1934 he had resigned from the NAACP, becoming what F. L. Broderick famously termed "a leader without followers."[10]

Far more popular than Du Bois's efforts were those of Marcus Garvey's

Universal Negro Improvement Association (UNIA). Garvey's personal charisma and message of race pride attracted thousands in the 1920s and early 1930s. UNIA's mission was comprehensive: through business, cultural, educational, political, and welfare activities, it would work for a free and independent African nation on African soil. Such separationist zeal ignored the assimilationist aspirations of many African Americans, yet the religious tone of UNIA rhetoric and the prescribed ritual core of its branch meetings found favor with many—especially the newer disillusioned urbanites who challenged the value systems of their grandparents (seeing Christian theology as part of the slaveholders' ideology) while recognizing the historical significance of the church as the first truly African American institution.[11]

This setting needs to be borne in mind when studying Zora Neale Hurston's *Moses, Man of the Mountain*. Its account of Moses and the exodus is written against a context of African American debates as to whether a leader should travel "before" or "with" his (or her) people. But *Moses* has other concerns, too. While the American discussion raged, on the other side of the Atlantic particular theories of leadership were being implemented practically with devastating results. Hurston wrote with an eye to affairs in Germany. Her Moses is at the same time both African American and truly international, a champion of black culture who also participates in the conversations of other communities.

The Bible and American Religion

The opening pages of Lincoln Steffens's *Moses in Red* betray its author's ambivalence toward the Bible. As was discussed in the previous chapter, Steffens suggests that the validity of the Bible story must be determined by weighing and testing it against life experience. In this respect, the Bible is no different in status from any other work of literature. Yet in spite of Steffens's professed relativism, *Moses in Red* is a testimony to the unique power of the Bible as America's iconic book, as a text that constructs America's sense of itself. In Hurston's introduction to *Moses, Man of the Mountain*, similarly mixed evidence emerges: "there are other concepts of Moses abroad in the world. Asia and all the Near East are sown with legends of this character. They are so numerous and so varied that some students have come to doubt if the Moses of the Christian concept is real."[12] Here is a seemingly unequivocal attempt to relativize the Bible text. Hurston's implication is that her story will evoke more exotic (and, she hints, more authentic) narratives. It is even more surprising, then, that immediately following this claim, Hurston quotes the biblical text as a frontispiece to the novel: "In all the signs and wonders which the Lord sent him to do in the land of Egypt to Pharaoh, and to all his servants and to all his lands, and in all that mighty hand and in all the great terror which Moses showed in the sight of all Israel! (Deuteronomy 34:11-12)." What, then, is the status Hurston accords the Bible in *Moses, Man of the Mountain?*

Janet Carter-Sigglow likens the positioning of Deuteronomy 34:11–12 in *Moses* to the preaching styles of African American Christians.[13] Hurston's anthropological researches (which continued alongside much of her literary career) led her to record the work of various preachers, most famously that of C. C. Lovelace of Eau Gallie, Florida, whose 3 May 1929 sermon featured in Hurston's contribution to the Nancy Cunard anthology, *Negro*, and reappeared in the same year in a fictional context in *Jonah's Gourd Vine*.[14] These sermons open with a biblical text from which they are formally derived; what follows may be a seemingly independent work of poetic creativity. As a text, the Bible is at once both valued and transcended. It is a source of inspiration and strength, which can at the same time be manipulated for the purpose of admonishment or affirmation. In its simultaneous recognition of and freedom with the biblical text, Hurston's novel evokes the sermon style, which she recorded as an anthropologist and knew from childhood: "my father and his preacher associates told the best stories in the church."[15]

One recurrent feature of much Hurston scholarship is its tendency to emphasize her experience of the rural black south at the expense of other influences on her writings. At worst, this tendency can go hand in hand with a characterization of her work as second-rate, folksy, or homespun; at best, it results in a sympathetic but still one-dimensional account of works that are complex and subtle. Hurston's use of the Bible in *Moses* not only is informed by the familiar preaching styles of C. C. Lovelace and others but it also employs theoretical insights on narrative and myth, drawn from Hurston's anthropological studies. The Bible text is presented as both fundamental and relative in *Moses, Man of the Mountain*. Like her teacher Franz Boas, Hurston was something of a cultural relativist. Exodus-Deuteronomy was only one Moses story among many. It was also only one story of origins (or "myth") among many. Yet at the same time, the narrative's place within Jewish and Christian civilization makes it crucially important for American culture. Hurston's novel captures this, using what she called the "spy-glass of anthropology" to explore issues and delve deeper into the role of language and tradition itself in shaping the social and political concerns of a nation. In this light, the assessment of the Bible in the introduction and frontispiece to the novel are not indicative of the work's weaknesses or contradictions but are instead marks of its sophistication.

Preaching strategies and contemporary anthropological theory help to contextualize Hurston's approach to the biblical text but not the detailed content of her departures from the biblical Moses story. Much of this chapter concerns the identification and analysis of the points where *Moses* deviates from the biblical account of the exodus. Some of the deviations are relatively unsurprising and represent Hurston's efforts to supplement rather than rewrite Exodus-Deuteronomy. Like DeMille's *Ten Commandments*, *Moses* embellishes the scant contents of Exodus 2 with an account of Moses' youth and early adult life in Midian. However, other changes are more radical. Hurston's Moses is a racially ambiguous hero with a Machiavellian streak. Prepared at first for strategic reasons to "adopt" Aaron as his brother, he slaughters him when he appears likely to thwart Moses' plans for the wilderness community. To what ends are these and other changes made, and how did Hurston's readers receive them? What insights, if any, do they offer to the attempt to make sense of the Bible's ongoing formative influence over culture and society in mid-twentieth-century America?

When Hurston came to assemble her Moses story, she drew on a range of extrabiblical sources. Most critics focus on her use of oral folklore traditions, but she also worked with other texts, including Josephus's *Jewish Antiquities*, from which she drew an account of Moses' military conquests in Ethiopia.

Hurston's use of *Antiquities* is readily demonstrated. Like Josephus, she recounts Moses' victorious campaign as commander in chief of Egypt's armies against Ethiopia (and in Hurston's version, the ancient Near East generally). She also has him seal the success by taking an Ethiopian bride.[16] Likewise shared is Moses' unhappy fate on his return to Egypt. In *Moses, Man of the Mountain*, his successes and subsequent attempts to institute domestic reforms arouse the jealous fears of crown prince Ta-Phar and see Moses denounced as a Hebrew, events that resonate with *Antiquities:*

> Now the Egyptians, after they had been preserved by Moses, entertained a hatred to him, and were very eager in compassing their designs against him, as suspecting that he would take occasion, from his good success, to raise a sedition, and bring innovations into Egypt; and told the king he ought to be slain. The king had also some intentions of himself to the same purpose, and this as well out of envy at his glorious expedition at the head of his army, as out of fear of being brought low by him; and being instigated by the sacred scribes, he was ready to undertake to kill Moses.[17]

It may strike the contemporary reader as strange that an African American woman writer working in the middle of the twentieth century used, or even knew of, a first-century Jewish account of biblical events. But until relatively recently, Josephus's works were phenomenally popular in the Western Christian world. For medieval and early modern Christians, his *Jewish War* (a personal account of the ill-fated revolt against Rome, 66–74 C.E.) was a record verifying the fulfillment of Jesus' prophecy on the destruction of Jerusalem (Mark 13:2). The longer *Antiquities* (twenty volumes on Jewish history from creation to Josephus's own day) was deemed to illustrate and confirm the events of the Bible. In particular, book eighteen was prized for the so-called *Testimonium Flavium*, a passage in which the author appears to make reference to a divine Jesus.[18] Indeed, *Antiquities* was the first (nonbiblical) work by a Jewish author to be printed in America. Hurston shared her peers' familiarity with the ancient author. She even used Josephus (together with Livy, Eusebius, Strabo, and Nicholas of Damascus) when in later life she constructed a life of Herod the Great, a work unpublished at her death, but one in which she had hoped Cecil B. DeMille might be interested.[19]

Josephus's account of Moses' life is lengthy and detailed, occupying parts of book two and all of books three and four of *Antiquities*. It could have furnished Hurston with a great deal of extrabiblical material. Yet apart from this one incident Hurston opts not to use Josephus and prefers to work more closely with African American and Afro-Caribbean oral tradition. It is therefore important to ask why she selected this particular passage as being (uniquely) helpful to her in her attempt to re-present Moses.

The answer perhaps lies in the incident's succinct blending of the heroic and the tragic. Moses performs a service for his nation but fails to reap recognition or personal happiness. This combination of nationalist-inspired conflict and personal political intrigue embodied in Josephus's story is in sympathy with the exploration of the fraught politics of leadership found elsewhere in *Moses* (see later). Victory or leadership is for Hurston at best bittersweet, carrying with it the weight of responsibility and risk that one's enlightened goals may be jeopardized by petty jealousies.

Hurston does not, then, allow the portrait of Josephus to drive her narrative but instead exploits her predecessor's work when it seems to furnish her with a ready example. This ad hoc utilization of Josephus is, however, mistakenly ignored. Early reviewers of the novel missed such references and played on the Africanisms they believed they had insightfully detected.[20] Yet, the presence of this intertextuality is a reminder that *Moses*,

Man of the Mountain, is firmly an African American book, a product of blending cultures and concerns.

It is a truism to say that without audience or community, there is no text. Modern historical criticism of the bible emphasized the objective recovery of the ancient context in which biblical texts were produced with the intent of finding a hermeneutical key. Postmodern readings have instead focused on the interpretation of the Bible by different communities of interest. Whichever type of approach is preferred, it is the case that without a "people of the book" there would be no book. Regarding Hurston's use of the Bible in *Moses*, it is important to locate her within the wider context of the African American religious community. As McDowell notes, "when Zora Neale Hurston turned to retelling the Exodus story in *Moses, Man of the Mountain*, she was building on a mountain of a tradition and anticipating its perpetuation."[21] Hurston stands in a chain of tradition, and, much to her chagrin, her account was certainly perceived in this way by early reviewers.

Historians have long emphasized the importance of religion as the ideological mainstay of African American slaves; it was an "invisible institution" that the slaveholders' regime could not subsume. Within the broadly Christian worldview of the slaves,[22] the story of Moses and the exodus was fundamental, as countless slave memoirs (and writings by their white contemporaries) attest. Slaves likened themselves to the Israelites in Egypt and drew from the exodus story a confidence to project a radically different future:

> The appropriation of the Exodus story was for the slaves a way of articulating their sense of historical identity as a people. That identity was also based, of course, upon their common heritage of enslavement. The Christian slaves applied the Exodus story, whose end they knew, to their own experience of slavery, which had not ended. In identifying with the Exodus story, they created meaning and purpose out of the chaotic and senseless experience of slavery.[23]

Once emancipation had been proclaimed, successive generations of free African Americans came to realize that there were pharaohs on both sides of the water. The exodus narrative was not superseded but retained its power. In Hurston's time and beyond, popular African American leaders from Marcus Garvey to Martin Luther King Jr. appropriated (or had thrust upon them) the mantle of Mosaic language and imagery.

As Raboteau suggests, the prime motivation for the use of the exodus imagery was its perceived resonance with African American experience. Slaves found common cause with the Israelites who cried out under the burden of bondage. They read the exodus as a story of liberation, a reading reinforced when, not unlike the biblical slaves, they gained freedom without the violence of a mass insurrection. Postbellum, the realization that emancipation was not complete and the biblical narrative's dual nature as text of liberation and inauguration struck a chord with those (Hurston included) who sought to actively construct a society in which they would be equal with their former owners.

For writers like Renita Weems, the close interaction between life experience and biblical narrative is unique to African American (more specifically to female African American) reading strategies. The previous chapter indicates that such claims to an exclusive hermeneutical position are ill-founded. A wealthy white American male, Lincoln Steffens, likewise privileged experience over text (as did Ransome). Indeed, numerous Christian groups throughout history have espoused similar beliefs.[24] There is no direct correlation between social position and hermeneutical strategy. However, the explanation that Weems offers for the primacy of experience in African American Bible reading strategies remains plausible. She notes how the illiterate slaves' reliance on aural and oral culture for their knowledge of scripture meant that they lacked an allegiance to any particular text or translation and were "free to remember and repeat . . . in accordance with their own interests and tastes." The survival of this selectivity within later written culture is famously depicted in Howard Thurman's story of his grandmother. She refused to hear or read biblical passages whose message she regarded as an affront to her humanity.[25]

Within a wider context of typological and experience-driven use of the Bible in African American religion, Hurston's seemingly capricious attitude toward the exodus story in *Moses* appears less remarkable. Her willingness to identify Moses as a character of fundamental programmatic importance for the African American community and at the same time adapt the story in a radical fashion, making bold alterations to heighten the association of the biblical story with her own social and political context, is in sympathy with these previously established approaches. However, Hurston's portrayal of Moses does not simply reflect this trend in African American use of the story. *Moses, Man of the Mountain* also contributes to one of the important debates surrounding African American religion in Hurston's time and since—that is, the issue of its preservation of African "survivals."

Anthropologists and religious historians debate the persistence of African elements within African American religious expression. Most would agree that the development of African American religion has entailed processes of innovation and tradition, continuity and change. It also seems possible to trace associations between the way in which an individual community was organized socially, the religious environment into which it was transplanted, and the level of African survivals that it was able to sustain. More survivals (beliefs and rituals) were in evidence in colonies such as Haiti, Cuba, and Brazil, where slaves lived in relatively large social groups and where the majority Roman Catholic faith, with its veneration of a number of saints in addition to the divine Trinity, provided a belief system that appeared not totally alien from the West African conception of a structured hierarchy of deities. In the north, there were fewer slaves, and conditions were less conducive to the retention of African culture. The strong internal slave market and the proportionately higher number of slaves who were American rather than born in Africa heightened the communities' dislocation from their heritage and subjected them to greater white influence and surveillance than was experienced by their counterparts elsewhere.[26] This is not to say, however, that no Africanisms persisted in North America. Melville Herskovits (like Hurston, a student of Franz Boas) traced African survivals in African American culture, and subsequent scholars see African elements in American worship, folklore, and traditional medicine. "Even as the gods of Africa gave way to the God of Christianity, the African heritage of singing, dancing, spirit possession, and magic continued to influence Afro-American spirituals, ring shouts, and folk beliefs."[27]

The most notorious expression of distinctive African American religiosity is voodoo (vodun in less anglicized form).[28] Voodoo is a comprehensive religious system found in the Caribbean (especially Haiti) and brought from there to some southern centers like New Orleans. It blends elements from traditional African religions with Christian ones and is characterized by ecstatic possession and sympathetic magic techniques through which followers seek to harness or divert the powers of deities and spirits. In voodoo are the clearest examples of Africanisms in African American religious life. For example, the Fŏn (the language of the Ewe people of Dahomey) word for a god, *vodu* and its Togolese variant, *vudu*, are plausibly supposed to be the source of the American term *voodoo* itself; slaves from those regions were mainly sent to Haiti and San Domingo (now Dominican Republic).[29] More important, scholars also see in the Haitian system an identification of African (or perhaps more accurately "African-style") deities with Catholic theology and iconographic tradition, so that the Haitian snake deity (Loa) known as *Damballah*, is associated with pictorial representations of both Saint

Patrick and Moses, which commonly include serpents (evoking Numbers 21:8–9).[30]

In the introduction to *Moses*, Hurston alludes to Haitian voodoo and to what she alleges is Dahomean religious tradition:

> In Haiti, the highest god in the Haitian pantheon is Damballa Ouedo Ouedo Tocan Freda Dahomey and he is identified as Moses, the serpent god. But this deity did not originate in Haiti. His home is in Dahomey and [he] is worshipped there extensively. Moses had his rod of power, which was a living serpent. So that in every temple of Damballa there is a living snake, or the symbol.[31]

Hurston's tone here is confident and authoritative. She presents her novel as an African story, the African "mouth" on Moses. (In many ways, her words prefigure Raboteau's account of African American religion as a manifestation of the West African worldview in a particular context of diaspora.)

The Moses-Damballah link Hurston makes in the introduction to *Moses* is expressed in more detail in *Tell My Horse: Voodoo and Life in Haiti and Jamaica*, a study published a year before *Moses* and based on fieldwork undertaken in the midst of the novel's creation:

> The Rada gods are the "good gods" and are said to have originated in Dahomey. . . . Damballah Ouedo is the supreme Mystere and his signature is the serpent. . . . All over Haiti it is well established that Damballah is identified as Moses, whose symbol was the serpent. The worship of Moses recalls the hard-to-explain fact that wherever the Negro is found, there are traditional tales of Moses and his supernatural powers that are not in the Bible, nor can they be found in any written life of Moses. The rod of Moses is said to have been a subtle serpent and hence came his great powers. All over the Southern United States, the British West Indies and Haiti there are reverent tales of Moses and his magic. It is hardly possible that all of them sprang up spontaneously in these widely separated areas on the blacks coming into contact with Christianity after coming to the Americas. It is more probable that there is a tradition of Moses as the great father of magic scattered all over Africa and Asia. Perhaps some of his feats recorded in the Pentateuch are the folk beliefs of such a character grouped about a man for it is well established that if a memory is great enough, other memories will cluster about it, and those in turn will bring their suites of memories to gather about this focal point.[32]

Moses is identified once more with the Haitian Damballah, and the latter characterized as a god rooted in Africa. However, whereas the introduction to *Moses* categorically states that the Moses-Damballah identification itself is African in origin, this second passage is at the same time both more cautious and more speculative, inferring an ancient African Moses tradition from the prevalence of African American Moses imagery. In reality, Hurston's knowledge of the African traditions to which she linked voodoo and hoodoo, a more definitely North American phenomenon in which a client-doctor type relationship exists between devotee and expert, was limited. At times, her portrayal of African religion (and therefore her assessment of the place of African survivals within African American religion) is insecure. Hurston's account of African and African American religion is dependent on Herskovits. Like Hurston, he had conducted fieldwork in Haiti in the 1930s; unlike her, he had also worked in West Africa some years earlier. By the time Moses was completed, Herskovits's findings would have been available to Hurston. In particular, his drawing of a link between Haitian and Dahomean worldviews and his study of the identification of voodoo Loa and Catholic saints seem to have been retailed (without credit) in Hurston's introduction to *Moses*, and in corresponding sections of *Tell My Horse*. This is not to accuse Hurston of blatant plagiarism. Rather, Herskovits's analysis provides a mental framework, within which Hurston reflects upon and interprets her observations. *Tell My Horse* comes close to acknowledging this when it describes Herskovits as the only man to have written intelligently on voodoo.[33]

When Hurston and Herskovits are compared, however, the limitations of Hurston's account are apparent. Whereas she identifies Damballah as the snake god in both Haiti and Africa, Herskovits presents a nuanced picture. The groups observed by Melville Herskovits (and his wife, Frances) in Dahomey referred to the deified Dã, the principle of mobility and sinuosity, associated with thunder and rainbows and generally less esteemed than feared. An individual was believed to be born with his or her own Dã; a male householder might establish or enshrine his Dã within the domestic compound to ensure the security of the household. The most powerful manifestation of Dã was in the form of Damballah or Dambada Hwedo, the Dã of unknown and undeified ("unestablished") pre-ancestors: "The Dã which are not established leave the individuals at death, manifesting themselves as a gaseous emanation from the head which can be seen by those who have the spiritual power. It ascends in spiral fashion and is deadly. . . . These Dã trouble human beings."[34] (Writing after Hurston, Geoffrey Parrinder similarly speaks of the spiritual principle of life, fluidity, and movement represented by and manifested in various phenomena including snakes, rainbows, and curling smoke, and known as Dã in the Dahomean interior.[35])

So, for Hurston and her Haitian informants, Damballah is a snake god, fundamental to both African and African American religion. But for Herskovits the Dã of the snake and that of ancestors, Damballah, are instead differing manifestations of an underlying spiritual principle, Dā. The difference between the two writers is most readily and convincingly explained by the suggestion that Hurston was familiar with Herskovits's work on Haiti and the Americas, but less aware of the Dahomean material. Some of Herskovits's later writing is relatively unspecific about African belief and practice. It is also on occasion ambiguously phrased and if read alone could at times be taken to imply a closer correspondence between African and American concepts than was the case.[36]

A second, clearer difference between Hurston and Herskovits arises in relation to the question of the ultimate origin of the Moses-Damballah association. Hurston believed the link began in Africa. For her, Africa had its own "voice" on Moses; indeed, the Moses story might be seen as an incorporation of African history into what eventually became Jewish and Christian tradition. Because this opinion is advanced not only in *Moses* but also in *Tell My Horse*, it seems to be her genuinely held view, not a strategic move to attract readers to *Moses, Man of the Mountain* by presenting it as an authentic, prebiblical account. It resonates with (but is not identical to) the work of some contemporary scholars who emphasize the African contribution to biblical text and tradition.[37] Herskovits disagrees. For him, a series of independent African-American contacts in the New World give rise to saint-Loa identifications (a view consistent with most general theory on the development of African American religious tradition). A pre–New World link would be plausible only if the identifications were identical in different locations, which they are not.[38]

The weight of scholarship against Hurston on the issue of the ancestry of the Moses-Damballah link underlines the derivative nature of her information on African belief. Reliance on the sometimes ambiguous writings of Africanists who turned their attentions to Haiti and on the views of Haitian informants for whom the assertion of the direct African nature of their Loa was in itself a (virtual) tenet of faith encouraged her to infer an African Moses tradition not found by those who undertook fieldwork in Dahomey and other parts of West Africa.[39]

Given Hurston's sustained involvement with a range of voodoo and hoodoo activities, it is unsurprising that, despite her claims, *Moses* is more representative of African American than of purely African tradition. However, even its presentation of a "hoodoo Moses" is not uncompromising.

Hurston certainly intends her readers to make connections between Moses and the great voodoo and hoodoo figures discussed in her anthropological writings. In the novel, a turning point in Moses' development is his visit to Koptos, where he wrestles a deathless snake to gain access to a legendary book. The contents of this volume give him great power and understanding. This incident echos the call experience of hoodoo conjurer Marie Leveau and the importance attached to books (especially the Bible) as part of the paraphernalia of voodoo and hoodoo.[40] Once empowered, Moses' behavior evokes his Haitian identity with Damballah—his day, too, is Wednesday.[41] Confronted by the returnee in the Egyptian royal court, Pharaoh Ta-Phar correctly identifies that Moses has been "messing around with hoodoo."[42]

But at times Moses' abilities appear limited and unremarkable in comparison with those attributed to the real-life hoodoo experts Hurston knew well. The ability to summon up plagues of frogs and snakes marks the zenith of Moses' talents as a hoodoo man in Midian. And in her account of the burning bush, Hurston tellingly prefers the Bible over hoodoo tradition. Her Moses is terrified by the divine presence, shying away from the snake-rod he is given as a staff.[43] Moses' actions embrace little of the detail of hoodoo practice that Hurston records in *Mules and Men* and *Tell My Horse*. Although he reads the book at Koptos and undergoes modest training under Jethro, Moses experiences none of the elaborate initiation rites in which Hurston herself participated.[44] His hoodoo achievements actually appear unimpressive in comparison with those attributed to twentieth-century figures like Anatol Pierre, whose rite to bring about the death of a client's enemy Hurston records, noting simply, "And the man died."[45]

Not only is Moses' hoodoo activity staid in comparison with that of the enigmatic figures recorded in Hurston's anthropological writings but also it appears tame when set alongside the summary she gives in *Mules and Men* of the hoodoo image of Moses. Common to the two accounts is the role of Jethro as the man who recognizes Moses' potential, but in *Mules and Men* Moses is less a recipient of revelation than a "two-headed man of power" who demands encounter with the divine:

> Moses talked with the snake that lives in a hole right under God's footrest. Moses had his head and a cloud in his mouth. The snake had told him God's making words . . . Many a man thinks he is making something when he is just changing things around. But God let Moses make. And then Moses had so much power he made the eight-winged angels split open a mountain to bury him in, and shut up the hole behind them.[46]

In conclusion, it is fair to say that Hurston's book is not a "window" into African or hoodoo images of Moses. It is a novel and should be regarded as "refracting" or resonating with African American traditions built around the biblical narrative, rather than replicating them. For some critics, Hurston's "failure" to provide a more convincingly hoodoo Moses is symptomatic of her inability to weave a coherent whole from the myriad of textual and contextual materials available. However, it may more convincingly understood as a function of her wider purposes and of her own personal context as an African American woman in prewar America.

Hurston was aware of the need to produce a work intelligible to an audience stretching beyond African America. White readers, even those willing to look at a work written in Southern dialect by an African American woman, might accept a slightly redrawn image of Moses but were likely to reject one that was too unfamiliar. Steffens's *Moses in Red* failed critically and popularly because the meanings it attributed to the biblical story could not be assimilated to the Moses myth as popularly conceived. As an anthropologist, it is likely that Hurston would have been conscious of the fact that despite the immense plasticity of biblical texts, there are limits to the variations a tradition may tolerate; as the introduction to this chapter showed, even Greenwich Village "radicals" regarded the ending of segregation with some unease.

In this respect, reviews from the white press of the day show that Hurston judged her audience well. *Moses* gave enough hints of the "mystery" and drama of African American religious life to entice its readers without demanding that they explore the detailed and complex theology of voodoo. But, although she was often reliant on white sponsors and faced recurring financial problems, Hurston's purpose in writing *Moses, Man of the Mountain* was not simply to produce a book that would sell. She also intended the novel to examine some important issues and dilemmas facing African Americans on the eve of World War II. Acutely aware of elite prejudice against popular cultural expression (including folk religion), Hurston recognized the need to tone down some of the more colorful elements of voodoo and hoodoo to guard against reinforcing sensational stereotypes of the religion. If encouraged, these might blind her readers to the book's more political message.

Ultimately, then, much of the ambivalence of the novel's relationship to the Bible and African American religion is traceable to the ambiguity of Hurston's own position as an African American woman operating in a society that deemed her inferior and second class, yet at the same time had offered her unprecedented opportunity, in (for example) the form of a Barnard College education. Like her peers, Hurston enjoyed an often difficult freedom. She found herself caught up in the tension of both privilege and marginalization. The result is a novel that negotiates first one community of interest, then another. This issue is considered in greater depth in the following section.

Race and Ethnicity

Moses engages issues that exercised Hurston's contemporaries and continue to tax present-day commentators. These include the leadership and direction of the African American community, war and antisemitism, and gender politics: Whereas Steffens's programmatic approach narrowed the range of issues dealt with in Moses in Red, the fictional form of *Moses, Man of the Mountain*, coupled with Hurston's strategic deployment of heteroglossia, permits allusion to a number of concerns and agendas.

In the opening chapter of *Moses*, the vocabulary of the terror to which the Hebrews are subjected immediately evokes the experience of African American slaves. They can expect "one hundred lashes for sassing the bossman."[47] Hurston's association of Hebrew and African American slavery was not new. However, her approach is at times distinctive. For African American slaves the exodus was the narrative by which they conceptualized their own fates. In *Moses*, the hermeneutical flow is reversed; African American experience informs the representation of the biblical story. When the slaves are finally instructed by Pharaoh to leave Egypt they respond with the cry, "Free at last! Free at last! Thank God Almighty I'm free at last!"[48]

In addition to drawing out similarities between the oppression of slaves ancient and modern (a radical claim, given the slaveholder belief that the abuse of Africans was divinely ordained), *Moses, Man of the Mountain* also tackles the thorny problems of racial definition and African American color prejudice. During the nineteenth and early twentieth centuries, white racists in North America sought renewed justification for their actions in the pseudoscience of eugenics and the new human sciences. The theory that there were distinctive "breeds" or races of humans was widely accepted as fact.[49] Moreover, popular (mis-)readings of Darwin's *The Origin of Species by Means of Natural Selection* (1859) and its various supplements, particularly *The Descent of Man and Selection in Relation to Sex* (1871), held that the various races (and the genders) should "naturally" occupy different spheres of activity. Discrimination and segregation found a rationale in the form of Darwin's theory of evolution by natural selection or "survival of the fittest" (Herbert Spencer's phrase). Nonwhites were regarded as examples of "low forms preserved" and treated as primitives (either childlike, to be patronized and belittled, or brutal, against whom white civilization needed to guard itself) with a clear conscience. Racists even claimed an altruistic motivation for their behavior. Just a few years before *The Origin*, the Comte de Gobineau wrote his *Essai Sur L'inégalité des Races Humaines* (1853–1855), a work popular in Europe and in North

America, which argued that the racial composition of a society determined its fate.[50] Certainly, Darwinism was not universally accepted. Among its opponents were biblical creationists. However, they, too, possessed a justification for racial discrimination. Although Genesis 9 spoke only of the cursing of Noah's son Ham, racist theology extended the judgment to his descendants, including Cush, identified as Ethiopia or the African peoples as a whole.[51]

As one of the relatively new human sciences, anthropology inevitably became embroiled in the debates around race and ethnicity, particularly as they related to establishing defining characteristics for each race and measuring their mental and physical capabilities. To this end, early physical anthropologists carried out tests and experiments, including intelligence tests and comparative studies of the cephalic index. Increasingly, however, scholars began to explore what is now know as cultural relativism—that is, the realization that norms, standards, and values vary with environment and even from person to person. In this respect, anthropologists came to challenge the basis of racist belief and practice. Race was shown to be a human construct rather than an absolute, self-evident category.

One of the best known early champions of cultural relativism was Franz Boas, under whom Hurston studied at Columbia (1925–1927). In 1894 he made his first public attack on prejudice in the lecture, "Human Faculty as Determined by Race." Arguing that historical circumstance rather than mental ability determined a culture's development, he went on to question the perceived culture-free nature of such physical measures as the cephalic index. Even this, he showed, could vary according to the environment. More fundamentally, Boas challenged the notion of races as objective categories. He stressed instead the plasticity of types and was also quick to suggest the possible implications of his findings for public policy makers: "More than any other anthropologist, he was responsible for a fundamental shift away from social Darwinism in support of equal rights."[52]

Hurston's intellectual debt to Boas was great. In *Dust Tracks on a Road*, she calls him "Papa Franz." Boas helped to arrange fieldwork fellowships for her and wrote a preface to *Mules and Men*.[53] Throughout *Moses*, her treatment of race bears traces of the Boasian legacy. The narrative champions the notion that it is impossible to distinguish one "race" from another. Many of the focal characters of the book themselves embody racial ambiguity. Although it is probable that Hurston had some awareness of this critique of racist propaganda long before her formal anthropological training (many African American families had within them the visible traces of differentiation; Hurston described her own father as a "mulatto"[54]), work with Boas formed an important reinforcement for earlier commonsense observations, enabling her to counter pseudoscience on its own ground.

Moses, Man of the Mountain constantly emphasizes the view that "no matter where two sets of people come together, there are bound to be some in-betweens."[55] The Goshen slaves, oppressed because of their supposedly distinct "Hebrew identity," are aware of the hollowness of this rationale. They all know of examples of intermarriage; Pharaoh has a Hebrew grandmother. As the heroine of Hurston's novel *Their Eyes Were Watching God* puts it, "'We'se uh mingled people and all of us got black kinfolks as well as yaller kinfolks.'" Moreover, the slaves' recollection of Joseph's achievements gives lie to Pharaoh's characterization (à la Gobineau) of their people as one that must be suppressed to prevent the destruction of all that is good in Egypt.[56]

While Hurston's Hebrews typify the responses of the victims of racism, she explores the motivations and mindset of oppressors in the shape of the Egyptian characters. Racists are shown to be inconsistent, even on their own terms. A Hebrew who has renounced his identity has gained a top position in the pharaonic administration, suggesting that cultural imperialism is the real motivating factor behind Pharaoh's actions. In this light, Pharaoh's racism toward the Hebrews assumes the character of a politically expedient philosophy. His own sister was evidently married to an Assyrian in the service of Egyptian foreign policy.[57] By contrast, Ta-Phar, the pharaonic heir apparent, is obsessed with race and breeding in a manner evocative of the more extreme social Darwinists of Hurston's day. Ultimately, this leads him to deny the humanity of those about him. Recalling the terminology of American slave auctioneers who advertised people as breeding stock, he thinks of his own sister as having been "mated with a foreign prince."[58] This prejudice is echoed by that of the Ethiopian princess, Moses' "treaty-wife." She is unable to see beyond her racist mythology about the Hebrews. Regardless of Moses' courteous behavior, she tells him that because of his heredity, "It is rape for you to even look at me."[59]

Hurston's attribution of racist hysteria to Moses' Ethiopian wife hints that although many aspects of *Moses, Man of the Mountain* may be understood as referring to the mistreatment of African Americans by whites, not all aspects of the book's handling of issues of race and ethnicity may be interpreted in this way. In chapter 26 Hurston attends to the incident in Numbers 12 where Miriam and Aaron criticize Moses because of his Cushite wife.[60] Given the general identification within the novel of the Hebrew slaves with African Americans, Hurston's treatment of the event has perplexed many readers, in that it seems to portray an African American woman (Miriam) criticizing someone on account of their being "dark complected."[61] Is this simply inconsistency on Hurston's part, a typical weakness in an overly ambitious book? For Janet Carter-Sigglow, Miriam's words mean that she herself cannot be black. Instead, "Hurston's narrative technique is to use Black English to make a political statement." She uses the language of an oppressed people to universalize the biblical message.[62] Other commentators, also unable to countenance the thought that Hurston could have meant to present black-against-black prejudice in the Miriam-Zipporah altercations, have offered alternative explanations. Davis suggests that at this point the African American–Hebrew analogy in the book is (uniquely) suspended. Hurston is instead striking a blow at "the Jewish color prejudice." Miriam, as Hebrew, now represents twentieth-century Jews; her words against Moses' wife represent the racism that they direct at African Americans.[63]

Neither of these readings of the Miriam-Zipporah incident seems to "fit" easily, either with what is known of Hurston's personal biography or with more holistic interpretations of the novel. Carter-Sigglow's and Davis's theories both require a rather inelegant temporary suspension of the Hebrew-African American identification at this point in the narrative. But while Hurston uses Moses to comment on a variety of power structures and systems of oppression, she generally does so in a more sophisticated and "economical" manner, weaving a set of allusions together, as in the opening chapter of the novel. Davis's reading is further questionable in that it seems to infer or require that Hurston herself had a strong sense of having suffered at the hands of Jews, something for which there is no evidence. In fact, Hurston's closest relationship with a Jew, Franz Boas, seems genuinely positive.

It is possible to provide a simpler (and in relation to the novel as a whole, more consistent) explanation of the passage, simply by engaging more willingly with the "surface meanings" of Hurston's text. Because Miriam is identified as African American elsewhere throughout Moses, and as she continues to use African American dialect in this chapter, there is no obvious reason to suspend reading her character as African American in the Miriam-Zipporah confrontation. The implication of this assertion— that in portraying the incident Hurston is presenting her readers with a clear example of black-black prejudice—may appear unappealing to modern critics, but such a reading of the passage is supported by evidence found in Hurston's other works. Their Eyes Were Watching God describes African American characters who express similar attitudes. When the book's heroine, Janie, who is light in color and has flowing hair (the result of her grandmother's rape during slavery), marries the darker Tea-Cake, their relationship meets with the disapproval of Mrs. Turner, who believes that "mulattos" should separate themselves from the rest of the African American population:

> "Ah jus' couldn't see mahself married to no black man. It's too many black folks already. We oughta lighten up de race." . . . "Look at me! Ah ain't got no flat nose and liver lips. Ah'm a featured woman. Ah got white folks' features in mah face. Still and all Ah got tuh be lumped in wid all de rest. It ain't fair. Even if they don't take us in with the whites, dey oughta make us uh class tuh ourselves."[64]

Practicing her own variant of Jim Crow, she will be treated only by white doctors, and she buys from only white-owned stores.[65]

Elsewhere, Hurston criticizes those who look down upon those of lighter coloring. Like Janie, John Pearson in *Jonah's Gourd Vine* is the product of rape in slavery. However, his light coloring attracts resentment; his mother's husband eventually throws him out of the family home, saying, "git dat punkin-colored bastard outa dis house . . . dey say deses half-white niggers got de worst part uh bofe de white and de black folks."[66] Finally, *Dust Tracks on a Road* provides a rationale for the equal condemnation of the positions Turner and Pearson represent:

> Light came to me when I realized that I did not have to consider any racial group as a whole. . . . Therefore I saw no curse in being black nor no extra favor by being white. . . . I am a mixed-blood it is true, but I differ from the party line in that I neither consider it an honor nor a shame. I neither claim Jefferson as my grandpa, nor exclaim, "Just look how that white man took advantage of my grandma!"
>
> After all, the word "race" is a loose classification of physical characteristics. It tells nothing about the insides of people. Pointing at achievements tells nothing either. Races have never done anything. What seems rare achievement is the work of individuals.[67]

Both white racists (and their African American imitators) and African American "race men" ("somebody who always kept the glory and honor of his race before him"[68]) are equally misguided. For Hurston, the achievements and failures of individuals are important; when groups or races become the focus of concern, inhumanity results. Mrs. Turner chastises Janie; John Pearson is made homeless. In *Moses, Man of the Mountain*, the Hebrews are enslaved, and Moses suffers the racist taunts of his Ethiopian treaty wife and his sister Miriam.

In view of Hurston's preference to speak in individual rather than racial terms, it is perhaps not surprising that, like her other novelistic heroes Janie and John, Moses is an example of a racially ambiguous individual; that is, he is what Hurston and her peers termed a "mulatto." In contrast to the biblical story, Hurston deliberately clouds the identity of Moses' natural parents. But whether the son of Amram and Jochebed (described as being of white face and red hair) or of the Egyptian princess and her dead Assyrian husband, he is the child of an interracial marriage.[69] Constant reminders of Moses' "doubtful" origins occur throughout the narrative. To Ta-Phar he is a misfit in the royal household; observers at the Pharaoh's military maneuvers suspiciously liken his riding skills to the Hebrews'. However, when the daughters of Jethro first encounter him, they judge him to be an Egyptian nobleman, and once disillusioned in the desert, the former slaves speculate that Moses is "a pure Egyptian" who "toled us off so his brother could butcher us in the wilderness."[70]

The illusive ancestry of Moses is fundamental to Hurston's aims in recasting the biblical story. Like Freud's *Moses and Monotheism*, Hurston's *Moses* is a book that challenges Moses' traditionally accepted racial identity, written against a backdrop of mounting racism-inspired conflict on the European continent. But whereas Freud, perhaps projecting his own ambivalence toward his Jewish identity, worked to establish the Egyptian identity of the biblical hero, for Hurston the presentation of Moses as a mulatto functioned quite differently. In the novel, Moses' very person becomes the statement par excellence of Hurston's denial of race as an objective category. He also serves the author's purposes in relation to other political themes running through the narrative. Creating a Moses who (depending on one's viewpoint) could be seen as either an unfortunate paradox or a liminal figure with unrivaled potential to mediate between and reconcile different communities provided opportunities to explore and expose issues of loyalty and obligation. Because he is a mulatto rather than a "pure" Hebrew, Hurston's Moses is a community leader differentiated from the Garveyite race men she despises elsewhere for their claims to lead the African American people toward separatism. His efforts on the slaves' behalf, motivated by revulsion at their suffering, and then by divine call, become selfless acts rather than unthinking reflexes: "He didn't have to pay us no mind if he didn't want to," discerns Joshua at one crucial moment in the story.[71] Hurston uses her novel to advocate a philosophy of individualism over tribalism and, in the person of Moses, shows how even leaders and community builders can champion values over pride in the group. Ultimately, then, *Moses, Man of the Mountain* is perhaps bolder and more radical than Freud's more sensationally received study.

Hurston's shaping of her Moses character not only made statements about the nonreality of race, but it also advocated a model of leadership at a time when many African Americans were asking profound questions about the future direction and headship of their communities. As outlined earlier, the positions adopted by African American leaders may be located along a spectrum between the twin poles of accommodation and protest.[72] They might, like Booker T. Washington, accept middle-class white norms and endeavor to shape their fellow African Americans accordingly. Alternatively, in a form of protest most famously articulated by Marcus Garvey, they might reject the dominant culture and work for racial segregation (ideological and actual). To function effectively as intermediaries between two communities of interest, however, they all had to seek and gain from both some kind of recognition of their status and claims. The necessary ambiguity with which the leaders therefore presented themselves and their ideas engendered suspicion. Strong words to the beleaguered African American community could be perceived by the white majority as rabble-rousing. Likewise, advocacy of caution or gradualism could be seen to suggest that one was in the pay of segregationists and perhaps willing to abandon the good of the community in favor of self-aggrandizement. As Ralph Bunch commented, "There are few Negro leaders who are not suspect immediately they attain any eminence."[73] Hurston's leader similarly suffers suspicion and criticism. On the banks of the Red Sea, the people accuse Moses of trickery and lies.[74]

However, Hurston's Moses differs from African American leaders of the early twentieth century in that, although a liminal figure of ambiguous origins, he is able to exercise considerable power, in many instances independent of communal approval and support. It is Aaron and the Hebrew who works as an overseer of slaves (in chapter 9), who in their relation to the dominant power structures most closely resemble real-life African American leaders. The overseer advocates a firmly gradualist position. Having been appointed to a role of minor importance, he hopes that by performing his duties in a manner pleasing to the Egyptians, he may be able to rise through the ranks and take a few other Hebrews with him.[75] Similarly, but with less altruistic ends, Aaron conceives of power and leadership in Egyptian terms. Once in the wilderness, he attempts to cultivate the style of the pharaonic court. Moses "looked at Aaron's face and he noticed the way he walked. His face looked like Ta-Phar's. . . . he was conscious of the envy of men."[76]

In contrast, Moses does not accommodate to Egyptian norms (nor does he need to). His "right hand" of power secures the slaves' liberation, rather than an ability to ingratiate himself with Ta-Phar. Hurston's Moses has no need of the manipulation that Washington, DuBois, and Garvey all had to employ. While Aaron assumes Egyptian guise, he aligns himself with the mass of the people, quite literally speaking their language.[77] In these respects, Hurston's Moses is something of an idealized African American leader, a hero unburdened by the need for realpolitik. His powers enable him to avoid the dilemmas and pitfalls faced by lesser figures such as Aaron—or the African American leaders of Hurston's own day.

The most visible prewar advocate for African Americans was, of course, Marcus Garvey. Moses' racial ambiguity means, however, that he cannot be regarded as a Garveyite figure. As Myrdal observed, "The Garvey Back-to-Africa movement appealed systematically to the darker Negroes [sic] and tried to impute superiority to an unmixed African heritage."[78] Moses' power as a leader is instead drawn possibly from the divine, certainly from roots in the culture of the folk for whom he works. His path to power begins with the folktales told to him by the Hebrew stablehand Mentu. Hoodoo greatness follows his familiarity with the legendary Book of Thoth, and the real work of nation building commences once he has adopted the ways of the people.[79] In this way, Hurston's Moses accords with the model advocated by members of the Harlem Renaissance, whose ideas Garvey both used and spurned. Their advocacy of the continuation and celebration of strong links with the folklore of the rural South created a sense of cultural pride that could (but did not have to, and in most cases did not) support Garveyism.[80] That Hurston was aware of these debates concerning African American leadership and communal development is clear. Although she differed from DuBois and the NAACP concerning the focus of the efforts to win equality for African Americans (she championed folk culture rather than the talented tenth), Hurston's emphasis in Moses on the power of culture and art aligns her more closely with that stance than with any other of the day.

Hurston's program in Moses also differs from Garveyism in that UNIA featured a developed organizational structure to which members were expected to devote their mental and physical energies,[81] whereas the fostering of individualism is inherent in the community that Moses seeks to encourage. Like Steffens and DeMille, Hurston gives little of the detailed legal prescriptions found in the Hebrew Bible. Instead, Moses reflects on his achievements: "He had found out that no man may make another free. Freedom was something internal. The outside signs were just signs and symbols of the man inside. All you could do was to give the opportunity for freedom and the man himself must make his own emancipation."[82]

Freedom and individualism are fundamental to the novel. In a sense, its theme is that liberty is about much more than legal emancipation. African American or Hebrew, former slaves must overcome the tendency to internalize the norms of the dominant culture. They need to construct a sense of their own selves by reconnecting with the intellectual, emotional, and spiritual roots of their culture. As Ruth Sheffey hints, Moses' end of making former slaves as individuals "feel free and noble" inevitably leads to the leader's loneliness,[83] but distance between leader and led is shown to be necessary if the community as a whole is to reach social and political maturity.

"How small Sinai appears when Moses stands upon it!"[84] Franz Kafka's remark could be aptly applied to Moses as represented by Steffens, Hurston, and DeMille. All three create extremely heroic figures, leaders distant from and misunderstood by the masses with whom they work. In a world familiar with the consequences of totalitarianism, such emphasis on the role and right to power of a single figure disturbs. The Western world has seen the terrors that can ensue from the *Führerprinzip* and (for the most part) does not wish to risk similar happenings again. However, Hurston differs from Steffens and DeMille because in *Moses* it is possible also to trace a critique of nationalism-inspired autocracy and a willingness to align with and humanize its numberless victims. Hurston not only encourages her contemporaries to read the biblical story through the lens of multiracial America but also suggests an analogy between Pharaoh's victims and their "Hebrew" descendants in the middle of the twentieth century. Nazism casts a shadow over the novel.

Little has been written on *Moses* in relation to Adolf Hitler's rise to power on mainland Europe in the early 1930s, but both the text itself and Hurston's own personal and professional concerns suggest that she wrote with an eye to Germany. The Nazi regime's interest in eugenics in the service of the "Aryan race" was, perhaps, likely to attract the interest of an African American writer with a background in anthropology, particularly one whose interests in race and culture had developed under the guidance of a scholar who consistently attacked race prejudice and argued for the equipotential of all peoples.

Franz Boas, a German Jew whose fieldwork took him to the Americas in the 1880s, joined or contributed to virtually every anti-Nazi organization in the United States. He was quick to condemn the regime in pronouncements against Hitler and his pseudoscience ("since a remote period there have been no pure races in Europe") and to procure aid for Jewish academics and students expelled from continental universities. He died while giving an antiracism address at a luncheon hosted by refugee Paul Rivet.[85] Significant for this study in particular is Boas's likening of antisemitism to prejudice against African Americans.[86] Numerous references in *Moses, Man of the Mountain* imply that Hurston, too, saw resonances between events in Europe and North America and the sufferings of the Hebrew slaves in Exodus. It was, after all, an American politician who declared, "The utter extermination of a race of people is inexpressibly sad, yet if its existence endangers the welfare of mankind, it is fitting that it should be swept away."[87]

The somewhat anachronistic terminology of fear Hurston deploys in the opening chapters of *Moses* evokes the twentieth-century oppression of Jews, possibly in a deliberate attempt to evoke the dislocation and disturbance of the age. The slaves are ghettoized, "driven out of their well-built homes and shoved further back in Goshen." In this environment they fear secret police and spies, agents of a regime that is constantly described as "new," a caesura in Egyptian history.[88] As the terror is specified, its detail mirrors the Nazis' New Order. In 1935 the Reichstag passed a harsh legislative program against German Jewry, the so-called Nuremberg Laws. The first of these, the Reich Citizenship Law, limited German citizenship to those certified by the Nazi party to be of German or related "blood" and relegated Jews to the status of "guests" or "subjects." At the same time, marriage and sexual intercourse between Jews and *Staatsangehoerige* (citizens or state-members of German or cognate blood) were prohibited by the Law for the Protection of German Blood and Honor. To this end, the employment by Jews of German women of childbearing age was outlawed. Jews were also no longer allowed to display the German flag. The essential provisions in this program are echoed in Hurston's account of the rigors suffered by the Hebrew slaves. Like German Jewry, they lose their legal status as citizens overnight: "Hebrews were . . . prevented from becoming citizens of Egypt, they found out that they were aliens," and are effectively denied participation in the symbolic and spiritual life of the state by means of a ban prohibiting them from entering temples.[89]

There are reasonable grounds to argue that Hurston consciously drew on European events when describing the slaves' plight. Drafts of the novel were written during the period 1934–1935, and at this time the Nazi program was reported at length by the American press, making the detail of the Nuremberg measures readily available. The *New York Times* outlined the provisions of the program "that put Jews beyond the legal and social pale of the German nation" and reproduced in full a translation of Hitler's speech urging the Reichstag to adopt the measures. Reporters were quick to notice the symbolic power of the newly adopted swastika flag and the laws' different implications for "full Jews" and non-Jewish "non Aryans."[90] The tone of Hurston's Pharaoh (who charges the downtrodden Hebrews with conspiracy and portrays his brutality as a measured response to a disobedient people whom he is weary of indulging) also evokes Hitler's attempts to suggest that it is the Jews' own willful refusal to develop "amicable" relations with the German nation that necessitates their legalized persecution.[91]

Moses, Man of the Mountain does not simply utilize the horrors of Hitler's Germany to create a context of terror that enforces the necessity of a Moses type of leader. Hurston's understanding of racial divisions as idealized abstractions enables her to critique both American racism and the Nazi program. The ambiguity of race argues against the Ku Klux Klan, against the Nazi blood myths, and for those Jews who lost their lives to this mythology. The slaves' highlighting of the supposedly racially pure Pharaoh's possible Hebrew grandparents[92] evokes the 1933 definition of the "non Aryan" as a person who had a Jewish parent or grandparent and the detailed regulations determining the identification of first- and second-degree *Mischlinge*, who were (initially) subjected to less harsh treatment than those classified as full Jews.[93]

Finally, although *Moses* predates the implementation of the Final Solution, it is worth considering briefly Hurston's depiction of the outcome of Egyptian nationalism in relation to the course of the Holocaust on mainland Europe. American media observers of the new Germany were alert to the correlative development of nationalistic fervor and military capability. Here also, Hurston's juxtapositioning of these two aspects within the Egyptian state, marked by the inclusion of the events of Egypt's "bi-annual military maneuvers,"[94] seems informed by reports of "a realistic sham battle before hundreds of thousands of thrilled and cheering Germans" that marked the end of the Nuremberg rally in 1935.[95] Both are ostensibly domestic celebrations that also demonstrate power to potential opponents abroad and at home.

By the time the manuscript of *Moses, Man of the Mountain* was completed in early 1939, large-scale violent conflict in Europe seemed possible if not probable; Hitler had already annexed Austria and the Czech Sudetenland. In an interlude inspired by Josephus, Hurston's Moses likewise goes to war. But unlike Josephus, she does not present Moses' battles in Ethiopia as an occasion of glory and success, instead heightening their damaging effects on the hero's position in Egypt. Although unaware of the horrors yet to come, Hurston's 1930s version of events portrays the war as a destructive, nationalism-inspired project, which can result in only misery for conquered and conqueror alike.

Gender Politics

In the 1970s Alice Walker's account of her quest to find and mark Hurston's grave sparked considerable interest in a then little-known "genius of the south."[96] Soon afterward, the appearance of Hurston's picture on the cover of *Black World* established her as one of a select group of key "Black Women Image Makers" and asserted her identity as a literary foremother who had been neglected by African Americanists of the past but who was finally being recognized as a major figure in the tradition. To acknowledge Hurston's life and work was to acknowledge the validity of the experience of African American women. Feminists and womanists found precedent and inspiration in *Their Eyes Were Watching God*'s account of Janie's convention-flouting attempts to find fulfillment, the endurance of Lucy Pearson in *Jonah's Gourd Vine*, and the events in the writer's own checkered life as recounted in *Dust Tracks on a Road*.

By the 1980s, feminist and womanist theologians were drawing on Hurston's work, now established as a valuable resource for the articulation of a positive African American female identity. This work is exemplified by Emily Culpepper, who sees her approach as transforming the territory of traditional academic theology, requiring it to take account of the religious lives and reflections of those who by reason of birth and education were previously denied a voice within the discipline. Similarly, for Katie Cannon, Hurston's accounts of women's struggle to develop moral and spiritual lives despite white patriarchy form the basis for a new ethical system.

Given the current appeal of Hurston's oeuvre for feminist theologians, their relative lack of discussion of *Moses, Man of the Mountain*, her most obviously biblical work, is striking. Equally surprising is Carter-Sigglow's appraisal of the novel's female characters as powerless, ineffectual, and unpleasant.[97] Her view that the book contains no subtext of female empowerment, together with the reticence of other commentators, belies the view that sees Hurston as an uncomplicated feminist and hints at the ambiguities inherent in her writings' handling of gender issues. With the emerging status of Hurston's works as resources for feminist theology in mind, this section discusses how far *Moses, Man of the Mountain* critiques or reinforces the gender-related dynamics of oppression that feminist scholars trace in the biblical account of the exodus. Certainly, the book can be seen as an example of women's biblical interpretation. But is it usefully viewed as a proto-feminist work?

By the time that *Moses* was written, African American women had already been able to appropriate the exodus story with some success. Female as well as male slaves had "read" their lives through the lens of the biblical narrative (and vice versa), and in the mid-nineteenth century Harriet Tubman, whose Underground Railroad coordinated the escape of hundreds of slaves, was commonly known as "Moses."[98] The male name had become a descriptive referent. It could be applied to any person responsible for the liberation of his or her own people. However, as African American women gained literacy following emancipation, it became increasingly apparent to them that the biblical story as historically read and interpreted within mainstream Christian circles was a gendered text. As modern feminists have stressed, although Exodus-Deuteronomy places women's struggles at the inception of national liberation (Exodus 1:15–2:10), it subsequently denies their role in the development of that process. The attempts of Miriam the prophet (Exodus 15:20) to challenge Moses' status (Numbers 12:2) result in punishment and infamy (Deuteronomy 9). Moreover, the former slaves' God sometimes advocates violence against women. One writer recently compared the divinely commanded seizure of Midianite women (Numbers 31) with the use of rape as a weapon in the Balkan conflict.[99] Hurston's retelling of the Moses story indicates that she is aware of the problems inherent in regarding a text that (at best) only implies female liberation as paradigmatic for African American society. Her exploration of the difficulties can be traced by considering her treatment of four crucial elements of the story—namely, Moses' birth, his relationship with Zipporah, the giving of the Law, and, perhaps most important, the person and role of Miriam.

As noted earlier, the opening chapters of Exodus that deal with the circumstances surrounding Moses' birth, abandonment, and rescue from the Nile feature important actions by several women. The birth of Moses is in itself not heroic. It is the extraordinary actions of first the midwives and then Jochebed, Miriam, and the Egyptian princess that ensure the working out of the divine plan. In particular, Nahum Sarna stresses the pivotal role of Shiphrah and Puah, whose defiance of the pharaonic decree that male Hebrew offspring should be put to death becomes the first faith-inspired act of civil disobedience in defense of a moral cause. The story is remarkable for the prominent, fateful, and generally noble role played by women.[100]

Hurston likewise begins her Moses story with (literally) women's voices. The impact of the pharaonic dictate upon the lives of the women who must carry and birth the children it would destroy is starkly emphasized: "The Hebrew womb had fallen under the heel of Pharaoh." This general distress is personalized in the experience of Jochebed, and when Moses is born, her courage is clear. Following the Bible rather than her other textual source, Josephus, Hurston depicts a defiant mother figure determined to save her child despite her husband's fearful wish to kill it before the Egyptian soldiers do.[101]

However, *Moses* does not present a uniformly positive picture of the women associated with its hero's birth. When they believe too readily Miriam's dubious claim that the child has been rescued from the Nile by the Egyptian princess, the Hebrew women's faith is blind. Gone also from this account is the positive biblical portrayal of the midwives whose silence preserves Israel. Interrogated by Pharaoh's secret police, Hurston's midwives "talked and talked aplenty, from old Puah on down."[102]

Some feminists argue that the Bible's presentation of praiseworthy mothers, sisters, and midwives in Exodus 1 and 2 reinforces patriarchy. Its implicit message is that women belong in the domestic or private sphere. In the words of *The Women's Bible Commentary*, in Exodus, "within what appears to be an exclusively female sphere of birth and childrearing, women act without male authority. . . . from a perspective concerned with the political and religious spheres of men, however, women become subject to control and exclusion (e.g., 19:15; 21:7)."[103]

Hurston's narrative seemingly offers an endorsement of this view, denying women rights to full and equal participation in private and public life. Of the different female characters in chapters 1 through 5 of *Moses*, only Jochebed as mother achieves something of value, and (again in contrast to Exodus 2) even she needs the aid of Amram before she can complete the task of making a reed basket.[104] Women in professional roles (even childcare-related ones) are unreliable and bring disastrous consequences (death of male children) upon the community.

This notion that women's place is in the private sphere but men are fitted to assume communal and leadership roles is reiterated in the novel's depiction of Moses' relationship with Zipporah. Much of this is grounded in the Bible (Exodus 2:16–22; 18:1ff.). Zipporah needs Moses to rescue her when the two first meet, a reminder of the danger inherent in women's assumption of "masculine" occupations. Biblical scholars have also long commented on the seemingly secondary nature of Moses' relationship with Zipporah in comparison with that between Moses and Jethro, in some cases seeing Moses' Midianite marriage merely as a narrative device to account for the relationship between father and son-in-law. When, after the exodus, Moses is reunited with his Midianite family, the emphasis is on the meeting between the two men; Zipporah becomes a silent, inactive figure in the shadows of the biblical tradition. This is the last time that it will deem it necessary to mention her by name.[105]

Once again, *Moses* not only reinforces but also accentuates the androcentric nature of the biblical text. Such a development of the exodus narrative is by no means inevitable or even necessary: DeMille's Sephora shares her husband's virtues of forbearance and modesty. Yet Hurston persists in drawing a contrast between Moses and Jethro's spiritual concerns and Zipporah's self-centeredness. While Moses perfects his capabilities as a hoodoo conjurer, she complains that "If only Moses had the proper ambition, she might be mistress of the palace someone had pointed out to her. And her sons might be Princes near the throne."[106] Unlike Moses' male confidants, Zipporah is unable to comprehend the gravity of his mission. If Moses is the ambiguous but broadly positive role model of African American leadership, then Carter-Sigglow's verdict that "women in *Moses, Man of the Mountain* represent petty jealousies which must not be allowed to hold Moses back" is certainly true of his wife.[107] When Moses attempts to educate her concerning the solemnity of his new role as a leader, she thinks only of the trappings of royalty, and she takes the other women with her: "They had no more interest in prophecy and politics. They were . . . interested in the earrings of Mrs. Moses and her sandals, and the way she walked and her fine-twined colored linens."[108]

Feminists from different faith traditions have concentrated on different aspects of the Exodus-Deuteronomy cycle, often in relation to the prominence accorded to those different elements within their respective communities. However, Christian and Jewish feminists alike have, with varying emphases, paid much attention to Exodus 19 and 20, the account of the making of the covenant between God and Israel, and its most famous epitome, the Ten Commandments. For the former, the apposition between people and women at 19:15 shatters any image of the wilderness community as an ideal egalitarian society.[109] For their Jewish counterparts, the halakhah's definition of male as normative and female as Other is a fundamental problem. The account of the entry into the covenant at Sinai in Exodus 19, the root from which all subsequent halakhah is formally derived, is a particularly difficult text.[110] Judith Plaskow describes the horror attendant upon the discovery that the Otherness of women finds its way into the very center of Jewish experience: "Given the importance of this event, there can be no verse in the Torah more disturbing to the feminist than Moses' warning to his people in Exodus 19:15, "Be ready for the third day; do not go near a woman." For here, at the very moment that the Jewish people stands at Sinai ready to receive the covenant . . . Moses addresses the community only as men."[111]

The Ten Commandments, for many Jews and Christians the epitome of the covenant, do not just imply a male audience; they rank women with other chattel—real estate, livestock, and slaves.[112]

As with *Moses in Red* and *The Ten Commandments*, the main focus of

Moses, Man of the Mountain does not lie in the detailed prescriptions of Exodus, Leviticus, Numbers, and Deuteronomy. Steffens, Hurston, and DeMille are more interested in the function of the law than in the content of a particular system of laws. Hurston recounts Moses' musings on this function—but not the contents of any of the laws themselves. He descends from Sinai secure in the belief that: "Now men could be free because they could govern themselves. They had something of the essence of divinity expressed in order. They had the chart and compass of behavior. They need not stumble in to blind ways and injure themselves. . . . Israel could be a heaven for all men forever, by these sacred stones."[113]

Straightforward or ironic, Hurston's mirroring of the gender-exclusive language of the biblical regulations ("men could be free") in this passage stands in contrast to her handling of Exodus 19:15. When the bible says, "And he said to the people, 'Prepare for the third day; do not go near a woman,'" she has Moses admonish the crowd, "And now don't nobody sleep with your husbands and wives until God done been here and gone."[114] Intentionally or not, the text of *Moses, Man of the Mountain*, with its move from inclusivity before the fixing of the covenant to Moses' patriarchal assumptions afterward prefigures the views of contemporary feminists who detect behind the Bible's final form the traces of the development of patriarchal order as a corruption of the divine ideal. Perhaps in this respect at least, Hurston can provide precedent for feminist readings, hinting at the Bible's potential for ending the diminution of women, in spite of that potential's being hidden behind an androcentric exterior.[115]

Thus far, examination of Moses' birth, his relationship with Zipporah, and giving of the Law as recounted in *Moses, Man of the Mountain* yields troubling results for those who, like Culpepper or Cannon, would use Hurston's work as an exegetical or theological resource. Setting aside the possible criticism of the wilderness order's male-centeredness, the novel's depiction of its individual female characters as weak-willed, dangerously unreliable creatures who attain worth only through motherhood seems far removed from the independent women who populate Hurston's other works. It is in a close examination of a final element of the Exodus-Deuteronomy collection as recounted in *Moses* that it may be possible to explain (while not, however, totally explaining away) some of these aspects of the novel that have rendered it so problematic for contemporary women readers.

Without doubt, the female figure in the Moses story who most intrigues feminists is Miriam. The woman whom the Bible both champions as (almost) equal to Moses and uses as a symbolic warning against disobedience has interested scholars such as Trible and Burns, as well as the writers of more meditative, devotional pieces.[116] Miriam is possibly the only woman in the Bible whose life is recounted from childhood to death. Although her genealogy is confused (interpreters, not the Bible itself, identify her with Moses' sister in Exodus 2:4; 2:8 and 6:20 suggest some doubt as to her relation to Moses and Aaron), the wilderness sees her established as a virtual coleader of the new community in the making (Exodus 15:20f.) until, on speaking out with Aaron against Moses' Cushite wife and his exclusive leadership, she is struck with leprosy (Numbers 12) and silenced for the rest of her life (Numbers 20:1). Crucially for a feminist readership, the fact that Miriam is punished and Aaron is not is a discriminatory decision against her, that has the effect of ending Miriam's public aspirations.[117] Debate continues as to the real nature of her challenge to Moses and whether the version of the incident as reported in the biblical text evidences the process of patriarchal redaction of an original narrative in which she once featured more prominently, possibly in some form of cultic role (as Phyllis Trible suggests.)[118]

It is in the feminists' figure of Miriam the prophet and freedom leader that Hurston would surely have had the most scope for presenting her readership with an unambiguously confident female personality, a woman not bound by society's presuppositions. However, *Moses* heightens the negative aspects of the biblical presentation of Miriam. Unlike the watchful sister of Exodus 2, Hurston's Miriam falls asleep, only to wake and find the reed basket gone. Her panic on making this discovery is fleeting; seduced by the trappings of finery, she is more interested in the Egyptian princess who is bathing nearby.[119] The story of Moses' rescue from the waters of the Nile is just that, a tale told to avert parental wrath:

> Seeing her frenzied mother searching for something with which to strike her made Miriam come alive inside more thoroughly than she ever had done before in her life and suddenly an explanation flashed across her brain.
>
> "You see, mama, while I was asleep the basket with your baby in it floated down-stream and the Princess saw it and took him home to the palace with her."[120]

Miriam's childhood failure to understand the nature of leadership and power causes her to be more concerned with the interests of a member of the ruling class that would destroy her than she is with her own brother. This failing manifests itself again later in the narrative in the forms of racist behavior toward Moses' wife, Zipporah.[121] Some scholars have argued that Numbers 12 originates in an early account of opposition to Moses' marriage to a Cushite woman and was only later developed to become a tale of opposition to his status as mediatory (prophetic) leader of the people.[122] But whereas the Bible ties Miriam's attack on Moses' private life to a challenge to exclusive power structures, within which Moses as God's servant is accorded primacy over other prophetic (Miriam) and priestly (Aaron) figures in the wilderness community, in *Moses* the racism becomes a function of Miriam's petty resentment of another woman:

> When Miriam showed herself through the growing crowd of awe-struck women, it was her intention herself to welcome Zipporah and as the leader of Israel's womanhood, impress herself and her office upon the wife of Moses. But the glitter and glamour of Zipporah's entourage and the poise and elegance of Zipporah herself had balked Miriam. She burst through the crowd and just stood there staring and glaring.[123]

It is a testimony to Hurston's narrative art that despite all her snarling and spitting, Miriam endures as the most tragic character of the book. Broken physically and spiritually by her punishment for claiming that God "'speaks through my mouth and Aaron's mouth just as much as He speaks through yours.' . . . All the rest of her days, Miriam was very silent."[124] It is on her death that Moses (and Hurston) reflects on the true import of her life. Without Miriam's attempts years before to claim him as her brother (and therefore as a Hebrew), he might never have fled to Midian and received the divine commission that led to the exodus. And although she had been instrumental in making the exodus emancipation feasible, it had brought her few compensations—she had been "sunk in slavery . . . and snarled in freedom," her prophetic leadership role belittled and sidelined in the new postslavery order.[125]

Moses' remarkable assessment of Miriam's life can provide a key to Hurston's understanding of the gender-related dynamics of power in and behind the Moses story. Miriam's voice is crucially important. Just as the somewhat foolhardy and naïve optimism of Jochebed preserves the baby Moses from early slaughter at the hands of Amram, so without Miriam's words (however true or untrue) concerning the fate of the baby in the reed basket, "Moses" would not have been kept alive at the symbolic, legendary level. There would have been no Moses story. And yet despite this importance, Miriam is progressively silenced; Hurston's text charts the career of a woman who loses her voice, or rather has it taken away from her by a male-centered, male-dominated society. At one level, of course, this silencing of Miriam is done by the book's author, Hurston herself. *Moses* is qualitatively different from modern feminist interpretations of Exodus-Deuteronomy. The Miriam of what some today term feminist midrash is embattled but remains secure in the knowledge of the validity of her own experience;[126] Hurston's character clearly does not. But if Hurston silences her female characters, she is not alone in so doing. Throughout the book, male figures attempt to restrict and quiet them, to the extent that it can be argued that if its novelistic predecessor, *Their Eyes*, is (as critics claim) about women finding their own voices in a context of patriarchy, then *Moses*, which opens with the voices of women who then quickly recede in importance, charts the silencing of women with the establishing of patriarchy.

Evidence supports the view that *Moses* is to be read as an illustrative analysis of the biblical text's marginalizing of the female voice, rather than (as Carter-Sigglow wants to suggest) simply as an example of such a marginalizing text in its own right. Amram not only muffles his wife's birth cries, but also attempts to belittle her ideas about how to save the newborn infant, claiming that she does not possess the higher critical faculties needed to recognize the gravity of the family's situation.[127] Similarly, when Moses hatches a plan to rout the Midianite cattle thieves, Jethro predicts that his daughter Zipporah will be the cause of its failure because she is "'nothing but a woman.'" Once Moses and Zipporah are married, he cautions him against paying her too much attention. Women should stay in the domestic sphere; serious concerns are the realm of men.

The apposition between serious business and female presence is maintained and extended by males throughout the narrative. Miriam already has a privileged status as a prophet and hoodoo conjurer in Goshen before Moses' return to Egypt, but he fails to comprehend that she might possess any talent for leadership and will concede only that she might be useful in "handling the women," who are by implication not expected to be able to grasp the import of Moses' own message unmediated.[128] Slowly but surely, *Moses* shows how the biblical women find their potential denied and their actuality diminished in the wake of a supposed liberation event.

For feminists hoping to glean a model for action or easy inspiration in Hurston's work, this reading of *Moses, Man of the Mountain* offers both problems and hope. On the one hand, it renders implausible the kind of allegorical, programmatic use of the novel that has characterized some feminist critics' use of Hurston's work.[129] On the other, it offers much in sympathy with the modern feminist enterprise by laying bare the dynamics of patriarchy and subtly undermining the authoritarian and absolute claims of its product, the received, redacted biblical text. Prefiguring contemporary feminist attempts to create compensatory or restorative midrashim, *Moses* is both a folk narrative or legend and, at an implicit level, a study of how such texts arise—both an example and a critique of a genre.

To conclude, the treatment of the women by Hurston and her male characters in *Moses, Man of the Mountain* reflects the kinds of processes that feminists today also believe lie at the heart of the structuring of the Bible tradition. In this respect, Hurston assumes a double role as commentator on and participator in the processes of patriarchy, something that mirrors her twofold identity as a recorder and creator of African American folklore in her earlier anthropological works like *Mules and Men*.[130] *Moses'* image of the fates women suffer at the hands of a male-dominated culture also reflects Hurston's personal experience as an African American woman trying to carve out a life very different from that envisaged for her by mainstream society. Moses' dismissal of Miriam's complaints as stemming from the fact that she never married and had a husband's needs to occupy her evokes the prejudice that colored many early assessments of Hurston's work. It also prefigures the spurious charges of sexual impropriety that effectively silenced the author some years later.[131] Here, then, in the stark realism of *Moses'* portrayal of the experience of thwarted and belittled biblical women, is another example of the confluence of Hurston's concerns. The novel's exploration of their fates sheds light on the construction and evolution of faith traditions and on the potential implications for African American women of the predominantly male debates concerning the leadership and future direction of the community. There is a real resonance between the experience of the novel's not-so-equal women and those female former slaves and descendants of slaves captured narratively in the portrait of Nanny, in *Their Eyes*: "Ah wanted to preach a great sermon about colored women sittin' on high, but they wasn't no pulpit for me."[132]

The Politics of Language

One of the key means by which Hurston reinforces her discussion of the dynamics of ethnic-and gender-related difference is the deployment of a varied repertoire of ways of speaking to her readers, including African American dialect and standard and colloquial English. Language and voice are crucial to *Moses*. Pharaoh is described as having "sacred voice and lips," and God is "the Voice"; Moses' assessment of his career lists his having given the slaves' god "a voice and glory" and "called to their memories the forgotten words of love and family" as his greatest achievements. When Miriam commits the crime of speaking against Moses and Zipporah, her devastating punishment is silence. The rise of the biblical order as recounted in the novel entails establishing the male voice over the female voice.[133]

On several occasions, language functions performatively: Pharaoh issues decrees that have great import for the slaves, the power of the girl

Miriam's story is such that it creates a Hebrew identity for Moses, and priests and conjurers use words to achieve mastery over nature and people.[134] In part, by emphasizing language and voice, *Moses, Man of the Mountain* is simply developing a trait already strong in the Bible story. Exodus-Deuteronomy is replete with performative language, and Moses is remembered as the prophet able to converse with both humans and God (see, for example, Exodus 19:7–9; 20:19). However, in the specifics of her language use, Hurston also demonstrates the extent to which anthropological perspective infuses her story. Hurston was acutely aware not only of the geographical, social, and ethnic variations in language and dialect but also of the politics of language. Her employment of African American dialect in her novels distinguished them from those of many of her Harlem contemporaries, who, in their self-appointed roles at the vanguard of an African American cultural renaissance, tended toward the norms of middle-class American or international English, and whose efforts were often implicitly informed by the conviction that explicitly high culture was capable of transcending racial division. As Bambara has observed: "At a time when most writers of the Renaissance theoretically acknowledged that all great art was/is derived from the folk and the folk base . . . was Blacksouth, even as they worked diligently to fashion big city literature and to spruce up their speech, Zora . . . in practice explored the rich vein and never ever ever cut those critical ties with the 'lowly down under.'"[135]

In part, Hurston's distinctive eagerness to employ Southern language is simply a reflection of the fact that her origins in Eatonville, Florida, meant that she had far more direct contact than some of her peers with the rural American South. Bruce Nugent and Langston Hughes were Washingtonians; Alain Locke was "born in Philadelphia, educated at Harvard and Oxford, and had never known the common run of Negroes [*sic*]."[136] In such a context, Hurston's choice to stick with the forms and dialect of her childhood, rather than use standard English, was an ideological statement. In an era when many African American intellectuals were attempting to facilitate assimilation, Hurston affirmed cultural difference.

Early anthropologists had been quick to appreciate the centrality of language—its dual identity as cultural communicator and component that both meets a need for a subtle, precise system of communications and at the same time is in itself a "cultural system of learned behavior, transmitted from generation to generation."[137] Boas's work on indigenous American language overturned the accepted wisdom that languages could be situated along an evolutionary continuum, with those of hunter-gatherers at the simple or primitive end and Western European ones at the advanced, complex end. The realization that all languages were complex phenomena (linguistic relativism) is explored by Hurston in one of her contributions to Nancy Cunard's *Negro Anthology* (1934), an essay on "Characteristics of Negro Expression." Like Boas, Hurston's essay discusses the distinctive elements of African American language, emphatically denying that it is derivative and unoriginal: "While he [the African-American] lives and moves in the midst of a white civilization, everything he touches is reinterpreted for his own use. He has modified the language, mode of food preparation, practice of medicine, and most certainly the religion of his new country."[138] She identified several types of linguistic modifications as being indicative of a general African American disposition to dramatize and adorn: the use of metaphor and simile, the double descriptive (e.g., "low-down," "kill-dead," "sham-polish") and the use of verbal nouns (e.g., "funeralize," "jooking," "she features somebody I know").[139]

Hurston's preoccupation with African American forms of verbal expression continued throughout her creative life, and she sought in her novels not only to replicate faithfully the linguistic structures she had considered in her anthropological work but also to demonstrate the social meanings inherent in certain types of language use, particularly those involved when an individual member of a speech community employs different languages (bilingualism) or varieties of the same language under different social conditions (a practice later termed *diglossia* by Charles A. Ferguson).[140] Writing in *Dust Tracks on a Road*, Hurston described how she learned the necessity of diglossia in order to achieve a desired end (to collect African American folklore). Her first fieldwork failed because "I went about asking, in carefully accented Barnardese, Pardon me, but do you know any folktales or folk-songs?" Success came when she adopted the vocabulary and style of her informants (and her own childhood). To them, folktales were "lies": "'Zora,' George Thomas informed me, 'you come to de right place if lies is what you want. Ah'm gointer lie up a nation.'"[141]

Linguistically speaking, *Moses, Man of the Mountain* is Hurston's most sophisticated work. In addition to stressing voice and the word, it uses language in ways informed by anthropological insight. In particular, two of the novel's central characters illustrate the symbolic importance of language and of linguistic code switching such as bilingualism and diglossia. Jethro serves as a linguistic (and ideological) go-between. His function as a conceptual bridge between Moses' time in Egypt and his future life as prophet of God is highlighted in *Moses*. Jethro's work in teaching Moses philosophical pretexts and conjuring techniques is instrumental in developing the younger man's leadership abilities, and he first suggests to Moses that he might return to Egypt and free the Hebrew slaves.[142] For the novel, his role is pivotal: "He [Moses] wished that the nation could know how much Jethro had meant to it,"[143] and this is, above all, symbolized by his bilingualism. Whereas Moses cannot at first understand Zipporah and her sisters, their father can speak Egyptian well, and his easy manner and dignity soon encourage Moses to feel able to adopt the Midianite way of speaking.[144]

Likewise, Moses himself comes to learn the importance of linguistic flexibility. On the bank of the Red Sea, Moses is faced with rebellion as the former slaves accuse him of being an Egyptian who has brought them out of Goshen to facilitate their slaughter by Pharaoh. In a crucial assertion of the power of diglossia, his adoption of the slaves' speech patterns enables him to reassert his identity with the Hebrew people and thereby win their continued trust and support: "He turned his back on the Egyptian horde and spoke to his people. Spoke to them in their own dialect as one of them."[145] Moses' identity with and distinction from the masses are simultaneously apparent. The requirement that leaders, however educated or "elevated" culturally, be able to speak (literally and figuratively) the language of the people is clear.

Hurston's attempt to embed within *Moses* her own anthropological understanding of language resulted in a complex piece of literature. Not surprisingly, in an age when nuanced theories of language and culture were not widespread (although some folktales of the period certainly indicate awareness of linguistic politics[146]), early reviewers found the work problematic. For some the use of African American dialect was a weakness that placed it in their estimation alongside folktales and other charming "frivolities," not worthy of serious analysis. However, the use of language within the novel is inseparable from its discussion of ethnic and gender politics in 1930s America. References to "spies" and "secret police," "christenings," and "sassing the bossman" are at one level anachronistic; at another, they enable the work to draw analogies between the world of the Bible, the experience of African American slaves and sharecroppers, and German Jews under the Nazis. In the context of biblical hermeneutics, Hurston's strategy ensures that at one and the same time the novel both stands in continuity with the biblical narrative and subtly subverts the authority of the voice of the "unmediated" biblical account, denying even that there can be such a voice. Hurston's baroque *Moses* ultimately argues that the biblical Moses is simply one among many, a single manifestation of a diverse and dynamic body of ever-growing tradition.

The Early Reception of *Moses*

Reviews of *Moses, Man of the Mountain* appeared in the national press as well as in publications aimed primarily at an African American readership. Those in the *New York Times Book Review* and the *New Yorker* were broadly positive but betrayed their writers' limited comprehension of both subject matter and author.[147] For the *New Yorker*, the novel was an enjoyable diversion: "the story of Moses as a great voodoo man, told in the American Negro folk idiom by a talented Negro writer. The real thing, warm, humorous, poetic."[148] In particular, the reviewer linked Moses and voodoo—strictly speaking, an inaccurate identification (Hurston likens the biblical leader to a practitioner of hoodoo, for her a phenomenon distinguishable from its Haitian counterpart), but one that indicates that the author's attempts to have her presentation accepted as the "African mouth on Moses" enjoyed some success. Tied to the depoliticized reading of the book is its characterization as "warm, poetic and humorous"—adjectives that can be applied with some accuracy to Hurston's text but also evoke white stereotypes of accommodating Southern African Americans. The reader associates Hurston with traditional images of the amusing "folksy" African American rather than with the articulation of any complex and radical social message.

Writing for the *New York Times Book Review*, Hutchison is alive to the presence of African American dialect in the novel. He notes that its use becomes less frequent as the book develops but sees this as a weak inconsistency rather than a politically significant aspect of Hurston's work. Like the reviewer for the *New Yorker*, Hutchison describes the narrative as "warm with friendly personality and pulsating with homely and profound eloquence and religious fervor." *Moses* is a "homespun book."[149] Most disturbing to the modern reader, though, is the willingness to see in the novel a representative account of the naïve credulity of the "primitive" African American:

> This is the story of Moses as the Negro sees and interprets the "man of the mountain." . . . All primitive peoples have an inordinate love of magic, or what appears to be magic, and the African most of all. . . . Moses seems almost to be greater than God. But this is not irreverence, for it is undoubtedly due to the fact that it was easier for a primitive mind to endow a human being with mystical powers than to grasp a purely rational deity.[150]

Hutchison assumes the guise of one who interprets the primitive Other to his own (by inference, more sophisticated) community. His readers can be reassured by his revelation that the African Americans who laud Moses are merely "primitive" rather than maliciously "idolatrous." Ironically, of course, Hutchison is unaware that Hurston's Moses is not narrowly African American and owes much to other influences, including Josephus and contemporary anthropological theory. Here perhaps Hurston's attempts to construct the reader's experience of her text backfire. Her ability to convince Hutchison that her Moses is directly representative of African tradition also allows him both to ignore her talents as a writer and to persist in unnuanced and inaccurate views of African America as a whole.

Hurston's work receives more sophisticated treatment in two reviews written from a Jewish perspective by Untermeyer and Slomovitz for *Saturday Review* and *Christian Century*. Perhaps aware (as members of another American minority) of the plurality of meanings applied to the biblical text, they are willing to admit their own biases in reading *Moses, Man of the Mountain*. Untermeyer (himself the writer of a novel named *Moses* in 1928) finds the book to be a not always wholly successful "series of compromises between the plausible and the bizarre, between the legend as we know it and the legend as it has been transplanted and recolored."[151] He does not, however, share the condescension of the *New Yorker* and the *New York Times*: The book has "dramatic intensity worthy of its gifted author" and African American folklore is placed on a par with the reworkings found in rabbinic tradition.[152]

Untermeyer's cultural relativism is taken further by Slomovitz in "The Negro's Moses."[153] While noting that for a Jewish readership, *Moses* would appear "weak in its interpretation of the ethical contributions of the prophet and in its treatment of the code of laws handed down by him," Slomovitz explains that the strengths of the book lie in its specifically African American character. *Moses* is "exceedingly interesting" because it sheds light on how a particular interpretative community in a postslavery context of oppression has shaped the Bible story. Hurston is "especially effective when she deals with Moses' miracle-producing powers" (his hoodoo conjuring); she has also "written a splendid study of slave emancipation. From this point of view her biography of Moses is invaluable."[154]

Although they sometimes betray failures and prejudices on the parts of their writers (even Slomovitz makes no attempt to discern how far Hurston's novel is representative of African American tradition), the reviews of *Moses, Man of the Mountain* for the mainstream white-controlled press were on the whole more positive than those appearing elsewhere. Writing for *Opportunity*, Hurston's former teacher, Alain Locke, dismissed the novel as "caricature instead of portraiture. . . . black Moses is neither reverent nor epic, two things I should think that any Moses, Hebrew, Negroid or Nordic, ought to be." In *New Masses*, Ralph Ellison, a fellow member of the Harlem Renaissance, uncharitably asserted that "for Negro fiction, it did nothing."[155] At first consideration, this seems surprising: By 1939 Hurston had become the most prolific African American woman writer ever. Why, then, did her own community not laud her?

As an independent woman prepared to divorce at least two husbands,[156] Hurston attracted the critical opprobrium of her Harlem Renaissance peers. In their reviews and biographical writings, she suffered for her refusal either to produce work that conformed to male radicals' definitions of political writings or to behaviorally please those who sought to gain acceptance by emulating white genteel norms (Locke had been educated with the white elite; the journal *Opportunity* for which he wrote was the organ of the Washingtonian National Urban League).[157] In particular, Wallace Thurman's novel *Infants of the Spring* and Langston Hughes's *The Big Sea* painted unflattering pictures of Hurston as a "perfect darkie" who self-seekingly pandered to the interests and stereotypes of her white patrons. These portraits downplayed her work and abilities as an author and anthropologist and failed to appreciate the harsh reality of Hurston's existence on the edge of poverty. They were also hypocritical. Most of those who accused her of playing the whites' game were dependent on the same white patron, Mrs. Osgood Mason.[158] Nevertheless, the tendency within some sections of the African American literary community to not acknowledge any worth in Hurston's work because of her refusal to accommodate to their norms of proper action and forms of political expression has persisted, in some cases until the present day.

In short, initial readings of *Moses, Man of the Mountain* assessed the novel as at best a folksy, apolitical diversion, at worst a damaging stereotypical product that could hinder the integrationist cause. The future for Hurston and her novel hardly looked promising.

Hurston Rediscovered

Zora Neale Hurston died in obscurity in 1960. Her funeral was paid for by the state, and she was buried in an unmarked grave in a segregated cemetery. For many years her writings were out of print. In the early 1970s, Alice Walker was able to describe her as "one of the most significant unread authors in America."[159] What criticism was produced during this period of neglect reinforces earlier tendencies to appraise Hurston's person instead of her work: "Always a colorful figure, Zora Neale Hurston was a popular Harlem personality during the early years of the Renaissance, one about whom many amusing anecdotes were told," writes Davis.[160] Hurston is passive object rather than creative, active subject here. This general failure to take her seriously as a writer manifests itself in an inaccurate and superficial treatment of *Moses, Man of the Mountain*. In Davis's cursory analysis, the former slaves' behavior in the wilderness—their dissent, whining, and endless complaint—is cited as an example of the way in which "the Bible story of Moses takes quite a beating" in the novel.[161] The carelessness of this remark is readily apparent. If Davis had actually compared *Moses, Man of the Mountain* with the Bible story, he would surely have noticed that this weakness of the former slaves is not Hurston's innovation.

More damning than Davis's lack of concern is Turner's dismissal of Hurston. For him, she is "an imaginative, somewhat shallow, quick-tempered woman," willing to exploit the culture of the rural South for personal ends. Turner even concludes that she deserved to die in poverty.[162] In the midst of this vitriol, *Moses* receives surprisingly positive treatment as Hurston's "most accomplished achievement in fiction." "If she had written nothing else, Miss Hurston would deserve recognition for this book."[163] Given Turner's general assessment of Hurston, however, his praise for *Moses, Man of the Mountain* is faint at best. The book's merit lies in its being "a good joke," and "a good joke, at best, is merely a joke. Miss Hurston's joke entertains readers but does not comment significantly on life or people."[164] For Turner as for some of Hurston's contemporaries, *Moses* cannot be of political or ideological import, because it fails to protest in the obvious and direct way that, for example, Richard Wright's *Native Son* does. Hurston's male contemporaries' definitions of politics are regarded as the norm. Turner's consequently narrow understanding of political writing and intolerance of any writer whose work does not fit that model leads him to fashion a reading of *Moses, Man of the Mountain* that is often unsustainable and inaccurate. A glance at the opening page of the novel reveals that it offers the reader much "more" than humor. And, of course, jokes frequently are profoundly political phenomena that do "comment significantly on life or people."[165]

Writing in 1990 of Hurston's fate in the immediate postwar period, Henry Louis Gates commented, "The dark obscurity into which her career then lapsed reflects her staunchly independent political stances rather than any deficiency of craft or vision." It is only comparatively recently, since Walker's rediscovery of her literary foremother, that Hurston's writings have attracted considerable attention, sparking what one writer has called "a Zora Neale Hurston cult."[166]

Given both the motivation for the rise of Hurston studies and their comparative newness, it is perhaps unsurprising that *Moses* has to date received only piecemeal treatment within the literary critical world. The use of Hurston's life and works by feminists and womanists has already been mentioned. Concentrating on the autobiography and the female characters in *Jonah's Gourd Vine* and *Their Eyes Were Watching God*, such approaches tell much about the experience of mid-century African American women as producers and consumers of fiction. However, the emphasis on Hurston's ability in these books to evoke the storefront life of the rural South of her childhood can lead to imbalanced readings. Too many critics consign Hurston to the Eatonville porch for eternity (in reality, she left as a child.)[167] Ultimately, the focus of their interest runs the risk of unintentionally reinforcing the 1930s and 1940s style of assessments of this remarkable individual as "apolitical" and homespun.

Moses, Man of the Mountain, although it explores issues of gender and race politics both within and without the Southern domestic sphere in a perhaps more sophisticated manner than Hurston's earlier novels, lacks obvious connection with the life experience of either author or reader. Its female characters do not possess the spirit of Janie Stark in *Their Eyes*, and its male ones, unlike John Pearson in *Jonah*, do not suffer for their refusal to accept the humanity of women. Narratively, *Moses* appears to replicate rather than remedy the silencing of women in biblical and African American society. As a result, many current Hurston scholars spend comparatively little time exploring the novel. As was noted earlier, even those whose study of Hurston is motivated by theological concerns ignore her work that is most obviously related to their sphere of interest.

The response of those new Hurston scholars who do address *Moses* is mixed. Although most agree that it should be viewed as her most ambitious project, few would differ with Hemenway's assessment of the end result as "a noble failure"[168] in which Hurston was ultimately unable to sustain her attempt at the fusion of differing styles, tones, and humor. Certainly, *Moses, Man of the Mountain* has its weaknesses, yet so do Hurston's other more (critically and popularly) "successful" works. *Jonah* ends abruptly and somewhat unsatisfactorily; in modern terms the feminist credentials of *Their Eyes* are slightly dubious; it is, after all, through a relationship with a man that Janie discovers herself. Why then is *Moses* so often deemed less pleasing than Hurston's other fiction?

Much as Steffens failed with *Moses in Red* because he contravened the American Moses "myth," so *Moses, Man of the Mountain* has fared badly at the hands of critics because it subverts modern criticism's construct that is the Hurston "myth." Present scholarly difficulty with *Moses, Man of the Mountain* stems from the assumption on the part of some critics that *Their Eyes* and *Jonah* represent (in terms of source, style, and motivation) that which is truly Hurston. Insofar as *Moses* differs from these earlier works (and it does so considerably), it is deemed problematic. Carter-Sigglow, for example, describes the novel as "a puzzling book," commenting that it lacks the (undefined) "richness" of the earlier novels.[169] Similarly, Wall praises *Moses, Man of the Mountain* where its hero seems to approximate models previously developed by Hurston. Like Janie, who abandons a repressive middle-class lifestyle for freedom through manual labor in *Their Eyes, Moses* achieves through identification with the folk. Where it enters less familiar territory though, Wall judges *Moses* a disappointing failure.[170]

Moses suffers from current overconcentration on Hurston's earlier fiction. Extended treatments of the work are still comparatively few in number, and the implicit assumption that the Eatonville fiction is normative works to prevent critics from approaching this complex book on its own terms. *Moses* is mistakenly regarded by its first critics as an interesting (but politically insignificant) diversion and by its more recent students as a deviation from its author's prime concerns: Hurston's fascination with the Bible and with its retellings by ancient writers like Josephus and within African American religion, including hoodoo, was both considerable and sustained.

A few recent readings of the novel have begun to provide a corrective to the earlier one-dimensional interpretations. Although holding that "finally . . . the book falls short of its mark," Lillie P. Howard's 1980 study is aware of several aspects to *Moses:* She touches briefly on the issue of the novel's allusion to intraracial tension and notions of leadership. Howard is most useful, however, in her explanation of Hurston's multilayered presentation as a technique designed to render the discussion of thorny political problems more palatable: "To achieve the kind of distance she needed to comment objectively on the question of slavery, Hurston transplanted American blacks to, and acclimatized them within, an Old Testament milieu."[171]

Elsewhere, notable advances have been made concerning the significance of anthropology within the book. Scholars now recognize that Hurston did not merely incorporate within her writings folktales or descriptive touches gleaned from fieldwork researches. Anthropological theory has an impact on her fiction, and her deployment of insights from cultural linguistics has recently been emphasized.[172] However, there is still much room for further research. For those interested in exploring the true breadth of Hurston's enterprise and for the current investigation of examining the history and politics of American representations of the biblical Moses figure, it is necessary not only to understand Hurston's creative techniques but also to expose the wide range of interests and concerns on behalf of which those techniques were implemented—something that this present study has, for the first time, attempted to do.

Conclusions

The internal complexity and changing fate of *Moses, Man of the Mountain* discussed in this chapter challenge consensus assessments of Hurston's recasting of the biblical story as "mere homespun" and a "joke." In *Moses*, the biblical story is reconfigured to engage racism and antisemitism, gender relations and the construction of patriarchy, and African American communal organization. As an educated, intelligent African American woman in the early twentieth century, Hurston was both party to and excluded from the majority society, and the impact that this had on her reading of the Bible text is clear.

Perhaps one of the more interesting findings of this chapter was the relative tolerance of Jewish reviewers toward a Moses very different from their own and the way in which this contrasts with the reception of the novel by Hurston's African American peers. Untermeyer and Slomovitz's apparent willingness to recognize diverse and competing images of Moses as being capable of possessing communally grounded authenticity is far removed from the association by other white reviewers (and those who wanted to assimilate to their norms) of "folk culture" and "inferiority." Perhaps the Jewish readers, used to operating in a context in which readings of the Moses story other than their own are dominant, share something of Hurston's awareness of the contested uses of the common myth. This once again demonstrates the necessity of drawing on the evidence of those on the periphery of society as well as of those at its center in trying to assess the place and function of the Bible and religious language in American culture.

It still remains to address the issue of why Hurston chose to work with this and not some other narrative. Perhaps the very polyvalency and eclecticism of *Moses* provide the key here? For Hurston, the story of Moses and the exodus was attractive because of the prior resonances of the story that have been identified in analysis. By reworking the Moses story, Hurston makes recourse to a text that her audience is already used to reading in a variety of ways. Hurston is in effect exploiting the history of the narrative so that she, too, can address an array of issues in fictional form. This approach is, of course, available to all those who re-present the Moses story. DeMille also uses it to popular effect in *The Ten Commandments*. Those who rework America's iconic book in this way stand, and build on, a vibrant and diverse tradition.

Coming in from the Cold (War)

Cecil B. DeMille's *The Ten Commandments* (1956)

In contrast to the relative obscurity of *Moses in Red* and *Moses, Man of the Mountain*, Cecil B. DeMille's 1956 film *The Ten Commandments* features one of the best known images of Moses. Starring Charlton Heston, with Yul Brynner as his pharaonic antagonist, it took in some $34 million dollars in the year of its release and ranked second to only *Ben Hur* (Wyler, 1959) in box office takings for the decade 1951–1960.[1] In later years, television and home video have ensured the continued life of the film, now part of an oft-repeated canon of Hollywood epics, rerun particularly during holiday seasons. Of course, such statistics and impressions are crude. They do not indicate how many cinema-goers are repeat viewers or who watches the film and how, but they do attest to the ongoing currency of DeMille's Moses.

In much "critical" discourse, biblical epics have typically either been reduced to a riot of statistics and anecdotes or ridiculed by those who dismiss them as cumbersome pieces of vulgarity. However, recent years have witnessed the development of considerable interest in films dealing with religious subject matter and themes. This trend is evident among scholars specializing in film (Babington and Evans; Uricchio and Pearson),[2] as well as those from the disciplines of religious and biblical studies (for example, Exum, Jewett, Kreitzer, Scott, and Telford).[3] At a popular level, there is also considerable interest in the use of film in evangelism and youth work.

Recent studies have tended to highlight the impact of production context upon story and the potential for film versions to suggest insights into the original biblical accounts, beginning what Scott terms "a conversation that will allow each partner, the bible and American movies . . . to hear different and new intonations in each other's voice."[4] It is as part of the move to undertake serious study of the biblical epic that this chapter examines the contribution made by DeMille's film to modern American discourse about Moses and the exodus. As Wood has suggested, "Moses now, for generations of people all over the world, looks like Charlton Heston."[5] We might go further and say that for many people Charlton Heston is Moses. But what sort of Moses is he, and why?

The Cultural Cold War

Journalist William Shannon described the 1950s as "the age of the slob," a decade of complacent materialism and political apathy.[6] In many ways it was, like the 1920s, a time of an expansion in suburban consumerism and increased efforts to create and maintain a unified American identity: "Americans have always struggled to accumulate goods and cultivate goodness. During the postwar era the nation again tried to do both."[7] Unlike the 1920s, however, Americans in the 1950s now perceived themselves as facing a common, clearly defined threat, both internationally and at home, in the shape of communism.

As Lincoln Steffens had believed it would, by the 1950s communism appeared poised to usurp the claim of the "American way of life" to present a paradigm of progress and action to other nations. Americans now felt insecure and defensive, for they had to contend not only with Russian power but also with a rival ideology of enormous appeal. In 1919, Woodrow Wilson had propagated the image of American soldiers as crusaders whose achievements in Europe "made all the world believe in America as it [believed] in no other nation organized in the modern world," but within ten years capitalism was rocked to the core by the 1929 crash and unemployment that rocketed to 15 million by 1933.[8] Postwar, the appeal and power of socialism seemed particularly striking in the light of the failure of the social and economic measures promised by the Truman administration in the late 1940s: Would a democratic state so unsure of itself be able to compete successfully against the Soviet Union in the race to fill regional power vacuums in Asia and Europe? Worse still, would Soviet domination abroad threaten living standards at home, helping to create the conditions for a popular uprising there?

Governmental policy addressed these concerns. Participation in the Korean War (1950–1953) can be understood partly as a practical experiment in American military opposition to communism. Domestically, the increased activities of the House Un-American Activities Committee (HUAC) and measures such as the Internal Security Act of 1950 (requiring communists to register with the attorney general) affected all areas of life. By 1954, security checks had been run on more than 6 million people. Sociologists claimed to detect an increase in pressure to conform to the ideal of the middle-class consumer as projected by television and the mass media. Compared with the 1920s and 1930s, this was also a weak time for radical movements like feminism.[9]

The worlds of cinema and religion were not unaffected by the emerging Cold War reality. Fifties films engaged in a cultural combat that was a reflection of the rhetorical campaign fought more widely in American society, but they did so in terms that were peculiarly their own. Despite (or perhaps in consequence of) its readiness to support the wartime antifascism program of the government, Hollywood came under the particular scrutiny of Senator McCarthy and the HUAC. Individuals who had been quick to sound the anti-Nazi alarm were labeled as suspiciously "prematurely anti-fascist" and hence communist (actual or potential). In the minds of those wary of the mass media, the success of wartime propaganda films also gave the lie to the industry's claims to provide "simple" entertainment. The pressures exerted on companies and individuals to reveal the identities of current and former communist sympathizers, or face the infamous blacklist, have been well documented.[10]

Statistics for the 1950s show an increase in religious affiliation and desire for participation in religious denominations. Suburbia in particular witnessed the emergence of the "organization church" (and its Jewish counterpart, the Conservative synagogue center), a voluntary community that engaged in a range of social, welfare, and recreational activities, as well as worship.[11] Ahlstrom attributes this growth to the transience of modern residential "communities" and, more important to the challenges to traditional values posed by fascism during World War II, and the USSR and its allies in the Korean conflict. As these latter opponents were officially and explicitly committed to atheism, the championing of religion and the church acquired additional importance as a means of affirming the American way of life.[12] Significantly, the 1950s was the decade in which a theological statement, the phrase "under God," was added to the Pledge of Allegiance (1954) and "In God We Trust" became the official national motto (1956). For Will Herberg, however, these sociopolitical dimensions to American religion were paramount to the extent that (despite healthy membership statistics) "true religion," in the sense of a deeply felt attachment to a set of beliefs, was under threat. Affiliation with one of the three major communities—Protestant, Catholic, or Jewish—was the means by which an individual was able to achieve a sense of belonging within a society in flux. The importance of the believer's genuine inner conviction and the traditional theological distinctions that distinguished the communities from one another was receding.[13]

It is in the light of this 1950s context that *The Ten Commandments* is here examined. Earlier discussions have shown how by retelling the Moses story Steffens was able to offer his own faltering contribution to the debates concerning the future of American society. Zora Neale Hurston used her novel to express views on a range of issues pertinent to an educated and aware African American woman. *The Ten Commandments* is similarly the aging DeMille's statement on the American-Soviet opposition, on the Bible, and (perhaps most significantly) on the place of the film industry in the Cold War world.

The Bible and American Religion

Bill Telford has highlighted the strengths that a biblical scholar immersed in the traditions of the historical-critical method may bring to a study of the Christ film. These strengths are the ability to establish, explore, and analyze intertextual links and an awareness of the impact of ideology and social context on the final product.[14] While the opening credits of *The Ten Commandments* stress its origins in "The Holy Scriptures" and in his autobiography DeMille described the Paramount executive's decision to "simply put the Bible story on the screen and let it speak for itself," at the same time he also somewhat contradictorily announced that the plot owed much to "the conclusions of some of the best modern authorities on the Bible and Egyptian history."[15] Bearing in mind Telford's concerns of intertextuality, ideology, and context, we shall try to discover in more detail the evidence in the film itself for the coexistence of the literal and critical approaches to the biblical Moses story that these comments suggest.

DeMille hinted that his motives in remaking *The Ten Commandments* were religious.[16] At a Manhattan luncheon with clergy and educators, he announced that the profits from the film were to be used to create a charitable trust and urged his listeners to "use this picture, as I hope and pray that God himself will use it, for the good of the world." According to Charles Higham, DeMille was "a devout believer in the Bible who saw himself in a missionary role, making the Scriptures attractive and fascinating to the masses in an age of increasing materialism . . . he literally accepted every word of the Bible without question."[17]

Higham's book is at time hagiographical in approach, but evidence of this sentiment can be found throughout *The Ten Commandments*. The film follows the Bible in theologizing the Moses story. Modern sociological approaches are ignored (contrast the 1975 DeBosio film *Moses*).[18] There is no attempt to deconstruct the exodus. For example, the servitude experienced by the Israelites at the hands of their Egyptian masters is unequivocally presented as unnatural and against God's plans for the world. A narrator describes the creation in language reminiscent of Genesis and the Johannine prologue: "And God said, 'Let there be light,' and there was light. And from this light God created life upon earth. And man was given dominion over all things upon this earth, and the power to choose between good and evil." The oppression into which Moses is born is cast as a violent intrusion upon the divine order.

The conservatism of approach to the biblical text in DeMille's film is further illustrated by *The Ten Commandments*' handling of miracles such as the burning bush, plagues, the crossing of the Red Sea, and the giving of the commandments themselves. Despite the financial and technological challenges to presenting these events on screen, they are all portrayed, as objectively "real" events. Finally, as if constructing an inclusio of piety, the film ends as it began, emphasizing the divine origins of the biblical order. An aged Moses is shown delivering to Eleazar the five scrolls, which (the viewer is told) he has written at divine behest.

The conservative attitude toward the biblical story implied by these elements is remarkable in view of DeMille's own desire to associate *The Ten Commandments* with "scholarship." By Lincoln Steffens's day, the historical-critical method of studying the Bible had been firmly established by scholars such as Duhm, Graf, and Wellhausen. Their identification of different sources behind the final form of the text challenged traditional belief in an inerrant, divinely revealed Bible. Contemporaneously, archaeology demonstrated that many of the stories and ideas found in the Bible were not unique but appeared similar to and influenced by the other religious cultures of the ancient Near Eastern world. The impact of these developments on attitudes toward the Moses story was far-reaching. As early as 1909, the Vitagraph film company had found the debates engendered by the development of scientific criticism impossible to avoid when it produced a silent *Life of Moses*.[19] The opening credits of DeMille's own 1923 *The Ten Commandments* (a quite different work, both formally and ideologically speaking, from its successor) attested to his awareness of similar debates, heightened by the postwar crisis.[20] As he planned to refilm the life of Moses, DeMille was aware that among biblical scholars and many ordinary believers in the 1950s, miracles like the plagues and the parting of the Red Sea were dismissed as the fanciful creations of "primitive" minds or rationalized as results of freak combinations of natural phenomena. More crucially, Mosaic authorship of the Pentateuch was disputed. The Law itself, including the Ten Commandments, had lost its connection with Moses and the exodus.[21] Set against such a context, *The Ten Commandments* can be seen as strikingly literal and pietistic in its attitude toward the Moses story.

However, *The Ten Commandments* does not take a uniformly consistent approach to the biblical account. One of the most curious aspects of the film's handling of the Moses story is its juxtapositioning of literalism alongside the exploitation of "scholarship" and the generation of elements designed to entertain a wide viewing public.

A cursory viewing of *The Ten Commandments* reveals more than half of the narrative content to be extrabiblical. Chief among the additions to the story is the romantic ménage à trois involving Moses, Rameses, and Nefretiri. The depiction of sexual tension between Moses and the Egyptian princess represents a departure from Exodus, in terms of both narrative detail and the spirit by which it is animated. At other points the biblical account is not merely supplemented but freely altered. Contra Exodus 2:15 and 32:25–28, Moses is forcibly exiled by Rameses, who wishes to punish but not kill him, and the worshipers of the golden calf are destroyed by fiery thunderbolts and earthquakes (rather than the swords of the Levites found in Exodus 32).

While the Moses-Nefretiri relationship did concern some reviewers of the film, at least an equal number found it to be spiritually uplifting.[22] This is not so surprising, perhaps, when it is noted that even where *The Ten Commandments* invents narrative, its style and language remain redolent of the biblical Moses story. In fact, even the most daring innovations ultimately function to assert the biblical account's primacy over subsequent re-presentations.

Many of the film's key additions are loosely derived from biblical verses. When DeMille's Moses decides to learn about his newfound family and participate in their Goshen slavery, the narrator quotes Exodus 2:11. Similarly integrated is Moses' spurning of Nefretiri. Her ire at his rejection of her advances causes her to "harden Pharaoh's heart" (cf. Exodus 4:21; 7:3).[23]

The influence of the Bible is present in the treatment of a number of other extrabiblical events in the film. Returning from his encounter with God at the burning bush, Moses tells the waiting Sephora and Joshua, "He revealed His Word to my mind and the Word was God. He is not flesh but spirit, the light of eternal Mind and I know that His light is in every man"—overt reliance on Johannine language.[24] Moreover, this speech is the culmination of an entire section of the film in which (as is explored later) the Gospels inform the construction of the story of Moses' life, from his discovery that he is a Hebrew to his domestic life in Midian. In this case, dependence on the New Testament does not simply demonstrate the filmmakers' awareness of the Bible's importance as a means of potentially validating their own elaborations. It can also be understood as an important aspect of the film's tendency to Christianize the Moses story.

In contrast to the lack of publicity concerning *The Ten Commandments'* use of biblical texts (especially the New Testament) to generate and justify departures from the Exodus account, DeMille made strenuous efforts to associate his novel material with biblical scholarship, particularly biblical archaeology. Even so, the film uses archaeological findings in a manner that subordinates them to the primary conviction of the importance and historical accuracy of the biblical text.

By the 1920s, investigative excavations at Jericho had seemingly disproved the historicity of the account of its overthrow by Joshua.[25] Although the most sensational and the most debated, this was not the only example of archaeological findings challenging the historical veracity of the Hebrew Bible. The general realization that, far from being unique, biblical law and prophecy had their parallels in the wider ancient Near Eastern world prompted an increasing number of scholars to consider biblical stories sociologically, understanding the Mosaic law as the humanly created and evolving requisite for the governance of a society as it developed from a nomadic to a more settled existence. However, DeMille's film rejects such suggestions and uses archaeology only where it may serve to enliven rather than challenge the biblical account. From archaeological study come the identification of Pharaoh and his wife as Rameses II and Nefretiri, respectively. It is also an inspiration for design—for example, the jackals and hounds game played by Nefretiri and Seti.[26] For DeMille, archaeology may be the servant of the Bible, but it may not attack its divinity by denying the historical reality of the plagues, the parting of the Red Sea, or the giving of the Ten Commandments.[27]

At first sight, then, *The Ten Commandments* seems fickle in its approach to the Bible, at times treating it literally and at others adopting a surprisingly free attitude. However, the nature of many of the departures from the biblical text means that ultimately they, too, assert the supremacy and overarching importance of scripture. Deviations from Exodus-Deuteronomy act to answer questions and resolve dilemmas posed by the biblical account in much the same way as did the postbiblical texts on which DeMille claimed to depend.

The Ten Commandments' trailer and title sequence allege a strong reliance on several ancient postbiblical Jewish texts (Philo, Josephus, the Midrash) and Eusebius, the fourth-century bishop. It is, DeMille asserts, to these ancient writers that he turned when seeking to supplement the biblical Moses story with accounts of incidents from the hero's youth. Noerdlinger similarly writes:

> For the picture *The Ten Commandments*, the facets of Moses' life that are not recorded in the Bible could have been invented and written in to scenes harmonious with the Old Testament story. However, Mr. DeMille . . . did not have to invent them. They had been set down in writing some 1,600 to 2,400 years ago. The missing years of Moses' life have survived in this very ancient literature.[28]

What DeMille and Noerdlinger fail to mention is that works by Philo and Josephus are historically irrelevant as far as attempts to construct the original, complete Moses story are concerned. More interesting in this context, though, is the extent to which DeMille's public appeal to these documents is more significant than the film's actual reliance on them.

Among the writers named by the film, Philo and Josephus are particularly highlighted, both in the trailer and in DeMille's remarkable appearance at the start of the film. DeMille identifies them as "ancient historians" who had access to traditions about Moses like those found in forgotten or long-lost documents "like the Dead Sea Scrolls." Significantly, they are also oriented historically in relation to significant events in early Christianity. Philo lived in the time of Jesus of Nazareth; Josephus wrote some thirty to forty years later and witnessed the destruction of Jerusalem by the Romans. In describing his ancient "sources" in this manner, DeMille is not attempting to facilitate simply their chronological location. By associating his own project with the "ancient historians" and via them documents and traditions that many at the time believed could hold vital information about the events and persons of early Christianity and Judaism, he is using the appeal to the ancient texts as part of a wider aim to associate *The Ten Commandments* with a reverential but scholarly Christian faith.

This identification of DeMille's real purposes in linking the film with postbiblical texts is borne out by an examination of the film's actual use of such works as Philo's *Life of Moses* and Josephus's *Jewish Antiquities*. As one early reviewer noted, the use of ancient texts in *The Ten Commandments* is superficial and inconsistent.[29] As might be expected, given that the vast majority of the material in the first half of the film deals with the life of the precommission Moses, reliance is greatest there, but even then remains limited.

Although Exodus 6:20 names Moses' birth parents and 1 Chronicles 4:18, "Pharaoh's daughter, Bithiah," several of the other details surrounding Moses' birth in *The Ten Commandments* owe their origins to Philo and Josephus. The presentation of Moses' birth as a divine response to the cries of the slaves in bondage draws on *Antiquities*, book 2, chapter IX [2.210–223]. These appeals to God are in part fueled by the conviction among the slaves that a deliverer will come to release them from their subjection. However, the prophecy is also known to Pharaoh's advisers, and their reading of the stars that foretell the deliverer's birth prompts the decree that Hebrew babies be slaughtered—another detail taken from the same work. Josephus has supplied DeMille with a rationale for the events of Exodus 1 that coheres with two of the film's key aims. First, it places the figure of Moses at the dynamic center of the narrative as the figure to whom others react and respond. Second, it offers the predominantly Christian audience the potential for comparisons between the lives of Moses and Jesus.[30] One further element of DeMille's portrayal of Moses' infancy that may be gleaned from an ancient writer is the theme of Bithiah's concealment of Moses' true origin. Whereas *Antiquities* implies that Moses' identity was known to the pharaonic court, Philo's *Life of Moses* 1.19 refers to duplicity on the part of the (unnamed) Egyptian princess.

These examples of reliance on ancient writers must be set against the many instances where DeMille's presentation of Moses does not utilize material from the Hellenistic and Rabbinic texts. Many stories contained in these works are not found in the film. To mention a few examples, Josephus and Philo both relate a prodigious childhood in which Moses' intellect and stature far surpass that of his peers. Josephus additionally describes an incident in which the young child, in an act symbolic of future triumph, flings the pharaonic crown to the ground and tramples it underfoot.[31] Although these features in the ancient texts are in keeping with *The Ten Commandments'* presentation of a heroic Moses whose future mission is predicted and foreshadowed in numerous ways throughout his early life, they are not used in the film. Equally, many essential elements in *The Ten Commandments'* birth narrative (such as the Memnet subplot) do not owe their origins to an ancient work. DeMille's film is dependent upon postbiblical writers in only a limited sense.

Despite the inconsistent adoption of Philo and Josephus, the birth narrative remains the most significant example of DeMille's reliance on the ancient texts foregrounded in the promotion of the film. Just a few further elements may owe their origins to themes and details in the ancient writers. *The Ten Commandments* appears, for instance, to owe its characterization of Dathan as the unredeemed and irredeemable traitor to Rabbinic tradition. Developing Numbers 16, in which Dathan and Abiram are significant participants in Korah's rebellion against Moses, the Talmud asserted that Dathan was wicked "from beginning to end" (*Sanhedrin* 109b). Midrashim claim that he was responsible for denouncing Moses and revealing his Hebrew origins to Pharaoh, following Moses' killing of the Egyptian taskmaster (*Yal. Ex.* 167), and at the Red Sea incited the children of Israel to return to servitude (*Exodus Rabbah* 1.29). Thus aggadic tradition contains precedents for all of Dathan's major actions in *The Ten Commandments*, with the exception of his role in the manufacture of the golden calf and sexual exploitation of Lilia.

The ancient emphasis on Moses' success as a shepherd may also inform the film's idyllic portrayal of his time in Midian. When DeMille's Moses procures high prices for Jethro's flocks, demonstrating agricultural and financial acumen, he resembles Philo's hero, who "became more skilled than any of his time in managing flocks."[32] The thrust of both accounts is similar: Success in shepherding animals prefigures an outstanding career as a leader of people. Likewise, the sentiment (not the detail) of *Exodus Rabbah* 1.27 is evoked when Moses, in charge of the Goshen building site, orders the institution of a day of rest and the freeing of temple grain stores to feed the slave laborers. The Rabbinic text suggests a similar concern for the welfare of the people when describing Moses' allocation of work tasks according to abilities, so that the strong carried the greater burdens and the weak, lesser ones.

Finally, in one of the most fascinating scenes in the film, the viewer is introduced to the adult Moses as he returns from a successful military campaign in Ethiopia. Pharaoh Seti greets the conquering prince, saying that he has heard how Moses laid siege to a city and overcame the threat of dangerous serpents with the aid of a natural deterrent, the snakes' worst enemy, the ibis. In a somewhat stilted exchange, Moses makes no remark in response to Seti's statement and simply introduces to him the rulers of his new client state, the Ethiopian king and his sister, who makes clear her physical attraction to Moses.

DeMille's use of Josephus in this scene is intriguing. The text of *Antiquities*, book 2, chapters X and XI (2.243–253) clearly forms its basis. The tale of Moses and the ibises, found also in Artapanus, has long interested scholars, as has the mysterious Ethiopian princess whose desire for Moses prompts her to surrender her city.[33] However, a comparison of Josephus's story with that in the film indicates that typically the ancient material does not drive the film's plot but relates to it only tangentially, providing a motivation for its presentation of Rameses's deepening hostility toward Moses. Josephus's incident is only alluded to as an off-screen event, and its outcome never pursued. The suggested sexual attraction between Moses and the Ethiopian princess is never referred to again, and her name (it is Tharbis, again following Josephus) is mentioned only in the opening credits rather than in the dialogue.[34] Seemingly, the ancient story has been used to add a veneer of scholarship to the film. It is not permitted to influence or define the narrative. The result is an interesting but somewhat inconsistent and unsatisfactory integration of ancient and modern in *The Ten Commandments*.

DeMille's presentation of religion and religious community in *The Ten Commandments* must be related to wider trends in postwar religious activity. Commentators have debated the significance and origins of the apparent renewal in religious commitment in 1950s America. As noted earlier, one major cause was the importance of the new suburban churches and synagogue centers in providing a sense of community for the geographically and socially mobile middle classes. Church membership figures should, then, be set alongside others, which indicate a corresponding rise in involvement in secular organizations and clubs.[35] Also important was the willingness of the churches to exploit mass-marketing techniques. (In effect, the exponents of this type of religious promotion were heirs of Steffens's rival, Bruce Barton.) Billy Graham used radio and television to sell the message of his Evangelistic Association. Norman Vincent Peale's feelgood theology urged readers to think their way to confident lives and personal happiness as described in books like *The Power of Positive Thinking*.[36] Without doubt, the Cold War opposition to the officially atheist societies of the USSR and its allies also played a role in the 1950s surge in religious participation. The ideological stance of the Soviet bloc ensured that the championing of religion assumed an additional dimension as an assertion of commitment to the American way of life. For J. Edgar Hoover, the choice was plain: "Since Communists are anti-God, encourage your child to be active in the church."[37]

For some scholars, the redefinition of religious commitment as a kind of secret weapon against Communism threatened to degrade religion's spiritual core, fostering sentimental attitudes that possessed wide appeal but were shallow and uncritical in nature. For Will Herberg, in the now classic *Protestant, Catholic, Jew* (1955), it was

> only too evident that the religiousness characteristic of America today is very often a religiousness without religion, a religiousness with almost any kind of content or none, a way of sociability or "belonging," rather than a way of reorienting life towards God. It is thus frequently a religious-

ness without serious commitment, without real inner conviction, without genuine existential decision. What should reach down to the core of existence, shattering and renewing, merely skims the surface of life, and yet succeeds in generating the sincere feeling of being religious. Religion thus becomes a kind of protection the self throws up against the radical demand of faith.[38]

Although Herberg overstressed his case, seemingly discounting the impact of his own conservatism (and that of neo-orthodox Christians like Reinhold Niebuhr,)[39] he did illuminate a significant dimension of 1950s American religion. Peale's gospel affirmed the middle classes. It promised individuals success and popularity and often seemed to champion the personal quest for satisfaction over traditional Christian emphases. Even the more traditional revivalist broadcasts of Billy Graham included nationalistic hymns, and addresses referring to the need to save America, so that it might save "The World." Eisenhower's own call for Americans to return to God further supports the contention that it was the general notion of the worth of religious commitment, rather than the specifics of any particular religious worldview, that was to the fore: "Recognition of the Supreme Being is the first, most basic, expression of Americanism. Without God, there could be no American form of government, nor an American way of life."[40]

Hollywood was not immune from the religious revival, with celebrities joining politicians in stressing the value of faith. DeMille's own articulation of the motives behind the production of *The Ten Commandments* can be understood as part of this general trend. Furthermore, several elements of the film seem to uphold some of Herberg's claims about the lack of substance in 1950s religion.[41]

In contrast to the biblical story of the release of God's "peculiar people," DeMille's exodus participants are strikingly de-ethnicized and departicularized. The slaves' identity as a distinct ethnic group is muted by the pointed inclusion in their ranks of Nubians and sympathetic Egyptians, suggesting that membership in the Chosen People is above all a voluntary, self-selected identity. Although Moses and his followers are the "ancestors" of modern Jewry, the film implicitly denies any connection based on heredity. Likewise, the biblical origins of particular behaviors associated with Judaism are downplayed or even excluded from the film. *The Ten Commandments* ignores the specifics of Jewish observance, including *kashrut, tumah ve-toharah*, and festival observances, which feature so strongly in the Hebrew Bible. The Aaronic priesthood and the construction of the tabernacle in the wilderness are also unmentioned.[42] The only legislation treated in the film is the Ten Commandments themselves—

that is, that part of the biblical legislation shared historically (although differently interpreted) by Jews and Christians—and even they are dealt with in a way that departicularizes their content and form. When Moses receives the tablets, the writing on them is not Hebrew but a language of "the late Bronze age." In this way DeMille is able to combine his twin goals of presenting a universalized Moses story and allying himself with contemporary scholarly discourse on the Bible.

The closest example to the presence of a particular ritual in *The Ten Commandments* is the (anachronistic) celebration of a proto-seder by Moses and his family in Goshen.[43] After the recitation of a primitive Shema and blessing over bread, Moses' son Eleazar evokes Jewish practice by asking a variant of the traditional *Mah Nishtanah*:

> Why is everyone afraid?
> Why is this night different from all others?
> Why do we eat unleavened bread and bitter herbs?[44]

However, even this observance becomes a demonstration of ecumenical or interfaith possibilities. When Bithiah and her Nubian servants arrive at the door, Moses pointedly admits them to the proceedings. His declaration that "there are not strangers among those who seek God's mercy" and "all who thirst for freedom may come with us" not only denies conflict based on ethnic differences but also implicitly asserts the ideal of faith communities that are open to, and ready to learn from, one another (at this stage Bithiah may be disillusioned with the Egypt and its belief system, but she has not accepted that of Moses). The emphasis on ethical and abstract notions like freedom and divine mercy evokes Herberg's allegation that a commitment to shared principles was more important to a 1950s audience than the detailed specifics of a particular religion.

Like Bithiah and her servants, Moses and Rameses undergo changes in their religious orientation, coming to faith in God at different stages in the narrative. However, despite these portrayals of the ideal of openness and fluidity in religious identity and DeMille's own statements about the need for Jews, Christians, and Muslims to unite against Communism, *The Ten Commandments* narratively and symbolically prefers the journey of faith to arrive at a Christianized destination.[45] By departicularizing Judaism and ignoring the halakhic content of the Hebrew Bible, the film effectively denies the worth of a life ordered according to its demands and champions instead an identity that assimilates to the wider (secularized/Christian) society. Faiths that practice "idolatry" and the worship of a plurality of divinities are even more explicitly rejected when DeMille accentuates the punishment of the Israelites involved in the building and celebration of the golden calf: *The Ten Commandments* has an unequivocally divine thunderbolt and fiery earthquake swallow the sinners.

The most sustained example of the championing of Christianity in *The Ten Commandments* is in the scenes presenting the period from Moses' discovery of his Hebrew origins to his exile and arrival in Midian. DeMille utilizes language and narrative from the New Testament extensively, and Moses' quest for self-discovery reveals a distinctly Christianized identity.

His true birth revealed to him by Bithiah and Yochebel, Moses undergoes a series of "temptations" as Bithiah presents him with a range of options. His family could be sent away and his Hebrew origins concealed once more (ensuring a good life for himself and his close relatives but denying the truth and the needs of the wider community). Alternatively, Moses could do nothing until he ascended to the throne. Once there, he could use his position to benefit all, including the slaves (again, a choice involving duplicitousness on Moses' part). These suggestions are followed later by the attempt of Nefretiri, who beseeches Moses to rescue her (from Rameses), himself (from drudgery), and the slaves by returning to the Royal Palace. Are they not all his people? she asks. These temptation scenes evoke the testing of Jesus in Luke 4 and Matthew 4. Effectively, they serve the same purpose as the New Testament story, expressing the dilemmas faced by Moses and presenting him with a number of ways in which he may choose to live his new life. Like Jesus, DeMille's Moses must decide the perimeters of his new sphere of activity and has to consider whether he is willing to compromise with evil (Egypt) to achieve his goals. His final decision to resist both Bithiah and Nefretiri thus establishes that his mission will be achieved by working among the people (not from a palace) and that it is with Israel and not Egypt that his true place lies.

Moses' rejection (like Jesus') of temptation prompts a Lukan-like declaration from Yochebel. Combining the themes of the Magnificat and Anna's speech in the Temple (Luke 1:46-55; 2:36-38), she announces prophetically that in Moses she has beheld her deliverer and by virtue of him is blessed among all mothers. *The Ten Commandments* also has its own Simeon, in the form of an elderly mud treader who works alongside Moses in the brick pits of Goshen. In contrast to the Lukan visionary, however, DeMille's character dies believing that his prayer that he might see his deliverer before death is unanswered (cf. Luke 2:25-35). The irony is that although neither he nor Moses realizes it, the old man's request has been granted. The film's translation of Luke thus serves to heighten the narrative tension and piously asserts that, despite appearances, prayer is answered.

The Ten Commandments not only draws on the New Testament for its treatment of the gradual revelation of Moses' true identity and purpose but also conceives of his downfall (capture and exile enforced by Rameses) in Christianizing terms. Whereas the Hebrew Bible has Moses flee after impulsively killing an Egyptian taskmaster, in the film he is banished from Egypt on account of his identity as the long-promised deliverer.[46] Like Judas, Dathan seeks and receives financial reward for betraying Moses to Rameses (compare Mark 14:10-11 and parallels). When Moses is charged with being the deliverer of the slaves, his response, "I am the son of Amram and Yochebel, Hebrew slaves," evokes both the language and the enigmatic nature of Jesus' replies at Luke 22:66–23-9 (and parallels). Seti, like Pilate, realizes that in the face of Moses' intransigence he must order his death, but he cannot bring himself to pronounce the sentence and hands him over to Rameses for punishment (Matthew 27:24-26 especially).

The film's most striking use of the New Testament occurs in the scene in which Moses is cast into the wilderness by Rameses. In one sense, Moses' experiences in the desert, the place "where holy men and prophets are cleansed and purged for God's great purpose," recall once more the synoptic temptation narrative. His survival in the desert without sustenance (he is given only a single day's rations) will be like that of Jesus, miraculous (Matthew 4:2; Luke 4:2). Just as the biblical Jesus is mocked as "King of the Jews" and dressed to parody regal wear (Mark 15:16-20 and parallels; John 19:2, 5), so Rameses taunts Moses as "the slave who would be King" and "Prince of Israel." Rameses has him dressed in a Levite cloth, "his robe of state" handing Moses a binding pole, he tells him, "Here is your king's scepter, and here is your kingdom. You have the scorpion, the cobra, and the lizard for subjects. Free them as you will: leave the Hebrews to me." The irony here is that these comments are closer to the truth than Rameses imagines. DeMille's Moses will prove to be the Hebrews' true leader, just as for the New Testament writers Jesus really was king of the Jews.

Thus DeMille's presentation of religious identity in *The Ten Commandments* is contradictory. On the one hand, the de-ethnicizing and departicularizing of the exodus participants and their religion seemingly lends credence to Herberg's characterization of 1950s religion as open but indifferent. Despite its graphic assertion of the necessity and divinity of the Law, the film never takes the step of portraying its observance (the narrative leaps from the giving of the Ten Commandments to Moses' death). The worth of the laws in their abstract and generalized form is affirmed, but the specifics of the working out of their implementation is not of interest to the filmmakers. On the other hand, a close examination of *The Ten*

Commandments' reliance on the New Testament in constructing its Moses narrative offers further weight to the argument that in the 1950s the departicularization of Judaism entailed its effective assimilation to the wider context, which was not simply "American" but in rhetoric and praxis profoundly "Christian."[47] The film's use of New Testament themes and language ultimately denies the specificity of Moses' life and requires its interpretation as Christlike. Hence *The Ten Commandments* both supports and challenges Herberg's characterization of 1950s American "religionless" religion.

To close the discussion of DeMille's Moses and American religion and lead to the next section of the analysis, I note here the relationship between *The Ten Commandments* and the American religion par excellence, the Church of Jesus Christ of Latter-Day Saints (Mormons). *The Ten Commandments*, in fact, premiered in Salt Lake City, perhaps because of DeMille's personal friendship with the president of the church, David O. McKay.[48] Certainly DeMille was sympathetic to the Mormon cause, which is acknowledged by his granddaughter's decision to establish the DeMille archive at Brigham Young University in Provo, Utah.[49] He did, however, remain an Episcopalian. Moreover, there are no definite traces of Latter-Day Saints doctrine or scripture in *The Ten Commandments*; it cannot be regarded as a Mormon film. Yet in the community of the Saints, DeMille found a group whose theology appeared to resonate with his film's message. On the one hand, the America-Israel analogy sustained in *Commandments* (discussed in the following section) has its counterpart in the Book of Mormon's account of America as both the place to which the Israelites fled after the fall of Jerusalem in the sixth century B.C.E. and the true Zion. The notion that American experience is somehow illuminated by recourse to biblical imagery and themes is also common to both. In the case of the Mormons, their characterization of the nineteenth-century migration from Nauvoo to Utah as an exodus led by the Mormon "Moses," Brigham Young, and the subsequent efforts to implement theocracy based on a Hebrew Bible–style model in Salt Lake City have been well documented.[50]

Like Mormonism, DeMille's film finds a special relevance in the Bible story. Ancient and modern concerns blend to create a new American narrative with profound religious and political implications.

Politics

For DeMille, as for Steffens and Hurston, the religious and political aspects of the Moses story were inextricably linked. The dominant political context in which *The Ten Commandments* was produced and screened was the Cold War opposition between the United States and the Soviet Union. But other significant issues could not be ignored, either. One was the continued subordination of America's African-heritage population. Further questions were raised by Middle East politics. By the time DeMille retold the Moses story, there was once again a Jewish state in Israel; the region had been ripped open by military and diplomatic conflicts, not least by the Suez crisis.

In addition to the political and military conflicts with the Soviet Union and its allies, 1950s America prosecuted a cultural Cold War, "which preferred oblique cultural attempts to win the hearts and minds of nonaligned countries to overt political ones."[51] This campaign had as its origin a widespread concern that Soviet philosophy might prove irresistible to the inhabitants of America or other countries such as Britain, which to the dismay of the Washington administration had elected a socialist (Labour) government immediately after World War II. America's political, economic, and ideological ascendancy seemed questioned. In this climate, and given the recent history of Hollywood's work in support of the war effort in the 1930s and 1940s, many filmmakers and government officials alike saw the feature film as a key agent of American values. Hollywood could proselytize for the "American way." In the words of Eric Johnston, president of the Motion Picture Export Association, films were "messages from the free country."[52]

Many Hollywood professionals accepted their role as cultural combatants with genuine zeal. Scholars are undecided as to whether this enthusiasm stemmed from a personal commitment to "American ideals," a wish to exploit for profit a topical issue, or a desire to appease the HUAC.[53] In any case, the sometimes uncertain motivations of the filmmakers resulted in the production of a considerable number of anticommunist films. Among them were several blatantly propagandizing works, which tended to do poorly at the box office. More commonly, anticommunism was evoked and promoted in an indirect fashion. For instance, it has been argued that 1950s science fiction films expressed fears about the vulnerability of the United States to attack from a distant, powerfully technologized, and intellectual enemy.[54]

Produced at the height of cultural anticommunism, in the immediate aftermath of the Korean War, DeMille's 1956 *The Ten Commandments* is very much an anti-Soviet film. DeMille had a strong interest in politics; he once toyed with the idea of (like Steffens) writing on the Mexican revolution. In later life, he shared the opinion that American institutions overseas (including Hollywood) ought to promote American ideals there, and even served as a consultant to the U.S. Information Agency.[55] *The Ten Commandments* was a film that took the cinematic portrayal of the life and person of Moses to its logical Cold War conclusion. Put simply, Moses, as instigator and guardian of a divinely willed and ordered freedom, became representative of the American nation and the identity of the United States as Israel, in the sense of both promised land and light for the nations. Pharaoh Rameses, whose autocracy attempted to deny the divine order and subjected countless masses to lives of meaningless drudgery enforced by the threat of state backed terror, functioned as his powerful yet eventually defeated Soviet enemy.

The view that biblical epics may be seen as allegories of meanings central to American identity has long been argued by writers like Wood and, more recently, Babington and Evans. For the latter authors, Wood's suggestion that at the end of *The Ten Commandments* DeMille poses Moses to resemble the Statue of Liberty marks a watershed in the development of serious study of the genre.[56] When DeMille has Moses urge the Israelites (and the audience) "Proclaim liberty throughout all the land unto all the inhabitants thereof" (Leviticus 25:10), he is annunciating a specifically American model of freedom (the words are taken from the Liberty Bell in Philadelphia)—a freedom from slavery and racial discord, defined by shared belief in one supreme God, and obedience to a set of divine norms.[57] Alongside the biblical yearning for a land of milk and honey is the film's presentation of the promised land as a place of private property and free enterprise, "where every man shall reap what he has sowed." As the children of Israel go out of slavery, there are "among them planters of vineyards and sowers of seed, each hoping to sit under his own vine and fig-tree."

The Cold War counterpart of ideal America, the demonized Soviet regime, is evoked in several ways in *The Ten Commandments*. Just as Wood has suggested that in many Hollywood productions America's colonial past is recalled by casting English actors in negative roles, so in *The Ten Commandments* the Cold War identification of the Egyptian regime with that in the USSR is hinted at by casting the Eastern European–accented Yul Brynner as Rameses.[58] The film's heightening of the biblical portrayal of the slaves' struggle for freedom as a battle for supremacy between God and a human tyrant also functions to stress its nature as an allegory of conflict between the American nation "under God" and a state founded on the teachings of a philosopher who had famously declared religion to be the "opium of the people." Rameses's goals are shown to be in conflict with those of faith when he confesses to Seti that his failure to complete the building of a treasure city stems from resistance engendered by the slaves' belief in a coming redeemer. Later on, Rameses's atheism is restressed when he explains the plagues sent by God naturalistically and then describes the Egyptian belief system sociologically, claiming that "you prophets and priests made the gods that you may prey upon the fears of men." The specifics of this social-scientific account of faith echo Marxist critiques of religion as a social construct that not only provides comfort in a harsh world but also justifies inequalities of power and wealth.[59]

The Ten Commandments does not merely discuss in an oblique fashion the threat of communism as understood by America in the mid-1950s. Despite its sometimes wearing gargantuism, it is also a feel-good film that assures the American viewing public of an eventual triumph. When Rameses proclaims that "his [Moses'] god is God," the audience is reassured that in spite of current events the Soviet threat will be extinguished. Moses (and America) will win.

It is not sufficient to end an analysis of *The Ten Commandments'* role in the wider Cold War context, as some have done, by simply stating the existence of a Moses-America and Rameses–Soviet Union analogy. Further, more nuanced insights may be gained by relating the specifics of the film's narrative to the precise political conditions of its production.

The anticommunist blacklist persisted in Hollywood well beyond the final HUAC hearing in 1953. Kirk Douglas's insistence that Dalton Trumbo receive credit for writing *Spartacus* (1959) is often cited as marking the end of the period, but in reality many writers, actors, and production workers identified as Communists or Communist sympathizers found it impossible to obtain employment through the 1960s and beyond. The only solutions were to flee to Europe or, in the case of screenwriters, produce work secretly in America and have it submitted to companies pseudonymously or fronted by a sympathetic nonblacklisted colleague. In this environment, there were nevertheless increasing attempts to rehabilitate some of those motion picture professionals who had suffered at the height of anticommunist hysteria. DeMille himself was involved in the early days of this movement, most notably as president of the Motion Picture Industry Council. Although the council generally toed the HUAC line and assisted directors in checking the loyalty of potential employees, it also sought to further the prospects of former Communists who "repented" of previous involvements and those who had been blacklisted unfairly. This off-screen belief in the possibility of change and rehabilitation has its mirror in the on-screen treatment of the characters Rameses and Bithiah in *The Ten Commandments*. Although Egyptians (or, allegorically, Communists), they are not presented as irredeemable. To some extent, both are able to participate in the liberty proclaimed by Moses-America. Bithiah rejects her former life; her willingness to learn the truth of God's plan leads

Moses to welcome her into the circle of those celebrating Passover in Goshen. Later on, Bithiah's "conversion" is evidenced by good works as she gives up her chariot for the infirm and defends Moses' reputation against Dathan's taunts in the wilderness.

Although DeMille's Rameses can hardly be said to have been welcomed into the company of Israel-America, it is noteworthy that, in a detail exploiting the ambiguity of Exodus 14:28, he does not perish with his charioteers in the Red Sea. On his return to the palace, he is a broken man, but both his atheism and a short-lived reliance on the petty idol of Sokar, king of the underworld, have been broken, too. Rameses's final scene suggests that for him too, some form of redemption will be possible. The haltingly voiced confession that "Moses' god is God" hints that Rameses's deep despondency is a proverbial "dark night of the soul." He may emerge a changed and better man.

It seems, then, that DeMille goes to some lengths to assert the possibility of repentance and rehabilitation. Seemingly, the character of Bithiah is developed for the sole purpose of presenting a model of conversion and change. Likewise, if the declaration of his newfound faith were to be removed from the film, Rameses's survival would be redundant from the point of view of the developing narrative. In this context, the two characters who are not redeemed (Nefretiri and Dathan) are all the more interesting.

While the film suggests that for Rameses a new life is possible, Nefretiri's final scene suggests that her life is soon to end at the hands of her husband. DeMille's failure to rehabilitate her may be understood as wholly consistent with *The Ten Commandments*' identification of Nefretiri as the essence or epitome of Egypt. When she tells a beguiled Prince Moses, "I am Egypt," the statement does not simply refer to her constitutional role as throne-princess. Nefretiri's life of opulence and extravagance; her cruel manipulation of Moses, Rameses, and Seti; and her willingness to murder Memnet to avert thwarting her lustful desires epitomize what the film terms the "intoxicating beauty" of Egypt. These behaviors and attitudes, which figures like Bithiah and Rameses must deny to participate in God's plan, are the sum total of her being; Nefretiri represents the irreducible, intransigent core of Egypt that must be destroyed. She functions symbolically as that part of Communist identity that Europe and, in particular, Russia must forgo to facilitate an accommodation to the American worldview.

The character of Dathan, destroyed on-screen in *The Ten Commandments*, is complicated by DeMille's casting of Edward G. Robinson in the role. In the 1930s, Robinson had been one of the first Hollywood actors to condemn fascism, and he worked for the American government in broadcasting propaganda messages to Germany during the war. Following 1945, this "premature antifascism," together with Robinson's Jewishness and Communist associations (he had met the exiled Trotsky), made him a target for the right wing. Never actually summoned to testify before the HUAC, Robinson was blacklisted. He found it hard to obtain work, and numerous pamphlets, mostly from hysterical antisemites, railed against his alleged activities as a Soviet stooge. Given the situation, DeMille's employment of Robinson to work on *The Ten Commandments* in 1956 is striking. The actor himself later recalled his surprise at the decision. "No more conservative or patriarchal figure [than DeMille] existed in Hollywood, no one more opposed to communism or any permutation or combination thereof." Yet DeMille resisted his advisers and offered the part to an actor whom they considered "unacceptable."[60] DeMille had not just cast Robinson to appear in the film, however; he had specifically placed him in the role of Dathan. Consequently, Robinson was rehabilitated (by virtue of his appearance), and the right-wing charges against him were evoked by means of his on-screen identification with Dathan, a figure who, as the American Communists were alleged to do, spied and informed on his own people.

The conflation of meanings consequently suggested by the Edward G. Robinson subtext is emblematic of DeMille's ambiguity in regard to cinema's role vis-à-vis the Cold War. The broad identification of Israel-America and Egypt–Soviet Union allegorizes the Cold War. But the specifics of the film also suggest that change and redemption are possible and welcome. Redemption occurs narratively for Bithiah and Rameses and also extranarratively, through the employment of real-life "Communists" such as Robinson. Like his Moses, in *The Ten Commandments* DeMille offers liberty on his own terms, on or off the screen.

Race politics also casts a shadow over DeMille's Moses. Although almost a century had passed since the abolition of slavery, racial segregation and discrimination survived in 1950s America. In 1955, a huge bus boycott was undertaken to end the continued segregation of public transport in Montgomery, Alabama. African Americans walked to work, church, and school in preference to being required to sit in only the back seats of buses. In 1957, violent clashes arose over an attempt to desegregate Central High School in Little Rock, Arkansas, by enrolling nine African American students. Despite Abraham Lincoln's efforts, Jim Crow was alive, if not quite well.[61]

Although the profile of the civil rights movement was high, the film industry's output tended to avoid the issues of race and ethnicity. A few important films were made in the 1930s and 1940s, such as *Pinky* (Kazan, 1949), which drew on issues raised by *The Autobiography of an Ex-Colored Man* and dealt with problems of discrimination and identity experienced by many African Americans.[62] On the whole, however, such projects were rare. Nonwhites were generally absent from the screen and, when they appeared, had stereotyped and unsympathetic roles. As late as 1940, a remake of *The Birth of a Nation* was countenanced. Even a progressive production such as *Pinky* featured a white actress (Jeanne Crain) in the starring role as a pale-skinned African American.

Hollywood's failure to push forward the civil rights agenda had multiple origins. First, although a significant minority of those working in the industry were Jewish and had personal experience of negative discrimination, on the whole the industry was no less racist than the wider society. For the average Hollywood employee, making an antiracism film was not a primary goal. Second, as noted earlier, many of those with pronounced antiracist attitudes were regarded as potential Communists. Finding themselves the victims of blacklisting, they fled to Europe. (Included in their number was Donald Ogden Stewart, second husband of Steffens's widow, Ella Winter.) Further factors impeding the production of films discussing race and ethnicity were externally imposed regulations governing film content and a mistaken (but widespread) belief in the importance of the Southern box office. Of all movies made in the 1940s about African Americans, only *Intruder in the Dust* (1949) was uncut in the Southern states. Typically, *Brewster's Millions* (1945) was banned in Memphis, and *Island in the Sun* (1957) in Memphis, New Orleans, Jacksonville, and Montgomery, because they portrayed African American male characters as equal to, and too friendly with, white females.[63] Only in the late 1950s did legal rulings and market research studies finally establish that cinema should enjoy the same freedom from censorship as was extended to newspapers and other printed material and that the most avid film viewer was not the poor white Southerner but the middle-class, Northern city-dweller.[64]

In a context of a racist society practicing active censorship, it is not surprising that DeMille's *The Ten Commandments* failed to address the kind of race issues Hurston foregrounded in *Moses, Man of the Mountain*. As a conservative operating within a besieged and overcautious industry, DeMille was hardly likely to explore on the screen the biblical hint that Moses' marriage was interracial.[65] Had he done so, the decision would have both aroused the wrath of official bodies and repulsed racist elements within his potential audience. It was only in 1956, after filming for *The Ten Commandments* had been completed, that on-screen "miscegenation" was permitted.[66] (However, the very nature of the Moses story, in which babies are slaughtered at birth because they were born into one ethnic group and not another, has inescapable antislavery, antiracism resonances. It is possible that when DeMille's version was first screened, these connections were made by some viewers.)

As already noted, the film identifies slavery as contrary to God's purposes and unnatural. More specifically, those divine purposes are identified with freedom and equality in the ending of the film, where Moses proclaims an American-style liberty to the nations. The implication for African American and other liberal viewers is that freedom should be extended to all, regardless of ethnic origins. Such a conclusion is reinforced by the acceptance of Bithiah into the community of the people of God. Moses corrects those in the company who would exclude her on the grounds of her origins: The children of Israel are to be defined not by race but by shared beliefs and values. This lesson is reiterated by Bithiah's Nubian attendants acceptance into the company and their pointed inclusion in the party of those who partake of the exodus liberation.

An additional rejection of slavery can be seen in Prince Moses' decision to bring the defeated Ethiopians to Seti's court not as slaves but as allies. As stated earlier, DeMille drew on Josephus's *Antiquities* as a source for Moses' Ethiopian campaign. In Josephus's account, the implied consequence of the Ethiopian defeat is slavery and destruction, but the extent of this is mitigated by a marriage treaty between Moses and the Ethiopian princess Thebis.[67] *The Ten Commandments'* handling of Josephus here suggests that the filmmakers considered that the portrayal of Moses as a man with two wives, including one African one, would not be tolerated by American audiences, but that the ancient writer's theme of cooperation between two peoples was thought appropriate and so made its way (albeit in weakened form) into the film.

Discrimination against individuals on purely racial grounds is alluded to in the Memnet subplot. It is royal nursemaid Memnet's misplaced belief in the importance of the racial purity of the Egyptian ruling class that leads her to plot against Moses and eventually reveal his Hebrew origins to Nefretiri. Her actions bring exile and grief into the lives of Nefretiri, Moses, Seti, and Bithiah, and end her own life. They contrast starkly with the attitudes and behavior of Bithiah and Nefretiri, for whom Moses can be royal regardless of his racial origins. The thrust of the narrative is thus that whereas their acceptance is the route to life (Moses is rescued from the Nile by Bithiah; Nefretiri makes several attempts to secure his survival), Memnet's prejudice can engender only violence and death, and eventually it destroys even that which she so misguidedly sought to preserve.

The most explicit statement against slavery and exploitation on ethnic grounds is, however, predictably placed on the lips of Moses, about to be exiled from Egypt by Seti. Asked by Seti what has turned him against the Egyptian state, he replies that it is "the evil that men should turn their brothers into beasts of burden . . . only because they are of another race, another creed."

As mentioned earlier, uniquely among the three works considered in this study, *The Ten Commandments* represented the Moses story to a world in which a Jewish state in Israel was once more a reality. It was impossible for DeMille to ignore the resulting unrest in the Middle East and, in particular, the sporadic military conflict between Arabs and Israelis. In his autobiography, DeMille recalled how King Farouk was exiled and a new Egyptian republic proclaimed under General Mohammed Naguib just as the production team for *The Ten Commandments* decided to visit the Sinai for location shooting. While they were there, Naguib himself was deposed and placed under house arrest.[68] Two years later, the same issue of *Time* magazine that reviewed *The Ten Commandments* also carried reports of Israel's invasion of Egypt and of the Suez Crisis.[69]

This juxtapositioning of the biblical Arab-Israeli encounter with modern-day ones did not go unnoticed by the film's first viewers or by subsequent commentators. Writing for the *New York Times*, Crowther opened his review with the following assertion: "Against the raw news of a modern conflict between Egypt and Israel—a conflict that has its preamble in the Book of Exodus—Cecil B. DeMille's *The Ten Commandments* was given its world premiere last night at the Criterion Theatre, and the coincidence was profound."[70] As the film recounted a story that famously portrayed the Egyptians in an uncompromisingly bad light, it was hard for DeMille to avoid charges of political propaganda. "No one ought to be admitted unless accompanied by an Egyptologist, on account of the glamour and the anti–ancient-Egyptian bias," Hodgens joked on the occasion of the film's tenth anniversary re-release.[71]

DeMille later recalled the accusations he faced when he was about to commence location work, in particular the words of Alfred Lilienthal, a Jewish pro-Arab activist. "In his view of things, it seemed, *The Ten Commandments* was going to be a piece of pro-Israeli, anti-Arab propaganda."[72] Although DeMille's account of the discussion (in which he portrays himself as exercising a dignified mastery of the situation) may not be entirely reliable, the report of the accusations most likely is. Like the Korean conflict, the Middle Eastern disputes were widely recognized to be United

States–Soviet Union wars by proxy. The United States funded and supported the nascent Israeli state, while her Arab adversaries, Syria and Egypt, received Soviet aid.[73] Given such realities, Lilienthal's concerns are intelligible.

DeMille's Midianite characters in *The Ten Commandments* are overwhelmingly stock Arab figures such as sheiks (Jethro and his associates) and, when Sephora's sisters entertain the company at the shearing festival, belly dancers. Midian is presented as a land characterized by violence (shepherds who raid Jethro's well) and sensuality (Sephora's lascivious sisters); these images are in continuity with much older Western characterizations of the region. In this sense, DeMille's film rehearses the stereotypes of Arabs that served to reinforce the complex ideology of empire.[74]

Ultimately, though, the reality of the film does not entirely live up to Lilienthal's fears. Although its account of an ancient Arab-Israeli conflict was likely to invite comparisons with the present-day ones, the potential for straightforward analogies to be drawn was minimized by the de-ethnicized presentation of the Israelites and the Ten Commandments themselves in the film. The presentation of the Egyptian Princess Bithiah, as one who is admitted to the ranks of God's people on the basis of belief rather than ethnicity and subsequently becomes a model member of the nomadic exodus community, additionally argues against a clear demarcation of good and evil along Jew-Arab lines. Significantly, and unlike the later DeBosio film *Moses* (1975), *The Ten Commandments* also avoids reference to the specifics of the biblical battles against alien peoples and the military conquest of the promised land. "Conscious . . . of his internationalist role, DeMille avoids specific allusions to this area [the Middle East], preferring to invoke the grander clash of political-ethical systems."[75]

In contrast to the de-ethnicized portrayal of the exodus participants, it is clear that viewers are encouraged to see Jethro's family as the noble forerunners of modern Muslims. In a scene that greatly expands on that in the Exodus account, Jethro identifies himself as a Bedouin, a descendent of Ishmael, and one of "the obedient of God," thus alluding to Islam, "submission" to the divine will. The role of Jethro and Sephora in helping Moses realize his mission to free the slaves is similarly developed. What they tell him about the mysterious unnamed deity on Mount Sinai prepares him for religious encounter at the burning bush.

The positive expanded portrayal of Jethro and of Moses' marriage to Sephora prompts Babington and Evans to suggest that *The Ten Commandments* presents the Moses-Sephora-Jethro relationship as a paradigmatic treaty between two peoples of the book.[76] In view of the animosity between the two parties in the twentieth century, it is interesting to speculate as to DeMille's motives in offering such a model. In the light of circumstances both in America and abroad, something akin to the types of tensions Hurston described might have been more realistic. Was DeMille's portrayal of idealized Jew-Arab relations in *The Ten Commandments* then simply a piece of naïvely moralizing futility, or was it something else?

Explanation may be found in the general homogenizing thrust of the film. The presentation of a peaceful unity between two peoples of the book is in line with a retelling of the Moses story that de-ethnicizes the exodus participants, hints at the reform of Rameses, and closes with a proclamation of liberty and freedom unto all the nations. DeMille also shared the sentiments of one of the greatest supporters of his work as related in the autobiography. When asked whether Muslims might object to the portrayal of a character such as Moses on screen, he answered:

> that one of the strongest voices urging me to make *The Ten Commandments* had been that of the distinguished Moslem Prime Minister of Pakistan, Mohammed Ali, who saw in the story of Moses, the prophet honored equally by Moslems, Jews, and Christians, a means of welding together adherents of all three faiths against the common enemy of all faiths, atheistic communism.[77]

What is significant about these remarks is not the mistaken equation (DeMille's, rather than Mohammed Ali's?) of Jewish, Christian, and Islamic assessments of Moses but the stress on a need for a unity of faiths against communism. The anticommunism of American society generally and DeMille in particular has been discussed earlier in this chapter. Setting this sentiment alongside the involvement of the Soviet Union in Middle Eastern politics, it is possible to discern the motivation behind the treatment of the Midianites in *The Ten Commandments*. The Moses-Sephora alliance is not a simple plea for ethnic cooperation. It is DeMille's own attempt, in an age when regional disputes seemed increasingly to be fueled and sustained by the two superpowers, to promote the argument that as people of faith the place of Arabs and Jews is to unite against "Egypt"—that is, communism—and recognize the United States as the model of a society founded on freedom for all. Arab and Israeli energies are misdirected against one another; communism should be recognized as the common threat to all who worship the same God.

The Politics of Film

DeMille and his team were secure in their belief in the power of cinema to reflect and transform the zeitgeist. They shaped their Moses story to convey messages about both American life and the place of the film industry within it. In doing so, they were developing strategies already used by previous filmmakers who had worked with the exodus story. The history of the Moses film, like that of biblical epics generally, goes back almost as far as that of cinema itself. The first screen life of Moses was the now-lost *Moses and the Exodus from Egypt* (1907, Pathé), followed in 1909–1910 by the five-reel series *The Life of Moses* (Vitagraph Company).[78]

Urrichio and Pearson have suggested that such productions formed part of a clearly defined group of so-called quality films in which the motion picture industry invested disproportionately large amounts of money, time, and technological expertise. *The Life of Moses*, for instance, was five times longer and more than ten times costlier to make than the average film of the day.[79] The remarkable statistics of such films function as indices of the significance and meaning invested in them by the industry. In an age when the movie theater was perceived as a place of both moral and physical darkness and the content of films was frequently stereotyped as violent, vulgar, and likely to inculcate similar behavior on the part of audiences, the threat of severe, restrictive regulation loomed large. Companies turned to the quality film as a means of appeasing critics by associating a then-questionable medium with the symbols of respectability, decency, and high culture. "When the works of Dickens and Victor Hugo, the poems of Browning, the plays of Shakespeare and stories from the Bible are used as a basis for moving pictures," asserted Frank Dyer, vice president of the Motion Picture Patents Company in 1910, "no fair-minded man can deny that the art is being developed along the right lines."[80]

The Life of Moses aimed to better the status of the new medium in the eyes of potential regulators. More specifically, its biblical base was designed to pacify cinema's harshest critics, those clergy who sought to prohibit Sunday screenings and the operation of motion picture theaters in close proximity to schools and churches. By handling the Moses story in a reverential manner, the filmmakers hoped to persuade clergy that the film industry was not a threat but a guarantor of "proper" belief and action.[81] Urrichio and Pearson's work on the functions of the earliest biblical films offers insights that hold true for subsequent Moses films. It is noteworthy that the production of biblical films peaked when the motion picture industry most feared censure and regulation: 1910 to the 1920s, and the 1950s. The Moses film has functioned in such times as a means of countering perceived threats to the industry and as a way of reasserting its claim to be an ally of high culture and the respectable life rather than a threat to it.

DeMille himself was acutely aware of the precarious status of American cinema. In 1913, on hearing of his decision to abandon a stage career and begin film production, his brother William admonished him, stressing "you do come of a cultured family, two of whose members have made honorable names in the field of drama. . . . I cannot understand how you are willing to identify yourself with a cheap form of amusement which no one will ever allude to as an art."[82]

Faced with the need to mollify both his own family and the wider critics of cinema, DeMille quickly assumed a significant role in the Lasky Company's venture into quality film. Like Vitagraph, the Lasky team attempted to elevate the status of film by associating it with that which had already been validated by the arbiters of good taste. In practice, this meant producing screen adaptations of successful novels and plays and engaging established Broadway actors such as Theodore Roberts, who later played Moses in DeMille's 1923 *The Ten Commandments*. Such tactics would, they hoped, attract into the motion picture house the middle and upper classes whose patronage (economic and political) cinema desperately needed to ensure its survival.[83]

For DeMille, the special attention that the House Un-American Activities Committee paid to the 1950s film industry created many tensions and dilemmas. On the one hand, DeMille opposed the unionization of the industry, sharing the widespread belief that it was effectively communism by the back door. He was a member of the often reactionary Motion Picture Alliance for the Preservation of American Ideals (founded in 1944), which pledged to combat Communist influences in Hollywood and included in its ranks several arch-conservatives like Walt Disney.[84] On the other, the atmosphere engendered by the tactics of the committee—in which often groundless accusations were immediately granted the status of truth, guilt was assumed, and innocence had to be thoroughly documented—made all those in the industry nervous.[85] And given the tendency of committee chairs (Dies, 1937; Rankin, 1945) to equate Jewish heritage with Communist sympathy, DeMille may have felt particularly threatened, despite his postwar reputation for conservatism. The approach of DeMille's autobiography, which devotes only two lines to his maternal (Jewish) ancestors and nine pages to the paternal (Christian) line, supports this theory.[86] Additionally, DeMille's presidency of the Motion Picture Industry Council suggests a concern for others' perceptions.[87]

Remaking *The Ten Commandments* suited DeMille's needs in the mid-1950s. The repressive political climate pushed Hollywood generally back to its familiar forms. The biblical epic, the Western, and the musical all enjoyed revivals at this time. More specifically, as a genre film treating the story of a people who escape the wrath of a dictator in order to become free under God, *The Ten Commandments* was an ideal vehicle for the expression of anticommunist sentiment and, as such, both insurance against personal attack and a defense against the blanket charges of pro-Communist sympathies levied at the film industry as a whole. More pragmatically, it was also a means of demonstrating the special effects and other technological capabilities that television lacked.

In short, whereas Steffens used the Moses story to argue via an accepted medium for what was in 1920s America an unorthodox program, DeMille used the story and the argument for American orthodoxy ("faith" and "freedom") to demonstrate the merits of the storyteller (himself) and the medium (cinema) in a time when both were under suspicion.[88]

Reception

DeMille sought to predetermine his audience's reception of *The Ten Commandments*, just as Steffens and Hurston had attempted to construct readings of their books. In the trailer and opening scene of the film, DeMille suggests several approaches to his film. Its presentation of the Moses story is defined as an exciting narrative, as a scholarly and reverential treatment with precedents in the works of writers such as Josephus and Philo, and as a universal message illuminating the struggles between freedom and oppression, law and lawlessness, and good and evil, that occur in all times and places. The following section attempts to gauge how successful DeMille was in constructing responses to *The Ten Commandments* in the 1950s and later.

The primary sources for determining the immediate reception of *The Ten Commandments* are the reviews that appeared in religious and other journals in 1956 and 1957. Box office statistics and accolades awarded are also of use. DeMille's status as a successful director with a reputation in the field of biblical epics ensured that *The Ten Commandments* received substantial media coverage. Assessments were mixed. Its lavish sets, array of Hollywood stars, and three-and-a-half-hour duration prompted *Time* magazine to describe the film as "Something roughly comparable to an eight foot chorus girl—pretty well put together, but much too big and much too flashy." In the *New Republic*, Evett claimed, "If the movie of *War and Peace* is longer than the book, *The Ten Commandments* is longer than the forty years in the desert."[89]

Thankfully, these glib quips do not constitute the entirety of the reviewers' output. Among the pieces written for a host of current affairs and general interest journals, those in the *New Republic*, the *New York Times*, the *Nation*, the *New Yorker*, *Newsweek*, and *Time* all attempted to measure the film against DeMille's claims for it. The popular film periodicals also published reviews. Assessments in *Sight and Sound* and *Films and Filming* are considered here.

Newsweek judged: "Viewing his current three and a half hour work, they [the audience] may find a DeMille production a trying experience now and then, but a very educational one. They are bound to be, as their parents and grandparents were [by the 1923 version], impressed."[90] *The Ten Commandments* was a worthy endeavor. However, a couple of reviewers took issue with DeMille's claims to provide in *The Ten Commandments* a scholarly presentation of the life of Moses drawing on theBible and the fruits of textual and archaeological research. Writing for the *New York Times*, Crowther hinted that some "frank apocrypha" not traceable in history or legend had been added to the biblical Moses story to produce "a lusty and melodramatic romance."[91] Evett developed this point further, having recognized that while "screen credits begin with the Midrash and end with the Mishnah," the influence of the ancient texts on the film was at best superficial. The nonbiblical sources had been scanned to provide the names of additional characters, and little else. Specifically, he bemoaned the fact that DeMille had seemingly neglected the wealth of stories collected in Ginzberg's *Legends of the Jews*, many of which related incidents in Moses' Egyptian childhood and adulthood. Although the absence of action in the film might give it at times "an odd, almost highbrow patina," it possessed nothing deeper than that.[92]

It was the fruits of DeMille's not entirely successful attempts to combine religious experience with entertainment that most excited the first reviewers of *The Ten Commandments*. The uneasy compromises struck in the attempt to reconcile the competing demands of scholarship, piety, and spectacle were exploited by writers as examples of hypocrisy or sheer stupidity on the part of the director. "Cinemogul DeMille claims that he has tried 'to translate the Bible back to its original form,' the form in which it has lived. Yet what he has really done is to throw sex and sand into the moviegoers' eyes for almost twice as long as anybody else has ever dared to," declared *Time*. The editor of *Films and Filming* complained that DeMille had molded religion into a set pattern of Hollywood conventions, with the result that the film, although well intentioned, lacked true and elevated spiritual content.[93] In terms that frequently evoked the Christian opposition to early cinema far more strongly than do the remarks of 1950s clerics, "secular" reviewers protested the film's treatment of sexual desire and its perceived blasphemy. One writer, alluding to the Moses-Rameses-Nefretiri subplot and its portrayal of the rejected Nefretiri as responsible for hardening Pharaoh's heart against the slaves, suggested that "the Exodus itself seems almost a sort of Sexodus—the result of Moses' unhappy (and purely fictional) love life." In the *Nation*, Hatch dismissed the very notion of a romantic Moses story as ludicrous and irreverent. DeMille had "exercised heroic bad taste to create an epic of balderdash."[94]

DeMille's elaborations were held to have debased and trivialized the biblical account. "Is this blasphemy?" pondered *Time*. "Technically not; but it is sometimes hard to determine where the fine line between bad taste and sacrilege is to be drawn. . . . it is impossible to avoid the impression that the movie maker, no doubt without intending to, has taken the name of the Lord in vain." *Sight and Sound* was less reticent: "When Moses first says 'Let my people go,' *The Ten Commandments* gathers some momentum. . . . Dilute it with 'I belong to you, Moses,' or 'Worship whatever God you please, so long as I can worship you,' and a rooted vulgarity is exposed," claimed Kitchin.[95]

Ironically, special effects, the very elements of *The Ten Commandments* that current scholars often perceive to be the most piously conservative, and that the film industry recognized with an Academy Award, seemed to the professional reviewers to be the most potentially problematic for the general viewer. *Time* particularly objected to the burning bush scene, which, it was claimed, made God sound like a television advertising voiceover. Elsewhere the pestilential mist used to signify the death of the Egyptian firstborn was derided as "fit for a stage production of *Dracula*."[96] With characteristic wit, Evett queried the merits for believers and unbelievers alike of the film's decision to portray miracles on screen:

> For a film on the ten commandments, this is a splendid demonstration of how to violate the first three. In making the Almighty talk as if He were at the bottom of a well, and by showing Him as a sort of suburban show-off and spoilsport, determined to toss off miracles as if they were parlor tricks, DeMille has given us a vision of God so shocking in its naïveté that even an atheist must blanch at the idea of disbelieving in anything so inconsequential.[97]

If DeMille's attempts in the prerelease trailer and opening scene of the film to justify the extrabiblical elaborations of the Moses story betrayed an awareness of the difficulties in getting an audience to accept them, we can only conclude that his uneasiness was well founded. The attempts to associate his enterprise with that of previous storytellers only engendered the criticisms of those who recognized the film's use of ancient writers as inconsistent and superficial. It noticeably failed to deflect the ire of those for whom romantic accretions adulterated or obscured the meaning of the exodus. Interestingly, the film caused the same critics to dismiss it as naïve and facile when it was faithful to the biblical account and portrayed theophanies and miracles on screen. In addition to saying something about the reception of the film, the remarks of these general reviewers of *The Ten Commandments* also reveal the ambiguous status of the Hebrew Bible narratives in relation to the beliefs and values of 1950s middle-class America.

In his autobiography, DeMille recalled the discussions surrounding the presentation of the divine voice in *The Ten Commandments*. Bypassing the criticisms of the general reviewers, he conceded that "our solution of that whole problem was imperfect," but preferred to only mention the positive assessment by Maryvonne Butcher in *Blackfriars*.[98] Further apparent Christian support for *Commandments* came in 1958, when DeMille was named lay churchman of the year and the Salvation Army's man of the year.[99] Nevertheless, reception of the film in the religious press was not uniformly positive. There was a wide divergence in assessments, as is typified by the debate in the *Christian Century*, initiated by Union Theological Seminary's instructor in religion and drama, T. S. Driver.

Driver vehemently opposed *The Ten Commandments*. Like the reviewers in *Time* and the *New Republic*, he reviled the emphasis on sex in the film and the portrayal of the divine voice, declaring them to be not just irrelevant but idolatrous. The church did not necessarily have to protest if a film did not wholly adhere to the biblical narrative, "But it must object when the primary drive and thrust of a picture, its conception, idiom and style, are in a direction exactly opposite from that of the Bible."[100] For Driver, DeMille's film was such a production. Whereas religion was essentially an internal matter of personal faith, *The Ten Commandments*, with its star-studded cast and lavish sets, was dedicated to the public and the external. To some extent the source of this weakness was deemed to lie in the nature of Judaism and Christianity as historical religions, based on events linked to concrete times and places. This might tempt the believer to feel that the meaning and significance of a biblical event could be accessed by recreating those times and places in great detail. The result was a misrepresentation of God. "The DeMille God is imprisoned in the DeMille style, which means in the irrelevant minutiae of Egyptian culture and the costume director. He bears no resemblance to the Old Testament Lord of History."[101]

Driver expressed particularly strong convictions regarding DeMille's attempts to win the support of clergy by inviting them to previews of *The Ten Commandments*. The antireligious nature of the film as Driver understood it meant that ministers must on the grounds of faith refuse to support it; indeed, they should engage in opposition: "This three-hour-and-thirty-nine-minute god must be rejected quite as absolutely as the god of the Golden Calf was rejected by Moses, for he is, in fact, his latter day descendant. . . . When the minister is invited to participate in the advertisement of this film . . . he will be unwittingly invited to choose whom he will serve."[102] It is not surprising that Driver's forceful opinions stimulated a debate about the merits and faults of *The Ten Commandments*. He had, in effect, claimed that those who saw some religious or spiritual value in the film, like the Methodist and Baptist ministers and the rabbi quoted in a recent *Time* article, were idolaters and as such no better than those whom the Levites slaughtered at divine command in Exodus 32:27f.[103] The *Christian Century* printed correspondence from several who felt that Driver's anger was misplaced and inappropriate.

Kennedy, a Methodist bishop, was typical in his suggestion that "it does not seem quite fair to expect Hollywood to create on the screen the atmosphere of a seminar discussing neo-orthodoxy." There were problems with the film, but it did make Moses "alive and great" and stress the place of God as the foundation of human freedom. The Rochester churchman H. L. Clark expressed similar views, arguing that Driver had asked too much of a film produced for a general audience. Some perceptive comments on Driver's review were offered by Lindsay Young, representing the National Conference of Christians and Jews in Los Angeles, who felt that the piece had revealed more about Driver than about the film. He also denied that *The Ten Commandments* was totally "external," asking, "Was he [Driver] not moved by the unconquerable will to freedom on the part of the people, a will born out of faith in God? Was he unimpressed by the portrayal of a loyalty to God that transcended allegiance to any state?"[104]

Thus the evidence from the religious press resembles that found in the more general journals; DeMille receives only limited praise. Far from highlighting the common ground between faiths, *The Ten Commandments* engendered disputes concerning the nature of true religious sentiment and the desirability or otherwise of cinema-religion interface. Some viewers were prepared to embrace the medium of film and asserted the potential value of cinematic representations of biblical events. In the words of Lindsay Young, "I'm too engrossed with the message to be unduly concerned about the wrapping."[105] For others like Driver, the "wrapping" was inextricably linked with the well-publicized excesses of Hollywood and its star system. By attempting to portray on screen the events of divine history, the cinema industry created petty gods or idols, hindering the development of true religious sentiment.

Although the reviews and responses to them constitute valuable evidence concerning the reception of *The Ten Commandments* in the 1950s, they cannot provide a complete picture of how the film was received and interpreted. In the absence of ethnographic and audience-interview research, it is virtually impossible to gain a full appreciation of the reception

of a film like *The Ten Commandments* by the mass of those patrons who ensured its box office success.[106] The fact that interpretations of nondomi-
nant groups are particularly hard to construct is especially regrettable
when dealing with a film version of the exodus story. In recent years, the
reception of a cinematic representation of a Chicano interpretation of the
exodus (*Born in East L.A.*, Marin, 1987) has interested both the wider His-
panic and scholarly communities alike, tantalizingly suggesting that the
interpretation of *The Ten Commandments* by the oppressed of the 1950s,
including African Americans, may have been particularly distinct.[107] But
all that the available primary evidence verifies is that the film was incredi-
bly popular and that it was interpreted in a multiplicity of ways. DeMille
could put miracles on screen but was unable to prescribe readings of the
film.

Despite its phenomenal popularity, the biblical epic as a genre was the vic-
tim of a not always benign scholarly neglect until the beginning of the
present decade.

Scholars of film and religion, if they deigned to discuss the genre, frequently did little more than reiterate the tritest of the reviewers' sentiments, judging the output of DeMille in particular as banal and anachronistic. In a short work on Hollywood in the 1950s, Gow described *The Ten
Commandments* as "histrionic and star-crammed, multitudinous with ex-
tras, orgiastic in an old-hat romp around the calf of gold, but technically
maladroit" in its handling of the parting of the Red Sea, revealed as con-
trived and mechanistic by the newfound clarity of VistaVision (the new,
wider 70-mm film).[108] This type of approach is perpetuated in a more self-
conscious manner by Holloway in *The Religious Dimension in Cinema*
(1972). For Holloway, the biblical epic constitutes a low point in the history of the religious film, emblematic of an era in which audiences pas-
sively identified with screen stars and Hollywood flooded the market with
pietistic, moralizing products. "The gods of the screen were Valentino and
Garbo, and the high priest of the religious genre was Cecil B. DeMille."[109]
The films' very successes were indications of both a lack of sophistication
on the part of viewers and the pernicious hold of "movie moguls," who
"gradually rose in power to stifle all artistic expression in the American
movie."[110]

Holloway's assessment of DeMille and the biblical epic is problematic,
both logically and ideologically speaking; he links the filmmakers' alleged
stranglehold on the industry to their ethnic origins, claiming that they
were "mostly pint-sized (ave. height was about five foot four) and mostly of

Jewish origin (the orthodox Jewish immigrants had clawed their way to the top of the movie like the Irish in city politics and the Italians in the Mafia)" and that their ultimate motivation was the making of money "through the wanton blending of good and evil in the typical melodrama." Fear often drove them "to excesses of fervor and power," he adds.[111] His assessment of a film's popularity as indicative of passivity and a lack of discernment on the part of viewers is logically flawed (it cannot, for instance explain why in the 1950s some films were more popular than others, or why different types of films, or a single film, have enjoyed widely fluctuating levels of popularity over the decades) and suggests an attitude toward popular culture evocative of the condescension of Arnold or Leavis.[112] Holloway's stance implies that the scholar can function as arbiter of good taste and self-appointed identifier of "mature" religious sentiment in cinema. Popular preference for DeMille and Wyler over Dreyer and Bresson merely confirms their (audience and director) superficiality, rather than pointing to the resonances that the work of the former directors had for the mass American public. At a theoretical level, the last two decades in particular have seen the decline of this notion that "culture has always been in minority keeping"[113] and an increased willingness to take seriously the culture of nonelites. Beginning in the 1950s themselves, empirical studies have indicated that cinema audiences are active and critically assess what they see and hear.[114] Finally, it is important to stress the merits of less stereotyped accounts than Holloway's of the role of Jews in the American film industry.[115]

Historically, more sympathetic treatments of *The Ten Commandments* and epic films generally have tended to be uncritical, or even outright frivolous, and in effect share with the negative assessments a failure to consider seriously the content of the films and their relation to the wider context.[116] Perhaps the most superficial handling of epics is Cross's *The Bible According to Hollywood*, in which stills from numerous films including *The Ten Commandments* (1923 and 1956) are given "amusing" captions, such as (below a still from the scene featuring the orgy of the golden calf) "Momentary panic grips the Israelites as Aaron realizes that he has forgotten their packed lunches."[117]

The last decade, however, has seen a new willingness on the part of scholars in film and religious studies to take the biblical epic seriously. Moving beyond an account of the statistics of production, several writers have attempted to offer an analysis of the statistics' significance and the meanings of the films' contents. Kreitzer has suggested that by studying film one may not only observe an example of the hermeneutical process in action but also note that the hermeneutical "flow" may be reversed, and new insights into the biblical texts themselves may be gained.[118] While such an approach is not without problems (examples of its practical implementation are as yet limited; Kreitzer's understanding of the use of such a technique is slightly unclear), it is interesting because it admits the value and significance of popular cinematic presentations of Bible stories and thus represents a departure from the stance of Holloway or Driver.

Writing specifically on DeMille's 1956 *The Ten Commandments*, Kreitzer notes that "for a great many more people than we might care to admit, Charlton Heston is the dominant mental picture of Moses and [that] many people believe the Red Sea parted precisely as Cecil B. DeMille directed it to."[119] He also mentions, although not in any detail, the essentially Christian portrayal of Moses' story in the film, highlights the conservative literal approach to the biblical miracles, and suggests that when scholars attempt to consider the merits of *The Ten Commandments* against those of more recent films and film cycles like Kieslowski's *Decalogue* (1990), they should be aware that "the answer we give is probably itself an indication of our own cultural assumptions and expectations, a hint about what we expect film to be and what we want it to do."[120] Unfortunately, Kreitzer's assessment of *The Ten Commandments* does not always live up to the promise of these initial insights. He does not consider the reasons for the Christianizing of the Moses story or the inconsistencies of the film's approach to the biblical text. Moreover, despite the statement concerning the subjective nature of placing the value of one Moses film over that of another, Kreitzer himself makes these kinds of judgments. Following a discussion of DeMille's handling of miracles, he asserts that the DeBosio *Moses* (1975) is "much more believable." More believable for whom? Kreitzer also argues:

> in many ways Kieslowski's effort is, in my opinion, much to be preferred as a means of engaging the meaning of the Mosaic Law since it involves the audience in the all too human dramas depicted. . . . One can but hope that Kieslowski's *Decalogue* film cycle will have such a widespread distribution that it [too] will become part of our mental heritage and help frame our understanding of the Ten Commandments and their challenge to our lives.[121]

When these remarks are considered alongside a discussion of DeMille that dwells more on special effects technology than on meanings, it is hard to escape the conclusion that, once again, *The Ten Commandments* has not received treatment that takes seriously its nature as a twentieth-century re-presentation of the Moses story.

In the absence of a Mosaic equivalent to the monographs detailing the history and interpretation of the Jesus film, the most thoroughly analytical scholarly assessment of *The Ten Commandments* remains that of Babington and Evans.[122] In many ways, their emphasis on the cinema-culture interface can be seen as a successor to the work of Wood, who linked Hollywood products to the central meanings of American mythology. Their book *Biblical Epics* is informed by the view that: "Wood's claim that in the final image of DeMille's 1956 *The Ten Commandments*, Moses (Charlton Heston) is posed to resemble the Statue of Liberty is one of the few significant perceptions about the Biblical Epic; once seen in this way the image illuminates the furthest reaches of the genre."[123] Although the wider subject matter of the book limits the space available for discussion of *The Ten Commandments*, *Biblical Epics* takes seriously the status of the film as both cultural construct and agent. Babington and Evans challenge the critic to surrender to neither nostalgia nor the temptation to adopt past modes of discourse about epics, which should be exposed for what they are, stereotyped accounts possessing only a veneer of knowledge. It is not enough for the scholar to seek justification for a superficial approach in the fact that this is how Hollywood's rituals of publicity talked about them in the past.[124] The implications of and influences behind aspects of the film must be related to such factors as American religion, including American-Jewish self-presentation, and the Arab-Israeli conflict. In many respects, the preceding analysis has built on the approach of Babington and Evans. It has tried to develop a way of examining *The Ten Commandments* that acknowledges its cultural significance and respects its integrity.

Conclusions

It is fitting, perhaps, that this analysis of twentieth-century American images of Moses ends with a discussion of film, perhaps *the* medium of modern mythology. Twenty-first-century studies will no doubt include within their remit computer games, which are also significant agents of cultural meaning and values.

In studying *The Ten Commandments*, I have deliberately tried to break away from earlier, dismissive approaches to the biblical epic and to subject the film to a rigorous investigation. DeMille's presentation of Moses and the exodus emerges as rich and sophisticated. In this respect, it is typical of many 1950s films that tried to please mass audiences by mixing various elements that would appeal to the maximum possible viewing population.[125] But a good deal of *The Ten Commandments'* complexity is there by necessity rather than by contrivance or design. The same polyvalency that Hurston was able to exploit in her novel posed DeMille a tremendous challenge: How could he produce a broadly acceptable film that had as its basis a familiar and much interpreted text? His somewhat byzantine response is in fact part of the film's necessary "hermeneutic code." Like the Moses-Rameses-Nefretiri triangle, the Memnet subplot is designed to pose "questions" to generate the audience's desire to keep watching. *The Ten Commandments'* audience for the most part knew what would happen; De-Mille created a fascinating film because he shifted attention to *how* things happen—to questions of narrative theme and character relation.

Unlike Steffens's or Hurston's books (both of which had vocal critics), DeMille's film was accused of blasphemy, irreverence, and vulgarity. That this in part stems from the difference in *medium* emerges from consideration of *The Ten Commandments'* specific handling of the biblical text. As shown earlier, *The Ten Commandments'* attitude toward the Bible is less capricious than a casual viewing may suggest. "Deviations" from the biblical account are dependent on (and thereby acknowledge the authority of) that text. Moreover, the film resists the claims of scientific and social scientific approaches to the Bible, refusing to deconstruct Exodus-Deuteronomy. Yet DeMille's need to create a film in which compelling characters form believable societies and undergo intelligible life experiences results in his including much that appears to be sheer fabrication. A historical void or a significant narrative interruption like those found in the early chapters of Exodus cannot be portrayed on screen. And even though some literary texts such as *Moses, Man of the Mountain* dare to offer an account of Moses' youth, the profoundly affective nature of film (stemming from its use of both visual and verbal signifying elements) makes it more likely to incite acrimony than equally audacious suggestions made "only" on a printed page.

These problems are not unique to *The Ten Commandments*; they are at the heart of ongoing debates about the locus of "authenticity" in film. Historical films and literary adaptations (and biblical films straddle both of these categories) are often critiqued according to their perceived "fidelity" to a text or event. Yet in translating a story from one medium to another, "replication" is simply not possible. In this sense, the medium really *is* the message.

In addition to raising issues more generally applicable within film studies, scrutiny of *The Ten Commandments* suggests further points of relevance to this study as a whole. As R. L. Moore noted in his work on "religious outsiders," consensus approaches to American religion have proved remarkably enduring.[126] Some contemporary critics, while acknowledging present diversity of religious commitment and expression, often seem to regard this to be symptomatic of the recent breakdown of a previously common set of shared meanings. With more than a hint of nostalgia, Petersen writes that "relationships such as church and state, mission and identity, or faith and science are more complex at the end of the twentieth century than they were at the beginning."[127] Yet *The Ten Commandments* is a consensus-oriented film, which finds it impossible not to engage the kinds of difficult debates that Petersen and those like him regard as distinctive of the postmodern condition. On one hand, the dialogue of the film condemns slavery, yet there are no nonwhite actors depicted in significant roles. In a similarly ambiguous manner, the film attempts to advance a model of interfaith harmony but does so in a way that assumes and privileges Christianity. All this argues that "consensus" is frequently not the product of a neutral convergence of views but may be the consequence of a process of competition, the ability of one group or groups to gain dominance over others. Close reading of *The Ten Commandments* and contemporary cultural artifacts indicates that this is true not just today but also in the 1950s, popularly idealized as a golden age in which people shared common goals, in a unified, harmonious society.[128] Awareness of this, and of the way in which a mass medium (like popular cinema) can be the site of contest and controversy, indicates that the contemporary diversity in mode and content of discourse around the Bible is not new. Perhaps this more nuanced historical perspective can help to build the resources needed for a more reasoned response to the apparent fracturing of meanings and values in the present day.

Conclusions

This study of three twentieth-century reworkings of the Moses story is almost at an end. The previous chapters have articulated examples of what might be termed the American afterlives of Moses: Lincoln Steffens's *Moses in Red*, Zora Neale Hurston's *Moses, Man of the Mountain*, and Cecil B. DeMille's *The Ten Commandments*. In these works the biblical Moses is redivivus—not wholly re-created, but certainly renovated and renewed.

Much discourse on literary, cinematic, or other cultural forms that draw on biblical texts tends to focus on the perceived "fidelity" of product to text: To what extent has an artist or writer faithfully "depicted" or "represented" the details of the biblical story? However, "representation" is always "*re*-presentation" more than it is "replication." Sensitive to this reality, this study has therefore aimed not to judge the relative merits of Steffens's, Hurston's, and DeMille's Moses stories, but rather to ask why and how they recast the Moses story as they did and how the choices they made were encountered by audiences.

Whether the individual points made in the preceding chapters are found to be plausible or not, I hope that the analyses have demonstrated convincingly the fruitfulness of a cultural studies approach to biblical interpretation. This study has been influenced by a cultural studies perspective in two major respects. First, it has attended seriously to popular cultural forms—that is, to the texts (broadly defined) and practices of everyday life. Second, it has acknowledged that text and context are inseparable. The methodology followed rejects the extremes of auteurism and reader-response and instead admits both the objective existence of cultural forms and their constructedness, especially the extent to which they are constructed through reception or production-in-use. Audiences or consumers engage with books and films, producing interpretations and creating meanings that cannot simply be read off from the materiality of the artifact in question.

This twofold approach seems to be particularly rewarding in a study such as the present one, which deals with re-presentations of a biblical text to which authors, filmmakers, and audiences all bring some prior knowledge and interpretative assumptions. Steffens, Hurston, and DeMille are all "producers" as well as "consumers" of the biblical narrative, but so, too, are their audiences. During the study, it became clear that the activity of the creators was in consequence significantly circumscribed. DeMille played successfully with the audience's power, shifting interest from "What will happen in this story?" to "How will it happen?" and creating a compelling product. Conversely, Steffens (for all his acknowldgment of the power of lived experience in determining textual interpretation) took little account of the need to negotiate with his readership, and *Moses in Red* was a failure. In short, then, what this study has uncovered about the text-context–producer-consumer nexus is in sympathy with what has been suggested by other studies of popular cultural forms and practices: "This is a history that makes much of sharing, compromise, and interchange. But it is also a history of ordinary people and their powers to adapt, trespass, and subvert whatever is directed at them."[1]

It will have been apparent to readers that each study is, to a large extent, freestanding and capable of being read as a discrete unit. Because the film and books chosen have rarely been subjected to rigorous analysis, I wanted to create a text that would operate at several levels. The chapters are intended to make a worthwhile contribution to wider analysis of the individual work discussed. (In the case of *Moses in Red*, the first-ever thorough assessment is offered here.) But they are also intended to function cumulatively to argue for a shift in the concerns of biblical and religious studies. What conclusions arise, then, from a consultation of this study in toto?

Perhaps most obviously, the study adds yet further weight to Martin Marty's well-known characterization of the Bible as an iconic text, "enshrined in a vault in its [America's] archival heart."[2] For Steffens, Hurston, DeMille, and their interpreters, the exodus narrative is both powerful, influencing narrative, and one that Americans may in turn refashion in response to their own agendas and interests. In short, the Bible is a text that is good to think with.

It is also clear that the currency (or timelessness) of the biblical text goes hand in hand with its contestedness. In our chosen period, disagreement about the Moses story is not an indication that the Bible's formative function is weakened.[3] Common myths do not have to be read in the same way to preserve their status. On the contrary, it is in the very contestedness or malleability of the Moses story that its popularity is grounded. On the one hand, the ongoing manipulation of the image of Moses ensures his continuation as a popular hero. On the other, that complex interpretive history makes available to subsequent writers (such as Hurston) a variable and complex range of discourses and associations that can be activated for readers or viewers by any subsequently produced interpretation.

Practitioners of cultural studies will be aware that the ideas of studying popular or mass culture and of making one's work a "political" intervention have always been closely linked. Given the history of academic biblical studies, a work focusing on what DeMille, Hurston, Steffens, and their audiences (rather than, say, Coats, Gottwald, and Von Rad) have to say about Moses cannot shirk this task. I hope that in a modest way this volume will contribute to the discussion between all those who wish to grow the discipline of biblical studies.

First, investigating *Moses in Red*, *Moses, Man of the Mountain*, and *The Ten Commandments* has required me to take seriously the voices of those historically peripheral to the discipline of biblical studies, including members of ethnic minorities and other disempowered groups such as women, the politically heterogeneous, and those who, if not powerless, are historically peripheral to the concerns of the academy, such as Hollywood filmmakers like Cecil B. DeMille. Their readings of the Moses story have emerged as rich and sophisticated. Nonelite biblical interpretation (both in terms of actual examples of readings and in terms of general hermeneutic strategies) can and should be studied seriously.

However, a willingness to include the study of popular cultural expression within the remit of biblical studies will have far-reaching consequences. It will not involve a simple expansion in subject matter. It will also entail the alteration or even abandonment of many dominant theories, presuppositions, and structures. For example, the traditional boundaries between what is deemed "elite" versus "popular," or "academic" versus "lay" interpretation are weakened when one appreciates the complexity and the heterogeneity of the hermeneutical strategies deployed by writers like Hurston and Steffens. It is no longer clear that these (for the academy) empowering binary oppositions are other than political constructions. At a more fundamental level, the cultural studies understanding of the nature of the text-context relation differs significantly from the Enlightenment-grounded one assumed by much historical-critical interpretation of the

Bible. If there is to be any dialogue between the two, then each discipline will probably undergo profound but as yet unpredicatable transformation.

This change will not be easy, but biblical studies has always been an unfolding discourse, responding to changing political and social conditions, and always marked by debate and disagreement. And it is in an awareness of the paid interpreter's participation in the broader hermeneutical enterprise that the route to a more humane and a more discerning discipline lies.

Notes

Chapter 1. Introduction

1. Coats, "Humility and Honor," 88–98.
2. King's famous "I have a dream" speech, quoted in Washington, *Testament of Hope*, 286.
3. Roshwald and Roshwald, *Moses*, and Silver, *Images of Moses*, survey a range of literary portraits. Mannering, *Biblical Art*, reproduces paintings by Veronese, Fiorentino, and John Martin. Chapter 4 of this book refers to the work of Michelangelo, which informed Cecil B. DeMille's *The Ten Commandments*.
4. Riches, *The Bible*, 99.
5. Miles, *Seeing and Believing*; McDannell, *Material Christianity*.
6. McDannell, *Material Christianity*, 23.
7. Grossberg, "Is There a Fan?" 52–53.
8. For convenience I use "reception" widely in this book, but this should be understood as referring to fundamentally active processes, alternatively characterized as "secondary production" or "production-in-use." See Storey, *Cultural Studies*, 44–45.
9. Staiger, *Interpreting Films*, 212.
10. See briefly, Riches, *The Bible*, 82.
11. Drury, *Critics of the Bible*, 1.
12. Ibid., 20.
13. Garber and Walkowitz, *One Nation?* ix.
14. Brock, *Mosaics*, 12.
15. Wentz, *Religion in the New World*, 19.
16. Quoted in ibid., 196.
17. Moore, *Religious Outsiders*, viii.
18. Bellah, "Civil Religion in America," 168–189.

19. See also Gamoran, "Civil Religion," 235–256.
20. Moore, *Religious Outsiders*, 203.
21. Bodnara, *Remaking America*.
22. Turner, *Religion and Social Theory*, 59.
23. Moore, *Religious Outsiders*, 202.
24. Albanese, *America*, 502–533.

Chapter 2. Back to the Future: Lincoln Steffens's *Moses in Red* (1926)

1. Letters to Laura Suggett 6 July 1922, 5 July 1923, and to Laura and Alan Suggett, 17 June 1922. Lincoln Steffens Papers, Rare Book and Manuscript Library, Columbia University, Series III, Reel 3. Hereafter, "Lincoln Steffens Papers" will be abbreviated as "L.S." Material so referenced is otherwise unpublished. The papers consist of circa 37,500 items acquired by Columbia University in 1950, 1966, and 1978. This study makes particular use of the Series II papers, added in 1978, and not available to many earlier critics.

2, Letter to Steffens, 19 October 1926, L.S. Series II, Reel 1.

3. Winter and Hicks, *Letters*, 776–777.

4. Stinson, *Lincoln Steffens*, 112. Interestingly, fire also destroyed most copies of a novel by Josephine Bontecou, Steffens's first wife.

5. Barton, *The Man Nobody Knows*.

6. Ibid.

7. Brogan, *History*, 509, 519, 522; Tallack, *Twentieth Century America*, 15; Tindall and Shi, *America*, 1074–1085.

8. Ford forced car dealers to take his newspaper, the *Dearborn Independent*, which carried a series of articles, "The International Jew," similar in content to *The Protocols of the Elders of Zion* (see Dinnerstein, "Henry Ford," 181–193). He eventually retracted the publication and repudiated antisemitism, most publicly in a 1942 letter to the Anti Defamation League (Brown, *Religion in America*, 305.)

9. Carroll and Noble, *The Free and the Unfree*, 321.

10. Patterson, *America*, 173–178; Brogan, *History*, 638–640.

11. Carroll and Noble, *The Free and the Unfree*, 320.

12. Spencer, *Education*, 36.

13. Letter to Marie Howe, 3 April 1919, Winter and Hicks, *Letters*, 463.

14. Steffens, *Moses*, 9–45. This discussion occupies almost one-third of the text.

15. Ibid, 9–10. Arthur Ransome was a children's novelist and journalist. He left Moscow in 1919 with Steffens when he returned to Versailles with the Bullitt mission. Ransome received a copy of *Moses in Red* from Steffens in 1926. The book is now owned by Cambridge University Library. It bears Ransome's signature and a note, "sent by Lincoln Steffens, 1926," but no marginalia. For Ransome's account, see his *Six Weeks in Russia in 1919*, 151; *The Crisis in Russia*, and *The Autobiography of Arthur Ransome*, 266–267. A letter of his to Steffens is preserved at L.S. Series I, Reel 4.

16. Steffens, *Moses*, 10.

17. Ibid., 11–12, 14–16. "Fundamentalism" was in Steffens's day a relatively new designation, referring to the program advocated by conservative Christians at Niagara in 1895. Their five fundamentals of faith—scriptural inerrancy, the divinity of Jesus, the virgin birth, the substitutionary theory of atonement, and the bodily resurrection and imminent return of Jesus—were made widely known through a series of books and pamphlets (Barr, *Fundamentalism*, 2).

18. Steffens, *Moses*, 21.

19. See letters to Allen H. Suggett, 21 January 1911, and Laura Steffens, 15 June 1911, *Letters*, Winter and Hicks, 1:259–260, 269. See also Stein "Lincoln Steffens," 120.

20. See Rowland, *Companion*, or specifically Gutiérrez, *Theology of Liberation*; Pixley, *On Exodus*; Ellis, *Toward a Jewish Theology of Liberation*; and Cohn-Sherbok, *Exodus*.

21. Steffens, *Moses*, 12.

22. Winter and Hicks, *Letters*, 2:631–632.

23. Letter to Laura Suggett, L.S. Series III, Reel 3.

24. Letter to Laura Suggett from London, 28 December 1923, Winter and Hicks, *Letters*, 2:634.

25. Other date books can be seen at L.S. Series II, Reel 2.

26. For the schedule of lectures for 1923–1924, see the *Cambridge University Reporter*, 10 January 1924, 482–484.

27. McNeile's conclusions on the historical value of Exodus (*Exodus*, cvi–cxviii) are of particular interest: (1) the book is not by Moses but represents different literary strata, and it is the responsibility of the student to trace the underlying basis of fact; (2) the biblical account is animated by a strong national and religious bond based on belief in one God who has a special care for Israel; (3) the existence and character of such a people *requires* a person such as Moses to account for them: "in order to rouse them, and knit them together, and persuade them to escape from the country, a leader was necessary" (cx).

28. Kent, *Student's Old Testament*, vii, 48; Letter from Kent to Steffens, L.S. Series I, Reel 3.

29. Steffens, *Moses*, 26–27.

30. Grabbe, *Leviticus*, 12–18 provides a summary of views past and present on P. Historical-critical method is discussed in McKnight, *Post-Modern Use*, 44–53.

31. Steffens, *Moses*, 22.

32. Ibid., 115.

33. McNeile, *Exodus*, cix; Kennett, *The Church of Israel*, 1–72; Albright, *Archaeology*.

34. Steffens, *Moses*, 27.

35. Marsden, *Religion*, 123, and see 118–120 generally. Ahlstrom, *Religious History*, 796–798, discusses Ely and the sociologist Albion W. Small.

36. See Jones, *The Agricultural Social Gospel*.

37. Quoted in Bedell, Sandon, and Wellborn, *Religion in America*, 344. See also Handy, *Social Gospel*, 253–389, and Minus, *Walter Rauschenbusch*, 158–161.

38. Steffens, *Moses*, 14.

39. Ibid., 15; Coser, "Chicago Sociology," 70–71.

40. Steffens, Moses, 13.

41. Stein, "Lincoln Steffens," 86.

42. Ibid. 103.

43. Palermo, Lincoln Steffens, 72, 75.

44. Steffens, Upbuilders, 152 and 46; see, too, p. 100 on Ben Lindsey.

45. L.S. Series I, Reel 2 "Lincoln Steffen [sic] in Ridgefield Park: Christianity the Remedy" article in unidentified Bergen County newspaper vol. XVI, no. 51; "Ideal Politics as Viewed by Lincoln Steffens," Greenwich Graphic, 18 June 1910, 1.

46. Steffens, Autobiography, 658–689; 669. Note the use of "scientific" vocabulary here.

47. Filler, Muckrakers, 351.

48. Letter from F. Kohler to Steffens, 1 March 1909, L.S. Series I, Reel 3.

49. Steffens, Autobiography, 690.

50. Steffens was forbidden to speak publicly in San Diego (Autobiography, 775–777.) The editor of the Sacramento Bee proclaimed, "The proper place for Lincoln Steffens is in jail" (J. Kaplan, Lincoln Steffens, 235, 266).

51. Steffens, Moses, 21.

52. Horton, Lincoln Steffens, 117.

53. See Iriye, The Globalising of America, 54–55, for the suggestion that opposition was not inevitable.

54. Steffens, Autobiography, 790–802.

55. Carroll and Noble, The Free and the Unfree, 331.

56. Cartoon by Art Young in Good Morning, 5 October 1919; see Steffens, Autobiography, 744.

57. Description applied by Oscar Cargill in 1951 (J. Kaplan, Lincoln Steffens, 330).

58. von Mohrenschildt, "Lincoln Steffens," 31.

59. Cohen, America in the Age of Soviet Power, 74–75.

60. On Steffens's influence, see Aaron, Writers on the Left, 159, 189, 355.

61. Hicks regarded the Autobiography as "possibly the most influential book of the 1930s" (Stein, "Lincoln Steffens," 337.)

62. Simon, As We Saw the Thirties, 76–101.

63. Walzer, Exodus, 4, 65.

64. Wildavsky, The Nursing Father, 130.

65. Stinson, Lincoln Steffens, 126–127. Steffens was engaged to Burgess in 1889 but ended their agreement when he married Josephine Bontecou. Following Josephine's death in 1911, the two embarked upon a long affair, finally terminated by Steffens's marriage to Ella Winter, who was expecting their baby. At Gussie's request, she was not mentioned in the Autobiography. Winter and Steffens stayed together until Steffens's death in 1936.

66. "A pro-Russian, pro-communist book is the one that's needed now" (May 1933, Winter and Hicks, Letters, 2:959). When Steffens wrote this, he and Ella were facing sustained pressure from neighbors who accused them of child abuse and espionage. The situation was so dangerous that Steffens considered emigration.

67. Letter to Bev Bowie, 19 November 1932, Winter and Hicks, *Letters*, 2:934; also letter to Joseph R. Boldt Jr., 2:1007–1008.

68. Art Young, in Aaron, *Writers on the Left*, 12.

69. Cruse, *Crisis* (22) credits Dodge with having launched an American renaissance from her rooms.

70. Steffens, *Autobiography*, 655–656.

71. Palermo, *Lincoln Steffens*, 84.

72. Winter and Hicks, *Letters*, 2:895.

73. On Mexico, see Steffens, *Moses*, 32; letter to the editor of the *Sacramento Bee*, 5 July 1927, Winter and Hicks, *Letters*, 2:1046.

74. Steffens, *Moses*, 24–25.

75. J. Kaplan, *Lincoln Steffens*, 218.

76. For typical passages, see Steffens, *Moses*, 36 (on dictatorship) and 39 (on liberty).

77. Ibid., 51–59, 60–81.

78. See ibid., 34–35.

79. Ibid., 32.

80. Ibid., 33.

81. Ibid., 33–34. Steffens's record of Lenin's characterization of "scientific men" bears strong resemblance to the Gramscian "organic intellectual" (See Joll, *Gramsci*, 120–123).

82. See Michael Gold's comments, Aaron, *Writers on the Left*, 189.

83. Steffens, *Autobiography*, 817.

84. Ibid., 853.

85. Following the rise of National Socialism in Germany and persecution of Jews there, Steffens spoke out against fascism. See letters to Ella Winter ("Peter"), of 6 December 1932 and November 1933, Winter and Hicks, *Letters*, 2:938–939, 2:970–971.

86. Steffens, *Moses*, 82.

87. Ibid., 35. Pipes, *Russia*, discusses the period.

88. Steffens, *Moses*, 34–35.

89. Steffens, *Autobiography*, 812; J. Kaplan, *Lincoln Steffens*, 266–267.

90. "The Great Expectation,"[?] 1918, L.S. Series I, Reel 9, 2, 9, 11.

91. Steffens, *Autobiography*, 786.

92. Steffens, *Moses*, 14.

93. Ibid., 22.

94. A 1923 letter describes a Christmas dinner attended by both men (Winter and Hicks, *Letters*, 2:634–635).

95. *Current History*, December 1926. For this notice and those in *Cincinnati Times Star* (18 December 1926), *New York Herald-Tribune* (26 December 1926), *Miami Herald* (5 December 1926), *Emporia (Kansas) Gazette* (14 December 1926), *St. Louis Star* (18 December 1926), and *San Francisco Call* (18 December 1926), see the collection sent by E. A. Filene to Ella Winter, 9 April 1927 (L.S. Series I, Reel 2).

96. *New York Herald-Tribune*, 26 December 1926 (L.S. Series I, Reel 2).

97. Wise, "Moses as a Revolutionist," 168–170 (L.S. Series I, Reel 2).

98. Winter and Shapiro, *The World of Lincoln Steffens*.

99. Winter and Hicks, *Letters*, 2:776–777.

100. Horton, *Lincoln Steffens*, 114.

101. Steffens, *Moses*, 123–124.

102. Ibid., 103–104.

103. J. Kaplan, *Lincoln Steffens*, 215.

104. Telegram from Glen Frank to Steffens, 6 October 1924, L.S. Series III, Reel 1.

105. Letter to Steffens from Glen Frank, 6 October 1924, L.S. Series III, Reel 1.

106. Letter to Steffens, 19 April 1926, L.S. Series III, Reel 1.

107. Letter to Steffens, 29 November 1926, L.S. Series I, Reel 4.

108. Memorandum to E. A. Filene, 13 January 1927, L.S. Series I, Reel 2; Letter to Steffens from E. A. Filene, 10 February 1927, L.S. Series I, Reel 1.

109. In addition to his writing career, Barton (1886–1967) led an advertising firm and was a Republican congressman. *The Man* led the list of nonfiction titles in 1926. See Montgomery, "Bruce Barton," 21–34; and Nuechterlein, "Bruce Barton," 293–308.

110. Barton, *The Man*, 131–157.

111. Ribuffo, "Jesus Christ," 207.

112. This stance contrasts with the wartime agenda, when a quest for Allied solidarity encouraged the portrayal of positive images of the Soviet Union and its leader, "Uncle Joe" (Stalin); see Neve, *Film and Politics*, 78.

113. Roshwald and Roshwald, *Moses*.

114. von Mohrenschildt, "Lincoln Steffens," 41, 38.

115. Rollins, "The Heart," 239–250.

116. Pipes, *Russia*, 209.

117. Tallack, *America*, 185–186.

118. Steffens, *Moses*, 22 (Steffens contrasts the illuminating image of Moses the revolutionary with the image of Moses the lawgiver).

119. Chartier, "Culture as Appropriation," 233.

Chapter 3. If Moses Was a Mulatto: Zora Neale Hurston's *Moses, Man of the Mountain* (1939)

An earlier version of part of this chapter has previously appeared as "'Sunk in Slavery. . . . Snarled in Freedom': Recent Feminist Analyses of Exodus-Deuteronomy and Zora Neale Hurston's *Moses, Man of the Mountain*," *Biblicon* 2 (1997): 39–49.

1. Cruse, *Crisis*, 23.

2. Luhan, *Intimate Memories*, 3:79–80.

3. Hurston's birth date is unknown; dates she claimed range between 1898 and

1903. More recently, a relative suggested 1891 as the likely birth date, and this has found some popular acceptance; see Hemenway, *Zora*, 13 and 32 n.8; and Shockley, *Afro-American Women Writers*, 450.

4. Van Vechten, *Fragments*, 56–57.

5. *Moses and Monotheism: Three Essays* appeared in English in 1939. Earlier English and German versions of its component parts were published 1934–1938 (Freud, *The Origins of Religion*, 239).

6. Barker and Jones, *African Americans*, 18; Wilmore, *Black Religion*, 139.

7. Barker and Jones, *African Americans*, 17f.; Patterson, *America*, 58.

8. B. Washington, *Up from Slavery*, 107.

9. For example, legal challenges to *Birth of a Nation* were mounted; see Staiger, *Interpreting Films*, 143.

10. White, *Black Leadership*, 65–70.

11. Ibid., 83–94.

12. Hurston, *Moses*, xxiii.

13. Carter-Sigglow, *Making Her Way*, 106–107.

14. Hurston, "The Sermon," in *Negro Anthology*, ed. Cunard, 50–54; Hurston, *Jonah*, 269. Hurston's strategy of simultaneously exploiting the same material in *Jonah* and the *Anthology* essay is repeated later in her career. *Moses* includes material on hoodoo and voodoo published only a year earlier in the fieldwork "report," *Tell My Horse*.

15. Hurston, *Dust Tracks*, 50.

16. Hurston, *Moses*, 55–62; Whiston, *Antiquities*, book 2, chapter X (II.238–253).

17. Hurston, *Moses*, 60–64; Whiston, *Antiquities*, book 2, chapter XI (II.254–255). Josephus's reference to the treachery of the "sacred scribes" also finds similarities in Hurston's earlier account of the priests' cynical manipulation of the royal household (43–44).

18. Whiston, *Antiquities*, book 18, chapter III (XVIII.63–64). One study identified at least 217 reprints or editions of this translation of Josephus (Feldman and Hata, *Josephus*, 14).

19. For extracts, see Hurston, *Spunk*, 99–106. The manuscript was damaged when, following Hurston's death in a state welfare home, a janitor tried to burn her effects (Hemenway, *Zora*, 4, 343–344).

20. The exception is Untermeyer, "Old Testament Voodoo," 11.

21. McDowell, "Foreword: Lines of Descent/Dissenting Lines," in Hurston, *Moses*, viii.

22. Slaves brought to America were followers of traditional religions or Islam. Oral testimonies indicate that some Muslims managed to observe prayer times and dietary laws for generations. Wilmore notes some evidence for the adoption of Christianity in the early sixteenth century; the first organized mission was undertaken by the Anglican church in 1701 (*Black Religion and Black Radicalism*, 6).

23. Raboteau, *Slave Religion*, 311.

24. Weems, "Reading Her Way," 31–50. There are other questionable elements

to Weems's thesis, including the undifferentiated portrayal of the "Anglo woman" as beneficiary and upholder of patriarchy. Among groups that have valued the experiential above the textual are the Religious Society of Friends (Quakers). See Steere, *Quaker Spirituality*; Scott, *What Canst Thou Say?*

25. Weems, "Reading *Her Way*," 34–35.

26. Raboteau, *Slave Religion*, 44–92.

27. Ibid., 96; Herskovits, *The Myth*.

28. For Hurston, voodoo is a coherent system involving elaborate ceremony and worship built around spirit possession. It is to be distinguished from hoodoo, a more definitely North American phenomenon in which a "client"-"doctor" type of relationship exists between the "devotee" and an "expert" who is paid to execute sympathetic magic and revenge work.

29. Parrinder, *West African Religions*, 35–36.

30. Herskovits, "African Gods," 324. (This article was first published before *Moses, Man of the Mountain*.)

31. Hurston, *Moses*, xxiv.

32. Hurston, *Tell My Horse*, 116–117.

33. Ibid., 204.

34. Herskovits, *The Myth*, 1951; Herskovits and Herskovits, "An Outline," 58. *Hwedo* is simply a different transliteration of Hurston's *Ouedo*.

35. Parrinder, *West African Religion*, 50–53. See also Argyle, *The Fon*, and Mercier, *African Worlds*, 210–234.

36. In "African Gods" (first published in *American Anthropologist* 39 [1937]: 635–681), Herskovits states that in African American religions "elements ancestral to the present-day organization or worship have been retained in immediately recognizable form" but does not carefully distinguish "recognizable" from "identical with."

37. For example, Copher, "The Black Presence," 146–164.

38. Herskovits, "African Gods," 328, charts how saint-*loa* identifications vary in Cuba, Brazil, and Haiti.

39. Hurston jumps from reporting informant opinion regarding the Moses-Damballah link (in *Tell My Horse*) to espousing it in *Moses*. This means that any attempt to rely on Hurston for an assessment of African survivals in America (as in Mulira, "The Case," 34–68) is problematic.

40. Hurston, *Moses*, 119–120. Compare (on Marie Leveau) Hurston, *Mules and Men*, 192, and (on the book) *Mules and Men*, 280.

41. Hurston, *Moses*, 150, 153–154, 162, 165, 172.

42. Ibid., 142.

43. Ibid., 113, 126.

44. *Mules and Men*, 191–205, 207–211, and 213–221.

45. Ibid., 211.

46. Ibid., 184–185.

47. Hurston, *Moses*, 1–2.

48. Ibid., 180.

49. See Dinnerstein, Nichols, and Reimers, *Natives and Strangers*, 219–223.

50. Thenen, "Gobineau," 163–164.

51. Swartley, *Slavery, Sabbath, War and Women*, studies pro- and antislavery hermeneutics.

52. Hyatt, *Franz Boas*, 33, 98, 108–109. See also Boas, *Anthropology*.

53. Hurston, *Dust Tracks*, 123; Boas, "Preface," in Hurston, *Mules and Men*, xiii–xiv.

54. Hurston, *Dust Tracks*, 7.

55. Ibid., 171.

56. Hurston, *Their Eyes*, 210; *Moses*, 19–20, 33–34.

57. Moses, 34.

58. Ibid., 37.

59. Ibid., 64.

60. Ibid., 242–246.

61. Ibid., 242. A similar contradiction may be present within the Numbers story if, as Copher suggests, Moses' family was black ("The Black Presence," 146–164).

62. Carter-Sigglow, *Making Her Way*, 118.

63. Davis. *From the Dark Tower*, 118.

64. Hurston, *Their Eyes*, 209, 211.

65. Ibid., 210f. Sociologist Myrdal also found African Americans who had adopted the white evaluation of light color as synonymous with superiority (*An American Dilemma*, 1382–1383, nn.13–16).

66. Hurston, *Jonah*, 23–24. Myrdal spoke of all African Americans as marginalized but noted that with the rise of race consciousness there was an increasing tendency to view light coloring as a hallmark of illegitimacy (*An American Dilemma*, 1384, n.24).

67. Hurston, *Dust Tracks*, 171, 239.

68. Ibid., 159.

69. Hurston, *Moses*, 11, 34, 49, 90, 189.

70. Ibid., 37.

71. Ibid., 203.

72. White, *Black Leadership*, especially 1–16.

73. Quoted in Myrdal, *An American Dilemma*, 774.

74. Hurston, *Moses*, 189.

75. Ibid., 69.

76. Ibid., 204.

77. Ibid., 178, 204.

78. Myrdal, *An American Dilemma*, 698; White, *Black Leadership*, 75–107.

79. Hurston, *Moses*, 38–44, 118–119, 204.

80. Myrdal, *An American Dilemma*, 750–751.

81. White, *Black Leadership*, 87.

82. Hurston, *Moses*, 282.

83. Sheffey, "Zora Neale Hurston's," 220.

84. Quoted in Goldstein, *Reinscribing Moses*, 31. For Freud, Moses' presence on Sinai is symbolic.

85. Hyatt, *Franz Boas*, 145–146.

86. Ibid., 85.

87. James Griggs (Georgia) on 17 April 1908, quoted in Carroll and Noble, *The Free and the Unfree*, 255.

88. Hurston, *Moses*, 2, 4, 8.

89. Mendes-Flohr and Reinharz, *The Jew*, 492–493; Hurston, *Moses*, 2, 5.

90. Hemenway, *Zora*, 256; Tolischus, "Reich Adopts," 1, 11; and "Reich's New Army." See also "Nazi War on Jews Hurts Christians," 3.

91. Hurston, *Moses*, 19–21; Tolischus, "Text of Hitler's speech to Reischstag at Nuremberg," The *New York Times*, 16 September 1935, 11.

92. Hurston, *Moses*, 34.

93. Rubenstein and Roth, *Approaches to Auschwitz*, 111. The Nuremberg laws of 15 September 1935 were originally directed against all non-Aryans [sic]; a swift amendment passed within a day limited their application to "full Jews" only (Tolischus, "Reich's New Army," 14).

94. Hurston, *Moses*, 47–50.

95. Tolischus, "Reich's New Army," 1, 14.

96. Walker, *In Search*, 93–116.

97. Carter-Sigglow, *Making Her Way*, 115–117.

98. See Hopkins and Cummings, *Cut Loose*, 36; and Bradford, *Scenes in the Life of Harriet Tubman*.

99. Hollyday, *Clothed*, 45–47.

100. Coats, *Moses*, 43; Sarna, *Exploring Exodus*, 25, 31. See also Setel, "Exodus," 30; and Phipps, *Assertive Biblical Women*, 31–37.

101. Hurston, *Moses*, 1, 4.

102. Ibid., 21; contrast the defiance of the women in Exodus 1:19.

103. Setel, "Exodus," 29.

104. Hurston, *Moses*, 24; compare Exodus 2:3.

105. Coats, *Moses Tradition*, 31.

106. Hurston, *Moses*, 112.

107. Carter-Sigglow, *Making Her Way*, 117.

108. Hurston, *Moses*, 217, 221.

109. Setel, "Exodus," 33.

110. As at *m. Aboth* 1.1 (Danby, *The Mishnah*, 446).

111. Plaskow, *Standing Again*, 25.

112. Exodus 20:17. See also Brenner, "An Afterword," 255–258.

113. Hurston, *Moses*, 233.

114. Ibid., 226.

115. For an articulation of this view, see Ozick, "Notes," 120–151.

116. See Burns, *Has the Lord*; Trible, "Bringing Miriam Out," 166–168; Hollyday, *Clothed with the Sun*, 139–144.

117. This reading contrasts with more conservative interpretations, which assert that Aaron suffers more than his sister, because he has to bear the pain of seeing Miriam suffer and to humble himself before Moses in order to lessen her punishment (for example, Plaut, *The Torah*, 1101–1102.

118. Trible, "Bringing Miriam Out," 173–179.

119. Hurston, *Moses*, 26–28.

120. Ibid., 29.

121. Ibid., 242–246.

122. For example, Coats, *Moses Tradition*, 88–98.

123. Hurston, *Moses*, 218.

124, Ibid., 246.

125. Ibid., 264f., and for the events Moses recollects, 26–35, 64–65.

126. See Bach, "With a Song," 251–254 for one example; and Plaskow, *Standing Again*, 54, 247 n. 73 for an account of others.

127. Hurston, *Moses*, 14.

128. Ibid., 135.

129. On further problems inherent in such an approach, see Birch, *Black American Women's Writing*, 66–67.

130. Hurston creates semifictional expansions and reorganizations of her fieldwork experience to contextualize her findings. The best known example of this blending of anthropology and fiction is *Mules and Men*. In *Tell My Horse*, Hurston's double identity as observer and initiate of voodoo is explicitly recounted.

131. Hurston's divorced status attracted censure. Suggestions that she was a lesbian abounded; she was charged with having committed sodomy with a minor. Although the charges were eventually dropped as groundless (Hurston was in Honduras at the time she had allegedly committed the offense in New York), they were a stimulus for the African American press to print inaccurate, lurid accounts of Hurston's private life; she despaired to the point of contemplating suicide (Hemenway, *Zora*, 319–322).

132. Hurston, *Their Eyes*, 31–32.

133. Hurston, *Moses*, 19, 127, 246, 248.

134. Ibid., 19–21, 29–35, 59.

135. Hurston, *The Sanctified Church*, 7.

136. Hemenway, *Zora*, 52 (quote from unpublished section of the manuscript for *Dust Tracks*).

137. Hickerson, *Linguistic Anthropology*, 1, 3.

138. Hurston, "Characteristics of Negro Expression," in Cunard, ed., *Negro Anthology*, 43.

139. Ibid., 39–40.

140. Hickerson, *Linguistic Anthropology*, 82–83.

141. Hurston, *Dust Tracks*, 127–128; *Mules and Men*, 19.

142. Hurston, *Moses*, 120.

143. Ibid., 267. See also Hurston, *Mules and Men*, 184 on the indispensability of Jethro.

144. Hurston, *Moses*, 87, 91.

145. Ibid., 190.

146. See the story about naming and code switching narrated in Hurston, *Mules and Men*, 79–80.

147. Hutchison, "Led His People Free," 21; *New Yorker*, 91.

148. *New Yorker*, 91.

149. Hutchison, "Led His People Free," 21.

150. Ibid., 21.

151. Untermeyer, "Old Testament Voodoo," 11.

152. Ibid., 11. See also Jackson, "Some Negroes," 103–107, where the reviewer emphasizes the legitimate right of the "Negro folk experience" to be regarded as "the reliable counterpart of every other human being's experience."

153. Slomovitz, "The Negro's Moses," 1504.

154. Ibid.

155, Locke, "Dry Fields," 7; Ellison, "Recent Negro Fiction," 211.

156. Hurston divorced Herbert Sheen in 1931 and Albert Price III in 1940. Hemenway, *Zora*, 32 n. 8, suggests that she may also have been married during the unaccounted-for decade of her life before she entered Morgan Academy in 1917, at the age of twenty-eight.

157. On the National Urban League, see White, *Black Leadership*, 77. De-emphasizing civil rights, it focused on manners and hygiene.

158. Cannon, *Black Womanist Ethics*, 105–106.

159. Walker, *In Search*, 93.

160. Davis, *From the Dark Tower*, 113.

161. Ibid., 117.

162. Turner, *In a Minor Chord*, 98, 100, 120.

163. Ibid., 109.

164. Ibid., 111.

165. On the politics of humor, see Durant and Miller, *Laughing Matters*; Bremmer and Roodenburg, *A Cultural History of Humour*, and for readings of Hurston that see humor as fundamental, Levecq, "'Mighty Strange Threads,'" 436–461; and Woodward, "Expressions," 431–435.

166. H. L. Gates, "Afterword. Zora Neale Hurston: 'A Negro Way of Saying,'" in Hurston, *Mules and Men*, 297; Shockley, *Afro-American Women Writers*, 450.

167. Hemenway, *Zora*, 16.

168. Ibid., 271. On the ambitious nature of the book, see Russell, *Render Me My Song*, 42; Howard, *Zora*, 113.

169. Carter-Sigglow, *Making Her Way*, 120.

170. Wall, "Zora Neale Hurston," 371–393.

171. Howard, *Zora*, 116, 123, 132.

172. Levecq, "'Mighty Strange Threads,'" 436–461.

Chapter 4. Coming in from the (Cold) War: Cecil B. DeMille's
The Ten Commandments (1956)

Earlier versions of parts of this chapter have appeared elsewhere as "Dialogue or Dominance? Interfaith Encounter and Cecil B. DeMille's *The Ten Commandments*." *Discernment: An Ecumenical Journal of Inter-Religious Encounter* 3 (1996):

10–19; and "Moses at the Movies: Ninety Years of the Bible and Film." *Modern Believing* 37 no. 4 (1996): 45–54.

1. Babington and Evans, *Biblical Epics*, 5–6.

2. Uricchio and Pearson, *Reframing Culture*.

3. Exum, *Plotted, Shot, Painted*; Jewett, *Saint Paul at the Movies*; Kreitzer, *The New Testament in Fiction and Film*; Scott, *Hollywood Dreams*; Telford, "The New Testament," 360–394.

4. Scott, *Hollywood Dreams*, x.

5. Wood, *America in the Movies*, 177.

6. Quoted in Patterson, *America*, 347.

7. Tindall and Shi, *America*, 1259. Most popular of the new consumer goods was the television.

8. Carroll and Noble, *The Free and the Unfree*, 319, 335.

9. Patterson, *America*, 335–341, 356.

10. See Sklar, *Movie-Made America*, 249–268; and Ceplair and Englund, *The Inquisition in Hollywood*. On the investigation of Jewish movie professionals, see Gabler, *An Empire of Their Own*, 351–386.

11. Winter, *Suburban Captivity*, 82–87; Sklare, *Conservative Judaism*.

12. Ahlstrom, *Religious History*, 950–951.

13. Herberg, *Protestant, Catholic, Jew*, 31, 260.

14. Telford, "The New Testament," 384–389.

15. Hayne, *Autobiography*, 337–378.

16. Ibid., 392; Noerdlinger, *Moses and Egypt*, 2.

17. "Mount Sinai to Main Street," *Time*, 19 November 1956, 82; Higham, *Cecil B. DeMille*, x.

18. See Wright, "Moses at the Movies," 46–54.

19. Urrichio and Pearson, *Reframing Culture*, 173–187.

20. See Babington and Evans, *Biblical Epics*, 44; Wright, "Moses at the Movies," 46–54.

21. Hayes and Prussner, *Old Testament Theology*, 126–142; J. Miller, "Archaeology," 51–56. For DeMille's somewhat defensive words on the difference between his task as film director and that of historians and archaeologists, see Noerdlinger, *Moses and Egypt*, 1–2, 5.

22. See later, "Reception."

23. On the tenuous reasoning behind the construction of Nefretiri's role, see Noerdlinger, *Moses and Egypt*, 61.

24. Compare John 1:1–5; 14.

25. Curtis, *Joshua*, 50, 54.

26. Noerdlinger, *Moses and Egypt*, 163: Then found in the Metropolitan Museum of Art, New York, Carnarvon Room, Exhibit 26.7.1287.

27. In this respect, *The Ten Commandments* follows the late-nineteenth-and early-twentieth-century lives of Moses. Compare, for example, the visual detail of DeMille's sets with the description in Ingraham, *The Pillar*.

28. Noerdlinger, *Moses and Egypt*, 13.

29. Evett, "There was a Young Fellow," 20.

30. Compare also presentations of Moses' birth in *Antiquities* and *The Ten Commandments* with that of Jesus in Matthew 2:1–7.

31. *Life of Moses* 1.18–24; Whiston, *Antiquities*, book 2, chapters X and XI (II. 230–231; 232–237).

32. *Life of Moses* 1.63.

33. See Collins, "Artapanus," 889–903.

34. A development of the Tharbis-Moses relationship would have weakened the film's presentation of the Moses-Rameses-Nefretiri nexus and contravened codes on screen "miscgenation."

35. Winter, *Suburban Captivity*, 83.

36. Ahlstrom, *Religious History*, 956; Tindall and Shi, *America*, 1273–1274.

37. Ahlstrom, *Religious History*, 951; Tindall and Shi, *America*, 1273–1273.

38. Herberg, *Protestant, Catholic, Jew*, 260.

39. See Brown, *The Essential Reinhold Niebuhr*.

40. D. Miller, "Popular Religion," 66–76; Tindall and Shi, *America*, 1273.

41. Related ideas have been previously explored in Wright, "Dialogue or Dominance?" 10–19.

42. For example Exodus 25–31, 35: 10–40; Leviticus; Numbers 6, 8–9.

43. A point also made in Segal, "*The Ten Commandments*," 38.

44. Compare the modern Seder: Why on this night do we eat unleavened bread? Why on this night do we eat bitter herbs? Why on this night do we dip our herbs? Why on this night do we recline?

45. In this respect *The Ten Commandments* represents in oblique fashion the supersessionist attitude toward Judaism that is overtly advanced in the 1923 version of the film (Babington and Evans, *Biblical Epics*, 45–46).

46. According to Noerdlinger, *Moses and Egypt*, 22: "In keeping with Moses' character we interpret his flight from the face of Pharaoh as a sentence of banishment."

47. Herberg speaks of the accommodation of American Judaism to the "American pattern of religious life" but does not emphasize its Christian character. For example, under Christian influence the festival of Hanukkah has assumed a prominent place in the religious calendar, institutionally the corporate structure of the synagogue resembles that of many Protestant churches, and features of the synagogue service in Reform Judaism are influenced by Christian practice (*Protestant, Catholic, Jew*, 191–192; see also Hilton, *The Christian Effect*, 15–17, 145–154).

48. Armstrong, *Rhetoric*, 6; Hayne, *Autobiography*, 433.

49. Usai and Codelli, *L'Eredità DeMille*, 16.

50. Melton, *Encyclopaedia*, 131–133; Arrington, *Brigham Young*; Gibbons, *Brigham Young*.

51. Wilford, "Winning Hearts and Minds," 315.

52. Swann, *Hollywood Feature Film*, 55.

53. See Gabler, *An Empire of Their Own*, 3–5; Jowett, *Film*, 364–368; and Neve, *Film and Politics in America*, 187.

54. Biskind, *Seeing Is Believing*, 4. Neve, *Film and Politics in America*, 181–198; Smoodin, "Watching the Skies," 35–40.

55. Edwards, *The DeMilles*, 48; Hayne, *Autobiography*, 387.

56. Babington and Evans, *Biblical Epics*, 10; Wood, *America in the Movies*, 187.

57. Noerdlinger, *Moses and Egypt*, 47.

58. Wood, *America in the Movies*, 183–184.

59. For summaries see Giddens, *Sociology*, 457–458; Haralambos and Holborn, *Sociology*, 652–655.

60. Robinson and Spigelgass, *All My Yesterdays*, 272.

61. Brogan, *History*, 648; Patterson, *America*, 372.

62. On the presentation of African Americans in Hollywood cinema see Cripps, *Making Movies Black*. The relatively positive portrayal of different ethnic groups in the 1956 *Ten Commandments* contrasts with the approach of its 1923 predecessor. In this film, postwar fears about the continuing tide of immigration are reflected in the character of Sally Lung, a Eurasian vamp who brings disease and disaster with her to America (Babington and Evans, *Biblical Epics*, 45). Johnson, *Autobiography of an Ex-Colored Man*, recounted the life of an African American and his experiences of "passing" for white in middle-class American society.

63. Cripps, "The Death of Rastus," 269.

64. Sklar, *Movie-Made America*, 269; Jowett, *Film*, chapter 15.

65. Numbers 12:1.

66. Biskind, *Seeing Is Believing*, 291.

67. Whiston, *Antiquities*, book 2, chapter X (II.253).

68. Hayne, *Autobiography*, 382, 386.

69. *Time*, 12 November 1956, 22–30.

70. Amberg, *The New York Times Film Reviews*, 306.

71. Hodgens, "*The Ten Commandments*," 59.

72. Hayne, *Autobiography*, 385–386.

73. The role of the superpowers in the region was widely recognized; see, for example, "The Middle East: The Threat of War," *Time*, 19 November 1956, 30–33.

74. On Western narration of the Middle East, see Kabbani, *Europe's Myths*.

75. Ibid., 54.

76. Ibid., 55.

77. Hayne, *Autobiography*, 385. See also Noerdlinger, *Moses and Egypt*, 86: "In the time in which we are living it may be well for western people to realize fully that the fundamental message of the Koran is identical with that of the Bible: Love of and obedience to the one God"; and Heston, *In the Arena*, 133: "He [DeMille] believed deeply in the message of the film and the power of the man, Moses, to reach across the millennia and move people of every faith, kind and condition."

78. Campbell and Pitts, *The Bible on Film*, 2–4.

79. Urrichio and Pearson, *Reframing Culture*, 164.

80. Dyer, "Moral Development," 11; Urrichio and Pearson, *Reframing Culture*, 41–64.

81. Urrichio and Pearson, *Reframing Culture*, 30–31, 165. In the early days,

movie theaters were urban phenomena, usually sited in the poorer districts and drawing their audiences from the ranks of the manual laborers. As such groups generally worked long hours for six days a week, Sunday screenings were particularly important for the survival of the industry.

82. Edwards, *The DeMilles*, 49. The DeMille family had strong links with the arts. William was a playwright but later followed Cecil into the film industry. Their father, Henry, was a teacher, playwright, and lay preacher, and their mother, Beatrice, ran a successful theatrical agency.

83. Higashi, *Cecil B. DeMille*, 184–185.

84. See, for example, Eliot, *Walt*, 128; 207 where Disney's antisemitism is discussed.

85. Sklar, *Movie-Made America*, 266.

86. Edwards, *The DeMilles*, 13.

87. Ceplair and Englund, *The Inquisition in Hollywood*, 359.

88. On the history of Moses films, see Wright, "Moses at the Movies."

89. "The Ten Commandments," *Time*, 12 November 1956, 122; Evett, "There Was a Young Fellow," 20.

90. *Newsweek*, 5 November 1956, in Ringgold and Bodeen, *The Films of Cecil B. DeMille*.

91. Crowther, "The Ten Commandments," 307.

92. Evett, "There Was a Young Fellow," 20.

93. "The Ten Commandments," *Time*, 12 November 1956, 124; Baker, "The Ten Commandments," *Films and Filming*, 23.

94. Hatch, "Theatre and Films," 506.

95. "The Ten Commandments," *Time*, 12 November 1956, 124; Kitchin, "The Ten Commandments," 149.

96. Kitchin, 149; McCarten praised the handling of the parting of the Red Sea but felt the film was a piece of "hokum" ("DeMille at the Old Stand," *New Yorker*, (17 November 1956, 101).

97. Evett, "There Was a Young Fellow," 20.

98. Hayne, *Autobiography*, 394–395.

99. Essoe and Lee, *DeMille*, 92.

100. Driver, "Hollywood in the Wilderness," 1390.

101. Ibid.

102. Ibid., 1391.

103. "Mount Sinai to Main Street," *Time*, 19 November 1956, 82.

104. Kennedy et al., "Through Different Eyes," 20–21.

105. Ibid., 21.

106. Staiger, *Interpreting Films*, 87.

107. Tafoya, "Born in East L.A.," 123–129.

108. Gow, *Hollywood*, 31.

109. Holloway, *The Religious Dimension*, 3.

110. Ibid., 93.

111. Ibid., 93–94.

112. Storey, *An Introductory Guide*, 21–33.

113. Leavis and Thompson, *Culture and Environment*, 3.

114. Jowett, *Film*, 369–373. Early studies focused in particular on such issues as whether audience attitudes could be shaped or reversed by film. They concluded that the viewer's context was important in determining the reception of any film and that an audience was likely to resist a cinematic presentation that contradicted or challenged prior convictions.

115. E.g., Gabler, *An Empire of Their Own*; Babington and Evans, *Biblical Epics*, 33–36.

116. For examples of this type of work that appeared at the time of the film's release, see Baker, "Showman for the Millions," 9–11, 14; and Gray, "New Testament for the Old Testament," 8.

117. Cross, *The Bible*.

118. Kreitzer, *The Old Testament in Fiction and Film*, 13.

119. Ibid., 14.

120. Ibid., 26.

121. Ibid., 26, 47–48.

122. Babington and Evans, *Biblical Epics*, 46–47.

123. Ibid., 10; Wood, *America in the Movies*, 187.

124. Babington and Evans, *Biblical Epics*, 2, 3, 9.

125. Staiger, *Interpreting Films*, 88.

126. Moore, *Religious Outsiders*, ix.

127. Petersen, *Christianity and Civil Society*, vii.

Chapter 5. Conclusions

1. Kaplan, *Understanding Popular Culture*, 13.

2. Quoted in Tucker and Knight, *Humanizing America's Iconic Book*, 3.

3. Compare Riches, *The Bible*, 137.

Bibliography

Aaron, D. *Writers on the Left: Episodes in American Literary Communism*. New York: Harcourt, Brace and World, 1961.

Ahlstrom, S. E. *A Religious History of the American People*. New Haven: Yale University Press, 1972.

Albanese, C. L. *America: Religions and Religion*, 3rd ed. London: Wadsworth, 1999.

Albright, W. F. *The Archaeology of Palestine and the Bible*. 1935. Reprint, Cambridge: Cambridge University Press, 1975.

Amberg, G. *The New York Times Film Reviews. A One Volume Selection, 1913–1970*. New York: Arno Press, 1971.

Argyle, W. J. *The Fon of Dahomey: A History and Ethnography of the Old Kingdom*. Oxford: Clarendon Press, 1966.

Armstrong, R. N. *The Rhetoric of David O. McKay: Mormon Prophet*. New York: Peter Lang, 1993.

Arrington, L. J. *Brigham Young: American Moses*. New York: Alfred A. Knopf, 1985.

Arthur, C., ed. *Religion and the Media: An Introductory Reader*. Cardiff: University of Wales Press, 1993.

Ateek, N. *Justice and Only Justice: A Palestinian Theology of Liberation*. Maryknoll, N.Y.: Orbis, 1991.

Awkward, M., ed. *New Essays on Their Eyes Were Watching God*. Cambridge: Cambridge University Press, 1990.

Babington, B., and P. W. Evans. *Biblical Epics: Sacred Narrative in the Hollywood Cinema*. Manchester: Manchester University Press, 1993.

Bach, A. "With a Song in Her Heart: Listening to Scholars Listening for Miriam," in *A Feminist Companion to Exodus-Deuteronomy*, edited by Athalya Brenner, 251–154. Sheffield: Sheffield Academic Press, 1994.

Bailey, T. A., and D. M. Kennedy, eds. *The American Spirit: United States History as Seen by Contemporaries*, vol. 2. Lexington, Mass.: Heath and Co., 1994.

151

Baker, P. "Showman for the Millions." *Films and Filming* 3, no. 1 (1956): 9–11, 14.
———. "The Ten Commandments." *Films and Filming* 4, no. 4 (1958): 23–24.
Bannister, R. C. *Social Darwinism: Science and Myth in Anglo-American Social Thought.* Philadelphia: Temple University Press, 1979.
Barker, L. J., and M. H. Jones. *African Americans and the American Political System.* Englewood Cliffs, N.J.: Prentice Hall, 1994.
Barlow, P. L. *Mormons and the Bible: The Place of the Latter-Day Saints in American Religion.* New York: Oxford University Press, 1991.
Barr, J. *Fundamentalism.* London: S.C.M. Press, 1981.
Barton, B. *The Man Nobody Knows.* London: Constable and Co., 1925.
———. *The Book Nobody Knows.* London: Constable and Co., 1926.
Beard, M., and J. Henderson. *A Very Short Introduction.* Oxford: Oxford University Press, 1995.
Bedell, G. C., L. Sandon, and C. T. Wellborn, eds. *Religion in America.* New York: Macmillan, 1982.
Bellah, R. N. "Civil Religion in America," in *Beyond Belief: Essays on Religion in a Post-Traditional World,* edited by R. N. Bellah, 168–189. 1967. Reprint, New York: Harper and Row, 1976.
———. *The Broken Covenant: American Civil Religion in Time of Trial.* New York: Seabury Press, 1975.
Berry, M. F., and J. W. Blassingame. "Africa, Slavery, and the Roots of Contemporary Black Culture." *Massachusetts Review* 18 (1977): 501–516.
Birch, E. L. *Black American Women's Writing: A Quilt of Many Colours.* London: Harvester Wheatsheaf, 1994.
Biskind, P. *Seeing Is Believing: How Hollywood Taught Us to Stop Worrying and Love the Fifties.* London: Pluto Press, 1984.
Bloom, H., ed. *Major Black American Writers Through the Harlem Renaissance.* New York: Chelsea House, 1995.
Boas, F. *The Mind of Primitive Man.* 1911. Reprint, New York: Free Press, 1963.
———. *Anthropology and Modern Life.* 1928. Reprint, New York: Dover Publications, 1986.
Bodnar, J. E. *Remaking America: Public Memory, Commemoration, and Patriotism in the Twentieth Century.* Princeton, N.J.: Princeton University Press, 1992.
Boi, P. "Moses, Man of Power, Man of Knowledge. A 'Signifying' Reading of Zora Neale Hurston (Between a Laugh and a Song)," in *Women and War: The Changing Status of American Women from the 1930s to the 1950s,* edited by M. Diedrich and D. Fischer-Hornung, 107–125. New York: Berg Publishers, 1990.
Bradford, S. *Scenes in the Life of Harriet Tubman.* Auburn: W. J. Moses, 1869.
Breidlid, A., F. C. Brøgger, Ø. T. Gulliksen, and T. Sirevag, eds. *American Culture: An Anthology of Civilisation Texts.* London: Routledge, 1996.
Bremmer, J., and H. Roodenburg, eds. *A Cultural History of Humour From Antiquity to the Present Day.* Cambridge, England: Polity, 1997.
Brenner, A. "An Afterword: The Decalogue: Am I An Addressee?" in *A Feminist Companion to Exodus-Deuteronomy,* 255–258. Sheffield: Sheffield Academic Press, 1994.

Brenner, A., ed. *A Feminist Companion to Exodus to Deuteronomy*. Sheffield: Sheffield Academic Press, 1994.

Brock, C. *Mosaics of the American Dream: America as New Israel—A Metaphor for Today*. Wheatley, England: Bayou Press, 1994.

Brogan, H. *The Penguin History of the United States of America*. London: Penguin, 1990.

Brown, G., ed. *Religion in America*. New York: New York Times, 1977.

Brown, R. McA., ed. *The Essential Reinhold Niebuhr: Selected Essays and Addresses*. New Haven: Yale University Press, 1986.

Buhle, M. J., P. Buhle, and D. Georgakas, eds. *Encyclopedia of the American Left*. London: St. James Press, 1990.

Buhle, M. J., P. Buhle, and H. J. Kaye, eds. *The American Radical*. London: Routledge, 1994.

Burke, P. *History and Social Theory*. Cambridge: Polity Press, 1992.

Burke, P., ed. *New Perspectives on Historical Writing*. Cambridge: Polity Press, 1991.

Burkett, R. K. *Garveyism as a Religious Movement: The Institutionalization of a Black Civil Religion*. Metuchen, N.J.: The Scarecrow Press, 1978.

Burns, R. J. *Has the Lord Indeed Spoken Only Through Moses? A Study of the Biblical Portrait of Miriam*. Atlanta: Scholars Press, 1987.

Bush, T. B. "Transforming Vision: Alice Walker and Zora Neale Hurston." *Christian Century* 105 (1988): 1035–1039.

Campbell, R. H., and M. R. Pitts. *The Bible on Film: A Checklist, 1897–1980*. Metuchen, N.J.: Scarecrow Press, 1981.

Cannon, K. G. "Resources for a Constructive Ethic in the Life and Work of Zora Neale Hurston." *Journal of Feminist Studies in Religion* 1 (1985): 37–51.

———. G. *Black Womanist Ethics*. Atlanta: Scholars Press, 1988.

Carby, H. "The Politics of Fiction, Anthropology, and the Folk: Zora Neale Hurston," in *History and Memory in African-American Culture*, edited by G. Fabre and R. O'Meally, 28–44. Oxford: Oxford University Press, 1994.

Carroll, P. N., and D. W. Noble. *The Free and the Unfree: A New History of the United States*, 2nd ed. London: Penguin, 1988.

Carter-Sigglow, J. *Making Her Way with Thunder: A Reappraisal of Zora Neale Hurston's Narrative Art*. Frankfurt Am Main: Peter Lang, 1994.

Ceplair, L., and S. Englund. *The Inquisition in Hollywood: Politics in the Film Community 1930–1960*. Berkeley: University of California Press, 1979.

Charles, M. M. "The Mormon Christianising of the Old Testament." *Sunstone* 5 (1980): 35–39.

Chartier, R. "Culture as Appropriation: Popular Cultural Uses in Early Modern France," in *Understanding Popular Culture: Europe from the Middle Ages to the Nineteenth Century*, edited by S. Kaplan, 229–253. New York: Mouton, 1984.

Coats, G. W. *Moses: Heroic Man, Man of God*. Sheffield: J.S.O.T. Press, 1988.

———. "Humility and Honor: A Moses Legend in Numbers 12." In *The Moses Tradition, edited by G. W. Coats*, 88–98. Sheffield: Sheffield Academic Press, 1993.

Cohen, W. I. *America in the Age of Soviet Power, 1945–1991*. vol. 4 of *The Cam-*

bridge History of American Foreign Relations. Cambridge: Cambridge University Press, 1993.

Cohn-Sherbok, D. *Exodus: An Agenda for Jewish-Christian Dialogue*. London: Bellew, 1992.

Collins, J. J. "Artapanus: A New Translation and Introduction," in *The Old Testament Pseudepigrapha*, vol. 2, edited by J. H. Charlesworth, 889–903. New York: Doubleday, 1985.

Collins, R. *Four Sociological Traditions*. Oxford: Oxford University Press, 1994.

Colson, F. H. trans. *Philo*, vol. 6. London: William Heinemann, 1935.

Combs, J., ed. *Movies and Politics: The Dynamic Relationship*. London: Garland, 1993.

Copher, C. "The Black Presence in the Old Testament," in *Stony the Road We Trod: African American Biblical Interpretation*, edited by C. H. Felder, 146–164. Minneapolis: Fortress, 1991.

Corrington, R. S. *The Community of Interpreters. On the Hermeneutics of Nature and the Bible in the American Philosophical Tradition*. Macon, Ga.: Mercer University Press, 1987.

Coser, L. A. "Chicago Sociology," in *Blackwell Dictionary of Twentieth Century Social Thought*, edited by W. Outhwaite and T. Bottomore, 70–71. Oxford: Blackwell, 1993.

Cripps, T. *Making Movies Black: The Hollywood Message Movie from World War Two to the Civil Rights Era*. Oxford: Oxford University Press, 1993.

Cripps, T. R. "The Death of Rastus: Negroes in American Films Since 1945," in *The Movies: An American Idiom. Readings in the Social History of the American Motion Picture*, edited by A. F. McClure, 266–275. Rutherford, N.J.: Fairleigh Dickinson University Press, 1971.

Cross, R. *The Bible According to Hollywood*. London: Ward Lock, 1984.

Crowther, B. "The Ten Commandments," in *The New York Times Film Reviews: A One Volume Selection 1913–1970*, edited by G. Amberg, 306–308. New York: Arno, 1971.

Cruse, H. *The Crisis of the Negro Intellectual*. London: W. H. Allen, 1969.

Culpepper, E. E. "New Tools for Theology: Writings by Women of Color." *Journal of Feminist Studies in Religion* 4 (1988): 39–50.

Cunard, N. ed. *Negro Anthology Made by Nancy Cunard 1931–1933*. 1934. Reprint, New York: Negro Universities Press, 1969.

Curtis, A. H. W. *Joshua*. Sheffield: Sheffield Academic Press, 1994.

Danby, H., trans. *The Mishnah*. Oxford: Oxford University Press, 1933.

Davies, P., and B. Neve, eds. *Cinema, Politics and Society in America*. Manchester: Manchester University Press, 1981.

Davies, P. R. *Whose Bible Is It Anyway?* Sheffield: Sheffield Academic Press, 1995.

Davis, A. P. *From the Dark Tower: Afro-American Writers 1900–1960*. Washington, D.C.: Howard University Press, 1981.

Davis, A. P., J. Saunders Redding, and J. A. Joyce, eds. *The New Cavalcade: African American Writing from 1760 to the Present*, 2 vols. Washington, D.C.: Howard University Press, 1991–92.

Davis, M. W. *Contributions of Black Women to America*, Vol. 1. Columbia, South Carolina: Kenday Press, 1982.

Deleuze, G. *Cinema: The Movement-Image*. Translated by H. Tomlinson and B. Habberjam. London: Athlone Press, 1992.

DeMille, C. B. "Forget Spectacle—It's the Story That Counts." *Films and Filming 3*, no. 1 (1956): 7.

Dinnerstein, L. "Henry Ford and the Jews," In *American Vistas: 1877 to the Present*, edited by L. Dinnerstein and K. T. Jackson, 181–193. 7th ed. New York: Oxford University Press, 1995.

Dinnerstein, L., R. L. Nichols, and D. M. Reimers. *Natives and Strangers: A Multicultural History of Americans*. New York: Oxford University Press, 1996.

Driver, T. S. "Hollywood in the Wilderness: A Review Article." *Christian Century* 73, no. 48 (1956): 1390–1391.

Drury, J., ed. *Critics of the Bible 1724–1873*. Cambridge: Cambridge University Press, 1989.

Duberman, M. B. *Paul Robeson*. London: Bodley Head, 1989.

Durant, J., and J. Miller, eds. *Laughing Matters: A Serious Look at Humour*. London: Longman, 1988.

Dyer, F. L. "The Moral Development of the Silent Drama." *Edison Kinetogram*, 15 April 1910, 11.

Dyer, R. *Only Entertainment*. London: Routledge, 1992.

Eagleton, T. *Literary Theory: An Introduction*, 2nd ed. Oxford: Blackwell, 1996.

Edwards, A. *The DeMilles: An American Family*. London: Collins, 1988.

Eliot, M. *Walt Disney: Hollywood's Dark Prince*. London: André Deutsch, 1994.

Elley, D. *The Epic Film: Myth and History*. London: Routledge and Kegan Paul, 1984.

Ellis, M. H. *Toward a Jewish Theology of Liberation*. London: S.C.M. Press, 1987.

Ellison, R. "Recent Negro Fiction." *New Masses* 5 August 1941, 22–26.

Elsner, J., and J. Masters, eds. *Reflections of Nero: Culture, History and Representation*. London: Duckworth, 1994.

Essoe, G., and R. Lee. *DeMille: The Man and His Pictures*. New York: A. S. Barnes, 1970.

Evett, R. "There Was a Young Fellow from Goshen." *New Republic* 135, no. 24 (1956): 20.

Exum, J. C. *Plotted, Shot, Painted: Cultural Representations of Biblical Women*. Sheffield: Sheffield Academic Press, 1996.

Felder, C. H., ed. *Stony the Road We Trod: African American Biblical Interpretation*. Minneapolis: Fortress, 1991.

Feldman, L. H., and G. Hata, eds. *Josephus, Judaism and Christianity*. Leiden: E. J. Brill, 1987.

Filler, L. *The Muckrakers*. University Park: Pennsylvania State University Press, 1976.

Fitzpatrick, E. F. *Muckraking: Three Landmark Articles*. Boston: St. Martin's Press, 1994.

Fletcher, R. *The Making of Sociology: A Study of Sociological Theory*, Vol. 1. New York: Charles Scribner's Sons, 1971.

Forrester, D. B. *Theology and Politics*. Oxford: Blackwell, 1988.

Freud, S. *The Origins of Religion: Totem and Taboo, Moses and Monotheism and Other Works*, edited by A. Dickson. Harmondsworth, England: Penguin, 1985.

Frye, N. *The Great Code: The Bible and Literature*. London: Routledge and Kegan Paul, 1982.

Gabler, N. *An Empire of Their Own: How the Jews Invented Hollywood*. London, 1979.

Gamoran, A. "Civil Religion in American Schools." *Sociological Analysis* 51 (1990): 235–256.

Garber, M., and R. L. Walkowitz, eds. *One Nation under God? Religion and American Culture*. London: Routledge, 1999.

Gardiner, J., ed. *What Is History Today?* London: Macmillan, 1988.

Genovese, E. D. *Roll, Jordan, Roll: The World the Slaves Made*. New York: Random House, 1974.

Gibbons, F. M. *Brigham Young, Modern Moses, Prophet of God*. Salt Lake City, Utah: Deseret Books, 1981.

Giddens, A. *Sociology*. Cambridge, England: Polity Press, 1989.

Ginzburg, C. *The Cheese and the Worms: The Cosmos of a Sixteenth Century Miller*. London: Routledge and Kegan Paul, 1980.

Goldstein, B. *Reinscribing Moses: Heine, Kafka, Freud and Schoenberg in a European Wilderness*. Cambridge: Harvard University Press, 1992.

Gorrell, D. K. *The Age of Social Responsibility: The Social Gospel in the Progressive Era 1900–1920*. Macon, Ga.: Mercer University Press, 1988.

Gottwald, N. K., and R. A. Horsley, eds. *The Bible and Liberation: Political and Social Hermeneutics*, rev. ed. Maryknoll, N.Y.: Orbis, 1993.

Gow, G. *Hollywood in the Fifties*. New York: A. S. Barnes, 1971.

Grabbe, L. L. *Leviticus*. Sheffield: Sheffield Academic Press, 1993.

Gray, A. *The Socialist Tradition, Moses to Lenin*. London: Longmans, Green and Co., 1947.

Gray, M. "New Testament for the Old Testament." *Films and Filming* 3, no. 1 (1956): 8.

Grossberg, L. "Is There a Fan in the House? The Affective Sensibility of Fandom." In *The Adoring Audience: Fan Culture and Popular Media*, edited by L. Lewis, 40–54. London: Routledge, 1992.

Gutiérrez, G. *A Theology of Liberation*. Maryknoll, N.Y.: Orbis, 1983.

Hadas, M. "Clio's Step Children." *Menorah Journal* 28 (1940): 337–349.

Hahn, E. *Mabel: A Biography of Mabel Dodge Luhan*. Boston: Houghton Mifflin, 1977.

Handy, R. T. *The Social Gospel in America*. New York: Oxford University Press, 1966.

Hansen, K. J. "Mormonism." In *The Encyclopedia of Religion*, vol. 10, edited by M. Eliade. New York: Macmillan, 1982.

Haralambos, M., and M. Holborn. *Sociology: Themes and Perspectives*, 3rd ed. London: HarperCollins, 1991.

Hatch, R. "Theatre and Films." *Nation*, 8 December 1956, 506.

Hayes, J. H., and F. C. Prussner. *Old Testament Theology: Its History and Development*. London: S.C.M. Press, 1985.

Hayne, D., ed. *The Autobiography of Cecil B. DeMille*. London: W. H. Allen, 1960.

Hemenway, R. E. *Zora Neale Hurston: A Literary Biography*. Chicago: University of Illinois Press, 1977.

Henking, S. "Sociological Christianity and Christian Sociology: The Paradox of Early American Sociology." *Religion and American Culture* 3 (1993): 49–67.

Herberg, W. *Protestant, Catholic, Jew: An Essay in American Religious Sociology*, rev. ed. New York: Anchor, 1960.

Herskovits, M. J. *Life in a Haitian Valley*. New York: Alfred A. Knopf, 1937.

———. *The Myth of the Negro Past*. New York: Harper and Bros., 1941.

———. *Franz Boas: The Science of Man in the Making*. New York: Charles Scribner's Sons, 1953.

———. "African Gods and Catholic Saints in New World Negro Belief." In *The New World Negro*, edited by F. S. Herskovits, 321–329. Bloomington: Indiana University Press, 1966.

Herskovits, M. J., and F. S. Herskovits. "An Outline of Dahomean Religious Belief." *Memoirs of the American Anthropological Association* 14 (1933): 7–77.

Heschel, S., ed. *On Being a Jewish Feminist: A Reader*. New York: Schocken, 1983.

Heston, C. *In the Arena: The Autobiography*. New York: HarperCollins, 1995.

Hickerson, N. P. *Linguistic Anthropology*. New York: Rinehart and Winston, 1980.

Hicks, G. "Writers in the Thirties." In *As We Saw the Thirties: Essays on Social and Political Movements of a Decade*, edited by R. J. Simon, 76–101. Chicago: University of Illinois Press, 1967.

Higashi, S. *Cecil B. DeMille: A Guide to References and Resources*. Boston: G. K. Hall, 1985.

———. "Cecil B. DeMille and the Lasky Company: Legitimating Feature Film as Art." *Film History* 4 (1990): 181–197.

Higham, C. *Cecil B. DeMille*. London: W. H. Allen, 1974.

Hilton, M. *The Christian Effect on Jewish Life*. London: S.C.M. Press, 1994.

Hodgens, R. M. "*The Ten Commandments*." *Film Quarterly* 20, no. 1 (1966): 59–60.

Hogan, L. *From Women's Experience to Feminist Theology*. Sheffield: Sheffield Academic Press, 1995.

Holloway, K. F. C. *The Character of the Word: The Texts of Zora Neale Hurston*. London: Greenwood, 1987.

Holloway, R. *The Religious Dimension in the Cinema: With Particular Reference to the Films of Carl Theodor Dreyer, Ingmar Bergman and Robert Bresson*. Hamburg: University of Hamburg, 1972.

Hollyday, J. *Clothed with the Sun: Biblical Women, Social Justice, and Us*. Louisville, Ky.: Westminster John Knox Press, 1994.

Homberger, E. *American Writers and Radical Politics, 1900–1939: Equivocal Commitments*. London: Macmillan, 1986.

Hopkins, D. N., and G. C. L. Cummings, eds. *Cut Loose Your Stammering Tongue: Black Theology in the Slave Narratives*. Maryknoll, N.Y.: Orbis, 1991.

Horton, R. M. *Lincoln Steffens.* Edited by A. W. Brown and T. W. Knight. New York: Twayne, 1974.

Howard, L. P. *Zora Neale Hurston.* New York: Twayne, 1980.

Hurston, Z. N. "Hoodoo in America." *Journal of American Folklore* 44 (1931): 320–417.

———. *The Sanctified Church: The Folklore Writings of Zora Neale Hurston.* Edited by T. C. Bambara. Berkeley, Calif.: Turtle Island Foundation, 1982.

———. *Spunk: The Selected Stories of Zora Neale Hurston.* Berkeley, Calif.: Turtle Island Foundation, 1985.

———. *Their Eyes Were Watching God.* 1937. Reprint, London: Virago Press, 1986.

———. *Jonah's Gourd Vine.* 1934. Reprint, London: Virago Press, 1987.

———. *Mules and Men.* 1935. Reprint, New York: HarperCollins, 1990.

———. *Dust Tracks on a Road.* 1942. Reprint, New York: HarperCollins, 1991.

———. *Tell My Horse: Voodoo and Life in Haiti and Jamaica.* 1938. Reprint, New York: HarperCollins, 1990.

———. *Moses, Man of the Mountain.* 1939. Reprint, New York: HarperCollins, 1991.

———. *Seraph on the Suwanee.* 1948. Reprint, New York: HarperCollins, 1991.

———. *The Complete Stories.* New York: HarperCollins, 1996.

———. *The Sanctified Church: The Folklore Writings of Zora Neale Hurston.* Edited by T. C. Bambara. Berkeley, Calif.: Turtle Island Foundation, 1981.

Hutchison, P. "Led His People Free." *New York Times Book Review,* 19 November 1939, 21.

Hyatt, M. *Franz Boas, Social Activist: The Dynamics of Ethnicity.* New York: Greenwood, 1990.

Ingraham, J. H. *The Pillar of Fire; or, Israel in Bondage.* 1859. Reprint, Boston: Roberts Brothers, 1874.

Iriye, A. *The Globalizing of America, 1913–1945.* Vol. 3 of *The Cambridge History of American Foreign Relations.* Cambridge: Cambridge University Press, 1993.

Jackson, B. "Some Negroes in the Land of Goshen." *Tennessee Folklore Society Bulletin* 19 (1953): 103–107.

Jewett, R. *Saint Paul at the Movies: The Apostle's Dialogue with American Culture.* Louisville, Ky.: Westminster John Knox Press, 1993.

Johnson, B. "Metaphor, Metonymy and Voice in *Their Eyes Were Watching God.*" In *Black Literature and Literary Theory,* edited by H. L. Gates, 205–219. London: Methuen, 1984.

Johnson, J. W. *The Autobiography of an Ex-Colored Man.* 1912. Reprint, London: Penguin, 1990.

Johnson, P. E., ed. *African-American Christianity: Essays in History.* Berkeley: University of California Press, 1994.

Joll, J. *Antonio Gramsci.* Harmondsworth, England: Penguin, 1977.

Jones, J. L. *The Agricultural Social Gospel in America: The Gospel of the Farm,* edited by T. E. Graham. Lewiston, Maine: Edwin Mellen, 1986.

Jowett, G. Film: The Democratic Art. Boston: Little, Brown, 1976.

Kabbani, R. Europe's Myths of the Orient: Devise and Rule. London: Macmillan, 1986.

Kaplan, J. Lincoln Steffens, a Biography. London: Jonathan Cape, 1975.

Kaplan, S. L., ed. Understanding Popular Culture: Europe From the Middle Ages to the Nineteenth Century. New York: Mouton, 1984.

Kawash, S. Dislocating the Color Line: Identity, Hybridity, and Singularity in African-American Literature. Stanford, Calif.: Stanford University Press, 1997.

Kennedy, G., H. L. Clark, D. M. Stowe, L. C. Moorehead, and W. Lindsay Young. "Through Different Eyes." Christian Century 74, no. 1 (1957): 20–21.

Kennett, R. H. The Church of Israel: Studies and Essays, edited by S. A. Cook. Cambridge: Cambridge University Press, 1933.

Kent, C. F. The Student's Old Testament: 1. Narratives of the Beginnings of Hebrew History from the Creation to the Establishment of the Hebrew Kingdom. New York: Charles Scribner's Sons, 1908.

Kitchin, L. "The Ten Commandments." Sight and Sound 27 (1957): 148–149.

Kreitzer, L. J. The New Testament in Fiction and Film: On Reversing the Hermeneutical Flow. Sheffield: J.S.O.T. Press, 1993.

———. The Old Testament in Fiction and Film: On Reversing the Hermeneutical Flow. Sheffield: Sheffield Academic Press, 1994.

Lasch, C. The New Radicalism in America (1889–1963): The Intellectual as a Social Type. New York: Alfred A. Knopf, 1965.

Leavis, F. R., and D. Thompson. Culture and Environment. Westport, Conn.: Greenwood, 1977.

Levecq, C. "'Mighty Strange Threads in Her Loom': Laughter and Subversive Heteroglossia in Zora Neale Hurston's Moses, Man of the Mountain." Texas Studies in Literature and Language 36 (1994): 436–461.

Lippy, C. H. Twentieth Century Shapers of American Popular Religion. New York: Greenwood, 1989.

Locke, A. "Dry Fields and Green Pastures." Opportunity 18, no. 1 (1940): 7.

Luhan, M. Intimate Memories. New York: Kraus, 1971.

Lundén, R. Business and Religion in the American 1920s. Westport, Conn.: Greenwood, 1988.

Lynd, R., and H. Lynd. Middletown. New York: Harcourt, Brace and Co., 1929.

Mannering, D. Great Works of Biblical Art. Bristol: Parragon, 1995.

Marsden, G. M. Religion and American Culture. New York: Harcourt Brace Jovanovich, 1990.

Marsh, C., and G. Ortiz, eds. Explorations in Theology and Film: Movies and Meaning. Oxford: Blackwell, 1997.

Martin, J. W., and C. E. Ostwealt, eds. Screening the Sacred: Religion, Myth, and Ideology in Popular American Film. Boulder, Col.: Westview, 1995.

Marty, M. E. Modern American Religion, 2 vols. Chicago: University of Chicago Press, 1991.

Mathisen, J. A. "Twenty Years after Bellah: What Ever Happened to American Civil Religion?" Sociological Analysis 50 (1989): 129–146.

May, J. R., ed. *Image and Likeness: Religious Visions in American Film Classics.* Mahwah, N.J.: Paulist, 1992.

McCarten, C. "De Mille at the Old Stand." *New Yorker* 32 (1956): 101–102.

McDannell, C. *Material Christianity: Religion and Popular Culture in America.* New Haven, Conn.: Yale University Press, 1995.

McFarlane, B. *Novel to Film: An Introduction to the Theory of Adaptation.* Oxford: Oxford University Press, 1996.

McKnight, E. V. *Post-Modern Use of the Bible: The Emergence of Reader-Oriented Criticism.* Nashville: Abingdon, 1988.

McNeile, A. H. *The Book of Exodus.* London: Methuen, 1917.

Mead, M. *Coming of Age in Samoa.* New York: Morrow, 1928.

Meier, A., and E. Rudwick. *Along the Color Line: Explorations in the Black Experience.* Chicago: University of Illinois Press, 1976.

Melton, J. G. *Encyclopedia of American Religions,* 4th ed. London: Gale Research, 1993.

Mendes-Flohr, P. R., and J. Reinharz, eds. *The Jew in the Modern World: A Documentary History.* Oxford: Oxford University Press, 1980.

Mercier, P. "The Fon of Dahomey." In *African Worlds: Studies in the Cosmological Ideas and Social Values of African Peoples,* 210–234. London: Oxford University Press, 1954.

Miles, M. *Seeing and Believing: Religion and Values in the Movies.* Boston: Beacon, 1996.

Millar, P. "The New Book of Revelations." *Sunday Times Magazine,* 27 August 1995, 16.

Miller, D. T. "Popular Religion of the 1950s: Norman Vincent Peale and Billy Graham." *Journal of Popular Culture* 9 (1975): 66–76.

Miller, J. M. "Archaeology (Old Testament)." In *A Dictionary of Biblical Interpretation,* edited by R. J. Coggins and J. L. Houlden, 51–56. London: S.C.M. Press, 1992.

Minus, P. M. *Walter Rauschenbusch: American Reformer.* London: Macmillan, 1988.

Montgomery, E. S. "Bruce Barton's *The Man Nobody Knows:* A Popular Advertising Illusion." *Journal of Popular Culture* 19 (1985): 21–34.

Moore, R. L. *Religious Outsiders and the Making of Americans.* Oxford: Oxford University Press, 1986.

Mosala, I. J., and B. Tlhagale. *The Unquestionable Right to be Free. Black Theology from South Africa.* Maryknoll, N.Y.: Orbis, 1986.

Mulira, J. G. "The Case of Voodoo in New Orleans." In *Africanisms in American Culture,* edited by J. E. Holloway, 34–68. Bloomington: Indiana University Press, 1990.

Musser, C. "Archeology of the Cinema, 8." *Framework* 22 (1983): 4–11.

Myrdal, G. *An American Dilemma. The Negro Problem and Modern Democracy.* New York: Harper and Row, 1962.

"Nazi War on Jews Hurts Christians Too," *New York Times,* 21 September 1935, p. 3.

Neve, B. *Film and Politics in America: A Social Tradition*. London: Routledge, 1992.

New Yorker, "Books. Briefly Noted: General." 11 November 1939, 91.

Noerdlinger, H. S. *Moses and Egypt: The Documentation to the Motion Picture* The Ten Commandments. Los Angeles: University of Southern California Press, 1956.

Nowlan, R. A., and G. W. Nowlan. *Cinema Sequels and Remakes, 1903–1987*. London: St. James, 1989.

Nuechterlein, J. A. "Bruce Barton and the Business Ethos of the 1920s." *South Atlantic Quarterly* 76 (1977): 293–308.

O'Donnell Setel, D. "Exodus." In *The Women's Bible Commentary*, edited by C. A. Newsom and S. H. Ringe, 26–35. London: S.P.C.K., 1992.

Ozick, C. "Notes on Finding the Right Question." In *On Being a Jewish Feminist: A Reader*, edited by S. Heschel, 120–151. New York: Schocken, 1983.

Palermo, P. F. *Lincoln Steffens*. New York: Twayne, 1978.

Parrinder, G. *West African Religion: A Study of the Beliefs and Practices of Akan, Ewe, Yoruba, Ibo, and Kindred Peoples*, 2nd ed. London: Epworth, 1969.

Patterson, J. T. *America in the Twentieth Century: A History*, 4th ed. Fort Worth, Texas: Harcourt Brace, 1994.

Petersen, R. L., ed. *Christianity and Civil Society: Theological Education for Public Life*. Maryknoll, N.Y.: Orbis, 1995.

Phipps, W. E. *Assertive Biblical Women*. London: Greenwood, 1992.

Pipes, R. *Russia under the Bolshevik Regime 1919–1924*. London: Fontana, 1995.

Pixley, G. V. *On Exodus: A Liberation Perspective*. Translated by R. R. Barr. Maryknoll, N.Y.: Orbis, 1987.

Plant, D. G. *Every Tub Must Sit on Its Own Bottom: The Philosophy and Politics of Zora Neale Hurston*. Chicago: University of Illinois Press, 1995.

Plaskow, J. *Standing Again at Sinai: Judaism from a Feminist Perspective*. New York: HarperCollins, 1990.

Plaut, G. *The Torah: A Modern Commentary*. New York: Union of American Hebrew Congregations, 1981.

Pondrom, C. N. "The Role of Myth in Hurston's *Their Eyes Were Watching God*." *American Literature* 58 (1986): 181–202.

Prickett, S., and R. Barnes. *The Bible*. Cambridge: Cambridge University Press, 1991.

Provenzo, E. F. *Video Kids: Making Sense of Nintendo*. Cambridge: Harvard University Press, 1991.

Raboteau, A. J. *Slave Religion: The "Invisible Institution" in the Antebellum South*. New York: Oxford University Press, 1978.

———. "Afro-American Religions." In *The Encyclopedia of Religion*, vol. 1., edited by M. Eliade, 96–102. New York: Macmillan, 1987.

Ransome, A. *Six Weeks in Russia in 1919*. London: George Allen and Unwin, 1919.

———. *The Crisis in Russia*. London: George Allen and Unwin, 1921.

———. *The Autobiography of Arthur Ransome*. London: Jonathan Cape, 1976.

Ribuffo, L. P. "Jesus Christ as Business Statesman: Bruce Barton and the Selling of Corporate Capitalism." *American Quarterly* 33 (1981): 206–231.

Riches, J. *The Bible: A Very Short Introduction*. Oxford: Oxford University Press, 2000.

Ringgold, G., and DeW. Bodeen. *The Films of Cecil B. DeMille*. New York: Citadel, 1969.

Robinson, E. G., and L. Spigelgass. *All My Yesterdays: An Autobiography*. London: W. H. Allen, 1974.

Rollins, A. B. "The Heart of Lincoln Steffens." *South Atlantic Quarterly* 59 (1960): 239–250.

Rosenstone, R. A. *Visions of the Past: The Challenge of Film to Our Idea of History*. Cambridge: Harvard University Press, 1995.

Rosenstone, R. A., ed. *Revisioning History: Film and the Construction of a New Past*. Princeton, N.J.: Princeton University Press, 1995.

Roshwald, M., and M. Roshwald. *Moses: Leader, Prophet, Man: The Story of Moses and His Image Through the Ages*. New York: Thomas Yoseloff, 1969.

Rouner, L. S., ed. *Civil Religion and Political Theology*. Notre Dame, Ind.: University of Notre Dame Press, 1986.

Rowland, C., ed. *The Cambridge Companion to Liberation Theology*. Cambridge: Cambridge University Press, 1999.

Rubenstein, R. I.., and J. K. Roth. *Approaches to Auschwitz: The Legacy of the Holocaust*. London: S.C.M. Press, 1987.

Russell, S. *Render Me My Song: African-American Women Writers from Slavery to the Present*. London: Pandora, 1990.

Sarna, N. M. *Exploring Exodus: The Heritage of Biblical Israel*. New York: Schocken, 1986.

————. *Exodus*. Philadelphia: Jewish Publication Society, 1991.

Scott, B. B. *Hollywood Dreams and Biblical Stories*. Minneapolis: Fortress, 1994.

Scott, J. *What Canst Thou Say? Towards a Quaker Theology*. London: Quaker Home Service, 1980.

Segal, A. F. "*The Ten Commandments*." In *Past Imperfect: History According to the Movies*, edited by M. C. Carnes, T. Mico, J. Miller-Monzon, and D. Rubel, 36–39. London: Cassell, 1996.

Setel, D. O'D. "Exodus." In *The Women's Bible Commentary*, edited by C. A. Newsom and S. H. Ringe. 26–35. London: S.P.C.K., 1992.

Sheffey, R. T. "Zora Neale Hurston's *Moses, Man of the Mountain*: A Fictionalized Manifesto on the Imperatives of Black Leadership." *C.L.A. Journal* 29 (1985): 206–220.

Shockley, A. A. *Afro-American Women Writers 1746–1933: An Anthology and Critical Guide*. New York: Meridian, 1989.

Silver, D. J. *Images of Moses*. New York: Basic Books, 1982.

Silverman, H. J. *Gadamer and Hermeneutics*. London: Routledge, 1991.

Simon, R. J. Ed. *As We Saw the Thirties: Essays on Social and Political Movements of a Decade*. Urbana: University of Illinois Press, 1967.

Sklar, R. *Movie-Made America: A Social History of American Movies*. New York: Random House, 1975.

Sklare, M. *Conservative Judaism: An American Religious Movement.* Glencoe, Ill.: Free Press, 1955.

Slomovitz, P. "The Negro's Moses." *Christian Century*, 6 December 1939, 1504.

Smith, T. H. *Conjuring Culture: Biblical Formations of Black America.* Oxford: Oxford University Press, 1994.

Smoodin, E. "Watching the Skies: Hollywood, the 1950s, and the Soviet Threat." *Journal of American Culture* 11 (1988): 35–40.

Spencer, H. *Education: Intellectual, Moral and Physical.* 1861. Reprint, Routledge/Thoemmes Press London, 1993.

Sperber, D. *Rethinking Symbolism.* Translated by A. L. Morton. Cambridge: Cambridge University Press, 1975.

St. Clair, J. "The Courageous Undertow of Zora Neale Hurston's *Seraph on the Suwanee.*" *Modern Language Quarterly* 50 (1989): 38–57.

Staiger, J. *Interpreting Films: Studies in the Historical Reception of American Cinema.* Princeton, N.J.: Princeton University Press, 1992.

Stead, P. *Film and the Working Class: The Feature Film in British and American Society.* London: Routledge, 1989.

Steere, D. V., ed. *Quaker Spirituality, Selected Writings.* New York: Paulist, 1984.

Steffens, J. L. *The Shame of the Cities.* New York: McClure and Phillips, 1904.

———. *Upbuilders.* New York: Doubleday and Page, 1909.

———. *Moses in Red: The Revolt of Israel as a Typical Revolution.* Philadelphia: Dorrance, 1926.

———. *The Autobiography of Lincoln Steffens.* New York: Harcourt, Brace and Co., 1938.

Stein, H. H. "Lincoln Steffens: An Intellectual Portrait." Ph.D. diss., University of Minnesota, 1965.

Stinson, R. *Lincoln Steffens.* New York: Frederick Ungar, 1979.

Storey, J. *An Introductory Guide to Cultural Theory and Popular Culture.* New York: Harvester Wheatsheaf, 1993.

———. *Cultural Studies and the Study of Popular Culture: Theories and Methods.* Edinburgh: Edinburgh University Press, 1996.

Stout, H. S. *The New England Soul.* New York: Oxford University Press, 1986.

Sundquist, E. J. *The Hammers of Creation: Folk Culture in Modern African-American Fiction.* Athens: University of Georgia Press, 1992.

Swann, P. *The Hollywood Feature Film in Postwar Britain.* London: Croom Helm, 1987.

Swartley, W. M. *Slavery, Sabbath, War and Women.* Scottdale, Pa.: Herald, 1983.

Tafoya, E. "Born in East L.A.: Cheech as the Chicano Moses." *Journal of Popular Culture* 26 (1993): 123–129.

Tallack, D. *Twentieth Century America: The Intellectual and Cultural Context.* London: Longman, 1991.

Tax, S., and L. S. Krucoff. "Social Darwinism." In *International Encyclopedia of the Social Sciences*, vol. 14, edited by D. L. Sills, 402–406. New York: Macmillan, 1968.

Telford, W. R. "The New Testament in Fiction and Film: A Biblical Scholar's Perspective." In *Words Remembered, Texts Renewed: Essays in Honour of John F. A. Sawyer*, edited by J. Davies, G. Harvey, and W. Watson, 360–394. Sheffield: Sheffield Academic Press, 1994.

———. "Jesus Christ Moveistar." In *Explorations in Theology and Film: Movies and Meaning*, ed. C. Marsh and G. Ortiz, 115–139. Oxford: Blackwell, 1997.

Thenen, R. "Gobineau, Joseph Arthur de." In *International Encyclopedia of Social Sciences*, edited by D. L. Sills, vol. 6, 163–164. New York: Macmillan, 1968.

Tindall, G. B., and D. E. Shi. *America: A Narrative History*, 3rd ed., vol. 2. New York: W. W. Norton, 1992.

Tolischus, O. D. "Reich Adopts Swastika as Nation's Official Flag; Hitler's Reply to 'Insult.'" *New York Times*, 16 September 1935, pp. 1, 11.

———. "Reich's New Army Shows Its Power to Army Leaders." *New York Times*, 17 September 1935, pp. 1, 14.

Trible, P. "Bringing Miriam Out of the Shadows." In *A Feminist Companion to Exodus-Deuteronomy*, edited by A. Brenner, 166–186. Sheffield: Sheffield Academic Press, 1994.

Tucker, G. M., and D. A. Knight, eds. *Humanizing America's Iconic Book: Society of Biblical Literature Centennial Addresses 1980*. Chico, Calif.: Scholars Press, 1982.

Turner, B. S. *Religion and Social Theory: A Materialistic Perspective*. London: Heinemann, 1983.

Turner, D. T. *In a Minor Chord: Three Afro-American Writers and Their Search for Identity*. Carbondale: Southern Illinois University Press, 1971.

Untermeyer, L. "Old Testament Voodoo." *Saturday Review*, 11 November 1939, 11.

Uricchio, W., and R. E. Pearson. *Reframing Culture: The Case of the Vitagraph Quality Films*. Princeton, N.J.: Princeton University Press, 1993.

Usai, P. C., and L. Codelli, eds. *L'Eredità DeMille*. Pordenone, Italy: Biblioteca dell'Immagine, 1991.

Van Vechten, C. *Fragments from an Unwritten Autobiography*, Vol. 2. New Haven: Yale University Library, 1955.

Vidler, A. R. *The Church in an Age of Revolution*, rev. ed. London: Penguin, 1990.

Von Mohrenschildt, D. S. "Lincoln Steffens and the Russian Bolshevik Revolution." *Russian Review* 5 (1945): 31–41.

Walker, A. *In Search of Our Mothers' Gardens: Womanist Prose*. London: Women's Press, 1984.

Wall, C. A. "Zora Neale Hurston: Changing Her Own Words." In *American Novelists Revisited: Essays in Feminist Criticism*, edited by F. Fleischmann, 371–393. Boston: G. K. Hall, 1982.

Wall, C. A., ed. *Changing Our Own Words: Essays on Criticism, Theory, and Writing by Black Women*. London: Routledge, 1990.

Walzer, M. *Exodus and Revolution*. New York: Basic Books, 1984.

Warrior, R. A. "A Native American Perspective: Canaanites, Cowboys and Indians." In *Voices from the Margin: Interpreting the Bible in the Third World*, edited by R. S. Sugirtharajah, 289–290. Maryknoll, N.Y.: Orbis, 1991.

Washington, B. T. *Up from Slavery*. 1901. Reprint, New York: Dover, 1995.

Washington, J. M., ed. *A Testament of Hope: The Essential Writings and Speeches of Martin Luther King*. San Francisco: Harper and Row, 1986.

Weems, R. J. "Reading *Her Way* Through the Struggle: African American Women and the Bible." In *The Bible and Liberation: Political and Social Hermeneutics*, rev. ed., edited by N. K. Gottwald and R. A. Horsley, 31–50. London: S.P.C.K., 1993.

Wentz, R. E. *Religion in the New World: The Shaping of Religious Traditions in the United States*. Minneapolis: Fortress, 1990.

Whiston, W., trans. *The Complete Works of Josephus*. 1737. Reprint, Grand Rapids: Kregel, 1995.

White, J. *Black Leadership in America: From Booker T. Washington to Jesse Jackson*, 2nd ed. London: Longman, 1990.

Wildavsky, A. *The Nursing Father: Moses as a Political Leader*. N.p.: University of Alabama Press, 1984.

Wilford, H. "'Winning Hearts and Minds': American Cultural Strategies in the Cold War." *Borderlines: Studies in American Culture* 1 (1994): 315–326.

Williams, D. S. "Black Women's Literature and the Task of Feminist Theology." In *Immaculate and Powerful: The Female in Sacred Image and Social Reality*, edited by C. Atkinson, C. H. Buchanan, and M. R. Miles, 33–110. London: Crucible, 1987.

Wilmore, G. S. *Black Religion and Black Radicalism: An Interpretation of the Religious History of Afro-American People*, 2nd ed. Maryknoll, N.Y.: Orbis, 1983.

Wilmore, G. S., ed. *African American Religious Studies: An Interdisciplinary Anthology*. Durham, N.C.: Duke University Press, 1989.

Wilson, C. P. "The Era of the Reporter Reconsidered: The Case of Lincoln Steffens." *Journal of Popular Culture* 15 (1981): 41–49.

Winter, E. *Red Virtue: Human Relationships in the New Russia*. London: Victor Gollancz, 1933.

Winter, E., and G. Hicks, eds. *The Letters of Lincoln Steffens*, 2 vols. New York: Harcourt Brace and Co., 1938.

Winter, E., and H. Shapiro, eds. *The World of Lincoln Steffens*. New York: Hill and Wang, 1962.

Winter, G. *The Suburban Captivity of the Churches: An Analysis of Protestant Responsibility in the Expanding Metropolis*. New York: Doubleday, 1961.

Witcover, P. *Zora Neale Hurston*. Los Angeles: Melrose Square, 1994.

Wood, M. G. *America in the Movies or, "Santa Maria, It Had Slipped My Mind."* London: Secker and Warburg, 1975.

Woodward, H. "Expressions of 'Black Humor': Laughter as Resistance in Alice Walker's *The Color Purple* and Zora Neale Hurston's *Moses, Man of the Mountain*." *Texas Studies in Language and Literature* 36 (1994): 431–435.

Wright, M. J. "Dialogue or Dominance? Interfaith Encounter and Cecil B. De-

Mille's *The Ten Commandments*." *Discernment: An Ecumenical Journal of Inter-Religious Encounter* 3 (1996): 10–19.

———. "Moses at the Movies: Ninety Years of the Bible and Film." *Modern Believing* 37, no. 4 (1996): 46–54.

———. "'Sunk in Slavery. . . . Snarled in Freedom': Recent Feminist Analyses of Exodus-Deuteronomy and Zora Neale Hurston's *Moses, Man of the Mountain*." *Biblicon* 2 (1997): 39–49.

Wright, R. *Native Son*. 1940. Reprint, London: Jonathan Cape, 1970.

Wright, T. R. *Theology and Literature*. Oxford: Basil Blackwell, 1988.

Wyke, M. *Projecting the Past: Ancient Rome, Cinema and History*. London: Routledge, 1997.

Zakai, A. *Exile and Kingdom: History and Apocalypse in the Puritan Migration to America*. Cambridge: Cambridge University Press, 1992.

Selective Filmography

Born in East L.A. (1987)
Directed by Cheech Marin
Produced by Peter MacGregor-Scott for Universal Studios
Screenplay by Cheech Marin
Leading players: Cheech Marin (Rudy); Daniel Stern (Jimmy); Kamala Lopez (Dolores)

Life of Moses (1909)
Directed by Charles Kent
Produced for the Vitagraph Company of America
Screenplay by Madison C. Peters and R. S. Sturgeon
Casting by C. P. Hartigan

Moses (1975)
Directed by Gianfranco DeBosio
Produced by Vincenzo Labella for Lew Grade
Screenplay by Anthony Burgess, Vittorio Bonicelli, and Gianfranco De Bosio
Leading players: Burt Lancaster (Moses); Anthony Quayle (Aaron); Ingrid Thurlin (Miriam); Irene Papas (Zipporah); Aharon Ipale (Joshua); Laurent Terzieff (Pharaoh)

The Ten Commandments (1956)
Directed by Cecil B. DeMille
Produced by Cecil B. DeMille for Paramount
Screenplay by Aeneas Mackenzie, Jesse Lasky Jr., Jack Gariss, and Frederick Frank
Leading players: Charlton Heston (Moses); Yul Brynner (Rameses); Anne Baxter (Nefretiri); Edward G. Robinson (Dathan); Yvonne De Carlo (Sephora); Debra Paget (Lilia); John Derek (Joshua)

Index